一百六十主要中成药

160 Essential Chinese Herbal Patent Medicines

一百六十主要中成药

160 ESSENTIAL CHINESE HERBAL PATENT MEDICINES

by

Bob Flaws

BLUE • POPPY • PRESS

Published by:

BLUE POPPY PRESS
A Division of Blue Poppy Enterprises, Inc.
3450 Penrose Place, Suite 110
BOULDER, CO 80301

First Edition November, 1999

ISBN 1-891845-12-8 LC# 99-73748

COPYRIGHT 1999 © BLUE POPPY PRESS

All rights reserved. No part of this book may be reproduced, stored in a retrieval system, transcribed in any form or by any means, electronic, mechanical, photocopy, recording, or any other means, or translated into any language without the prior written permission of the publisher.

The information in this book is given in good faith. However, the translators and the publishers cannot be held responsible for any error or omission. Nor can they be held in any way responsible for treatment given on the basis of information contained in this book. The publishers make this information available to English language readers for scholarly and research purposes only.

The publishers do not advocate nor endorse self-medication by laypersons. Chinese medicine is a professional medicine. Laypersons interested in availing themselves of the treatments described in this book should seek out a qualified professional practitioner of Chinese medicine.

COMP Designation: Original work using a standard translational terminology

Printed at Johnson Printing, Boulder, CO
Cover design by Anne Rue

10 9 8 7 6 5 4 3 2 1

Preface

Patent medicines are not the professional standard of care (SOC) for Chinese medicine in the People's Republic of China. The professional standard of care for Chinese medicine in China is orally administered, water-based decoctions made from bulk-dispensed, multi-ingredient prescriptions which have been individually written for each patient based on their individualized pattern discrimination. That being said, such polypharmacy, individually prescribed and dispensed, decocted Chinese medicinal formulas are not yet the professional standard of care for Chinese medicine in North America and Europe.

Because of various historical, sociological, and legal reasons, Chinese medicine has entered the Western world under the aegis of acupuncture. Acupuncture was the first Chinese medical modality to be practiced outside Asian communities in North America. Acupuncture was the first modality to be legalized in those states which have legalized any part of Asian medicine in North America. And acupuncture is still the main modality taught at North American schools and colleges of Asian medicine, which are generally thought of as "acupuncture schools." Only within the last two years has the National Commission for the Certification of Acupuncturists (NCCA) instituted a national certification exam in Chinese herbal medicine (and along with that changed its name to the National Commission for the Certification of Acupuncture & Oriental Medicine, NCCAOM). Because most professional practitioners of Asian medicine in the West primarily identify themselves as acupuncturists, so-called Chinese herbal medicine has largely been approached as an adjunctive modality to acupuncture in the West.

In Asia in general and China in particular, the situation is exactly reversed. Chinese herbal medicine is the main modality of Chinese medicine and acupuncture is the adjunctive or secondary modality. Acupuncturists in Asia typically play an analogous role to physical therapists in the West in terms of their relationship to those who prescribe "internal medicine." Furthermore, in the People's Republic of China, acupuncturists working in public clinics only do acupuncture (and the related modalities of moxibustion, cupping, and bleeding), while internal medicine practitioners only prescribe Chinese herbal medicine. Graduates of full-time, four year, Chinese entry level colleges of Chinese medicine only learn and are certified to do one or the other, not both.[1]

---

[1] A recent GMC ad on American tv says: "Do one thing. Do it well." At 53 years of age, I heartily subscribe to this philosophy.

In the West, the practice of Asian medicine is largely a second career. Most students of Asian medicine are adults between 25 and 60 years of age who attend Asian medical classes part-time on weekends and at night after work. Therefore, courses of study in the West are quite truncated in comparison to entry level training in the PRC. Westerners being as we are, having now found out about Chinese herbal medicine, most Western students are trying to learn and then go on to practice both modalities of acupuncture and internal medicine at the same time. This inevitably means that the quality of education in Chinese herbal medicine in the West is far below that of graduates of Chinese medical colleges in the PRC. In addition, Chinese herbal pharmacies are not commonly available outside of major Western cities with large Asian communities. Western practitioners, therefore, tend to sell whatever Chinese herbal medicines they prescribe from their own small dispensaries, and few have yet been able to afford to stock bulk Chinese medical dispensaries nor employ the help necessary to fill individually written, bulk-dispensed prescriptions.

For all these reasons, the majority of Western practitioners who do prescribe Chinese herbal medicine along with their acupuncture treatments do so in the form of ready-made medicines. In Chinese, such ready-made medicines are called *cheng yao*, manufactured medicines. In the West, we have adopted the name "patent medicines", meaning proprietary medicines, for these *cheng yao*. Such patent medicines mostly come in the form of pills, tablets, and capsules. However, in Chinese pharmacies both in China and in Chinatowns in the West, they also include powders, plasters, ointments, tinctures, oils, and liniments.

Typically in China, these ready-made medicines are purchased by consumers in the same way we buy over-the-counter (OTC) remedies at Western drugstores. Chinese consumers self-medicate themselves based on any combination of hearsay, common knowledge, and advertising. If such over-the-counter nostrums fail to get the intended effect, then the Chinese patient will typically see a professional practitioner for an individualized diagnosis and prescription. In that case, the professional practitioner will almost always write them a multi-ingredient, bulk-dispensed prescription to be decocted in water and drunk as a "tea" several times per day.

When professional Chinese medical practitioners in Asia do prescribe such ready-made medicines, it is most often for chronic, enduring conditions which require small, regular doses of medicine over a protracted period of time. The patient's condition is relatively stable and does not fluctuate widely. And, very importantly, their pattern fits one of the simple textbook patterns for which there is a standard ready-made medicine. Since the medicine must be taken for such a long, often indefinite time, it is important that it be easy to take, convenient to purchase, store, and carry around, and be affordably priced. If the patient's condition does not fit the above parameters, they will probably not be prescribed a ready-made Chinese patent medicine by a Chinese doctor in China.

Unfortunately, the majority of Western patients seeking professional Chinese medical care do not fit the above criteria for the use of ready-made Chinese patent medicines. They are typically seeking care for complicated conditions which no one else has been able to successfully treat, and they usually are currently ill. By this I mean that they want and need active remedial treatment, not simply the prevention of disease and maintenance of good health. After practicing Chinese medicine in the United States for 20 years, I would say that most Western patients seeking Chinese medical care are suffering from what are called "difficult to treat, knotty diseases" or *nan zhi jie bing* in Chinese. These are frequently chronic, progressive, and degenerative diseases which Western medicine is not so good at treating, such as chronic fatigue immune deficiency syndrome (CFIDS), multiple sclerosis (MS), rheumatoid arthritis (RA), systemic lupus erythamotosus (SLE), fibromylagia, and polymyositis/dermatomyositis. Since the majority of all patients are women, many patients are seeking treatment for endometriosis, functional uterine bleeding, uterine myomas, and infertility, typically the more difficult gynecological disease to treat with Chinese medicine. And even more unfortunately, a large number of Western patients of Chinese medical practitioners are suffering from various types of cancer or AIDS. In the PRC, ready-made or patent medicines are not the standard of care for the professional Chinese medical treatment of these diseases.

Therefore, a large part of my life's work has been dedicated to raising the level of education in and practice of Chinese herbal medicine in the West. Most of the books I have written and translated for professional practitioners of Chinese medicine in the West take individually written, bulk-dispensed, polypharmacy, water-based decoctions as their standard of care. This is what I have personally practiced for most of my 20 years in clinic, and this is what I primarily teach all over North America and throughout Europe. Thus many readers may be surprised that I have taken the time and spent the energy to compile this book on the prescription and use of Chinese patent medicines.

First of all, even though the prescription of patent medicines may not be the standard of care of professional Chinese medicine in the PRC, it is the current *de facto* standard of care in the West. Whether or not it should be, it is what is. Therefore, my writing of this book is an attempt to work skillfully with that reality, rather than futilely rail against it. If, for a variety of educational and economic reasons, this is what the majority of my fellow practitioners feel they need to do, I believe that I can help them do it even better. If one follows the step-by-step methodology presented in this book and then prescribes the right Chinese patent medicine based on the patient's pattern discrimination, I believe that medicine will have a far greater healing effect with less potential side effects than prescribing Chinese patent medicines on the basis of a Chinese or Western disease diagnosis. If one is careful to hew to the same step-by-step methodology used by Chinese doctors in China for composing and prescribing individually written, bulk-dispensed decoctions, one can often combine two or more ready-made medicines to come close to the same level of individualized prescription as with bulk-dispensed herbs.

Secondly, in the past couple of years, a number of Chinese medicinal suppliers and manufacturers, recognizing the unique needs and wants of Western consumers, have created a new generation of Chinese patent medicines. These suppliers and manufacturers understand that Western consumers want ready-made Chinese herbal medicines which are uncontaminated by heavy metals, chemicals, and pesticides and are free from adulteration by Western pharmaceuticals whose presence is not disclosed on the label. Until recently, when one purchased a Chinese patent medicine, there was no way of knowing if the medicine in question did contain the medicinals stated on the label, what other contaminants or adulterants it also contained, and in what kind of a facility and how it was made. In addition, packaging was shoddy, labels were written in "pidgin English", and many Chinese patent medicines contained medicinals made from endangered species, such as Cornu Rhinocerotis (*Xi Jiao*), Cornu Antelopis Saiga-tatarici (*Ling Yang Jiao*), and Os Tigridis (*Hu Gu*) to name but a few of the most famous (or infamous!).

Now, companies such as Mayway Corp. and Nuherbs Co. have searched out the best and most reliable manufacturers of Chinese ready-made medicines. They have weeded out formulas which contain the most egregious endangered species, and they have ensured that the medicines they are selling under their proprietary labels are free from contaminants and Western pharmaceuticals. These medicines are now packaged in sealed plastic bottles like other OTC medicaments in the West, with attractive labels designed specifically for Western tastes and sensibilities. In addition, these companies have created a number of new patent medicines in order to meet a wider range of Western clinical needs. Interestingly, many of these new patent medicines are not new formulas. For instance, *Ban Xia Xie Xin Tang* (Pinellia Drain the Heart Decoction) and *Xiao Chai Hu Tang* (Minor Bupleurum Decoction) are now available as ready-made pills. These are complex formulas suited for treating the typically complex combinations of vacuity and repletion, hot and cold, wet and dry which Western patients present.

My third and last reason for choosing to compile a book on Chinese patent medicines at this time has to do with terminology. As I have written in numerous other places, I believe that the professional practice of Chinese medicine greatly depends on the correct use of technically precise words. This system of medicine was created in the Chinese language, and the structure and logic of the Chinese language is very dissimilar to that of modern Indo-European languages. Therefore, the quality of the clinical practice of Chinese medicine in the West often hinges on the quality of the translational terminology which the practitioner is using. Many mistakes and defi-ciencies in the Western practice of Chinese medicine are functions of wrong or inac-curate understandings of the Chinese medical literature and the methodology it teaches.

I believe that the single most accurate, self-consistent English language terminology for translating the technical precision of Chinese medicine is that created by Nigel Wiseman and his associates. Till now, various authors on Chinese medicine have used whatever translational terminology they wished and there has been no way to A) gauge the accuracy and faithfulness of their translations or B) cross-reference terms from author to author. Because this medicine comes from China, Chinese is the linguistic standard of reference for this medicine. Ultimately, the identification and understanding of each technical term within this medicine is based on the Chinese word or words from which it was derived. Therefore, it is extremely important that readers be able to find out what Chinese characters are being translated by what English words. For instance, one author may call the *hua mai* a slippery pulse, another may call it a sliding pulse, and yet another may call it a rolling pulse. Until or unless we know that all three authors are speaking about the *hua mai*, we do not know if they are talking about the same or different pulses.

Nigel Wiseman has done a monumental piece of work by providing a philologically accurate standard translation for thousands of Chinese medical terms in his *English-Chinese Chinese-English Dictionary of Chinese Medicine*. This is not actually a dictionary (since it does not contain definitions) but is rather a glossary of suggested translational equivalents. Using Wiseman's translational terms, one can get as close as possible to understanding the technical precision of Chinese medicine in English. In *A Practical Dictionary of Chinese Medicine*, Wiseman has created a true dictionary of Chinese medical terms with definitions, although the number of terms it includes is less than his previously mentioned title.

Unfortunately, there has been much resistance to the adoption of Wiseman's terminology. A number of Wiseman's terms are different from those in common (though in many cases patently erroneous) use, and many of the terms are strange-sounding to the uneducated ear. Until or unless there is a relatively complete body of literature on all the various major aspects of Chinese medicine using this same, self-consistent terminology, students and practitioners are even more reluctant to have to switch back and forth between different systems of terminology. Therefore, this book is yet another step in the creation of a terminologically self-consistent Chinese medical literature in English. When students and practitioners can read and study all aspects of Chinese medicine in this same, self-consistent translational terminology, I believe that they will be more likely to adopt this terminology. Since I believe this is the best system of translational terminology available in English, I have taken it upon myself to create as many books using this terminology as possible.

The prescription of patent medicines is one way to begin the professional practice of Chinese internal medicine. It may not be the standard of care of professional Chinese medicine in the People's Republic of China, but it can be a valid step towards that standard of care. In addition, since most Chinese patent medicines in the West are prescribed as adjuncts to professionally administered acupuncture treatment, most patients prescribed Chinese patent medicines are receiving a combined therapy, whereas, in China, patients typically receive either acupuncture or internal medicine alone. I prescribed Chinese patent medicines for several years before "graduating" to bulk-dispensed, individually written prescriptions. When Chinese ready-made medicines are correctly prescribed based on the patient's Chinese pattern discrimination, they can be very effective, and they are effective without side effects. Therefore, if I can help my fellow Westerners prescribe Chinese patent medicines even more accurately, then this book will have been no small benefit.

Bob Flaws
April, 1999

Table of Contents

	Preface	v
1	Introduction	1
2	Choosing a Chinese Patent Medicine	7
3	Exterior-resolving Medicines	17
4	Draining & Precipitating Medicines	31
5	Harmonizing & Resolving Medicines	39
6	Heat-clearing Medicines	47
7	Interior-warming Medicines	61
8	Exterior-Interior Dual Resolving Medicines	65
9	Qi-rectifying Medicines	69
10	Blood-rectifying Medicines	81
11	Wind-treating Medicines	101
12	Dryness-treating Medicines	109
13	Dampness-dispelling Medicines	113
14	Phlegm-dispelling Medicines	131
15	Food-dispersing, Stagnation-abducting Medicines	137
16	Worm-killing Medicines	141
17	Spirit-quieting Medicines	145
18	Securing & Astringing Medicines	155
19	Supplementing & Boosting Medicines	161
20	The Five Most Important Chinese Ready-made Medicines	201
21	The Safety of Chinese Patent Medicines	205
	Bibliography	207
	Medicine Index	209
	General Index	211

1
Introduction

This book is a guide to the study and use of so-called Chinese herbal patent medicines. I say so-called for two reasons. First, Chinese "herbs" are not all herbs. Chinese medicinals are made from vegetable, animal, and mineral sources. In Chinese, the words *zhong yao* mean Chinese medicinals, not Chinese herbs. Secondly, the Chinese *cheng yao* means manufactured or ready-made medicine, while patent medicines refers to proprietary formulas upon which patents have been taken out. The term patent medicine is largely a nineteenth century convention.

Criteria for inclusion in this book

All of the medicines included in this book are distributed by companies who have consciously and deliberately made an attempt to sell only the best and safest Chinese herbal products. These companies have taken steps to insure freedom from contaminants, adulterants, and endangered species. Although the medicinals have been grown and gathered and the medicines have been manufactured in Asia, they have been manufactured according to Western standards of labeling and packaging. As far as I have been able to determine, the medicines included in this book only contain the ingredients listed on their labels in Chinese[1] and are safe and effective when prescribed according to a correct Chinese medical pattern discrimination.

In describing its Plum Flower and Min Shan brands of Chinese ready-made medicines, the Mayway Corp. catalog makes the following claims:

1. All [the medicines included under these brand names] are manufactured by well known manufacturers in China. Each product has obtained a production permit and surpasses the inspection codes of the Health Department of the People's Republic of China.

---

[1] I have qualified this statement by saying that the lists of ingredients are correct as stated *in Chinese* because I believe these Chinese companies have made some mistakes in terms of biological and pharmacological nomenclature when it comes to the Latinate identifications on their labels. These errors are due to honest mistakes and ignorance and are not due to any attempt to deliberately mislead Western consumers.

2. All products have been legally imported under the strict supervision of the U.S. Food and Drug Administration, the U.S. Department of Agriculture, and the equivalent thereof in most European countries.

3. All ingredients are completely listed, are 100% natural, and contain no pharmaceuticals.

4. All Mayway products are covered under product liability insurance.

5. All products have been recommended by physicians throughout China and have been proven safe and free from side effects.

6. All products make no claims or list indications. Please consult your herbal practitioner or patent formula handbook.[2]

Similarly, Nuherbs Co. has created its own Herbal Times brand of Chinese ready-made medicines. In their catalog, Nuherbs says:

> We have done everything to the best of our knowledge to comply with FDA regulations. We try to avoid confusion with adulterated formulas and products which have received negative publicity... In the past, many customers had [sic] asked for formulas without sugar coating. Herbal Times formulas are manufactured to satisfy those customers' requests... To protect quality of the product and avoid unwanted temparating [sic, *i.e.*, tampering], this new product is packaged in a plastic bottle with an inner and outer seal which follows the standard bottling method adopted by U.S. industries.[3]

Because of the growing popularity of Chinese herbal medicine, there are an increasing number of disreputable manufacturers, mostly in Asia. Called *shan zao chang* or "mountain bandit companies" in Chinese, many of the products of these "fly by night" companies are adulterated with undisclosed Western pharmaceuticals, such as acetaminophen and pulgeone, or contaminated by heavy metals, such as lead, arsenic, and mercury. Further, some Chinese ready-made medicinals contain medicinals made from endangered species, such as tigers, rhinoceros, Saiga antelopes, and musk deer, while others simply contain the wrong species of medicinals. Further, some of the medicines have been produced through incorrect or incomplete manufacturing processes. Although many of these other Chinese ready-made medicines are available in North America and Europe and may be useful in clinical practice, I have not discussed them in this book since I do not recommend nor endorse their sale and use.

---

[2] *Mayway USA 1998-1999 Herbal Catalogue*, p. iii

[3] *Nuherbs Catalog,* Spring 1997, p. 37

Introduction

This book is not meant to be an encyclopedia of Chinese patent medicines, discussing every patent medicine possible. I believe one of the big mistakes many Westerners make when trying to learn and practice Chinese medicine is attempting to learn and use too much. The formulas selected for inclusion in this book cover a wide range of patterns and conditions and are good ones for beginners to concentrate on mastering. There are medicines from almost every category of Chinese medicinal formulas. By combining two or more of these medicines together, one can craft a methodologically correct Chinese medical treatment for most diseases. If one learns and masters the use of this core set of ready-made medicines, one will have laid a good basis for going on to learn how to write individually-tailored, bulk-dispensed decoctions. This is because many if not most of the medicines included in this book are based on the main standard formulas of Chinese medicine.

Listed ingredients

I have worked closely for more than 18 months with the administrative staff of both Mayway Corp. and Nuherbs Co. checking and rechecking the ingredients in each of the medicines included in this book. However, it's a fact of life that the Chinese manufacturers of these medicines sometimes change the ingredients in their formulas for a number of reasons. These may include but are not limited to price fluctuations, availability, endangered species status, and processing problems and concerns. When such changes are made, they are usually the substitution of one Chinese medicinal with the same or similar functions and indications for another. Usually, these substitutions also only involve the messenger and adjunctive medicinals in a formula, not the ruling or ministerial medicinals.

Because of such medicinal substitutions and changes, I strongly recommend reading the ingredient list on every new batch of Chinese medicines to insure their suitability for your patient. The ingredients we list in this book reflect Mayway's, Nuherbs', and Blue Poppy's best efforts as of mid-1999.

Where to purchase the medicines included in this book

The Chinese ready-made medicines described in this book are available in the United States from two sources. They are:

Mayway Corp.
1338 Cypress St.
Oakland, CA 94607
Tel: 510-208-3113
Fax: 510-208-3069
Orders Tel: 1-800-2-MAYWAY
Orders Fax: 1-800-909-2828

Nuherbs Co.
3820 Penniman Ave.
Oakland, CA 94619
Tel: 510-534-4372
Fax: 510-534-4384
Orders Tel: 1-800-233-4307
Orders Fax: 1-800-550-1928

Not every one of the formulas described in this book is sold by both companies. Therefore, please refer to each company's latest respective catalog for the medicines that company has available. When both companies distribute a formula with the same Chinese name but different listed ingredients, I have noted this in a footnote.

Neither I personally nor Blue Poppy Press, Inc. are in any way related to either Mayway Corp. or Nuherbs Co. In addition, I have not received any financial aid or incentive from either of these companies in return for compiling this book. I have done so purely out of an interest in seeing Western practitioners correctly prescribe safe and effective Chinese ready-made medicines.

Prerequisites for using this book

This book is intended for students and professional practitioners of Chinese medicine. Before studying Chinese medicinal formulas such as those included in this book, students and practitioners are expected to have completed courses in basic Chinese medical theory, the four examinations, pattern discrimination, and materia medica. Chinese herbal patent medicines are not safe and effective because they are Chinese or because they are herbal. Many of the ingredients in these formulas did not originate in China, but were imported to China from India, Persia, Malaysia, Indonesia, and Europe. As mentioned above, these ingredients are also not all herbal, since some of them come from animal and mineral sources. Chinese ready-made medicines are safe and effective because of the prescriptive methodology with which they are used. In other words, they are only safe and effective when they are prescribed to the right person in the right dose for the right length of time. Otherwise, they are just as likely to cause unwanted side effects as any other medicine.

In order to correctly prescribe the medicines contained in this book, one must have a sound grounding in the basics of Chinese medical theory. One must know how to do a Chinese medical diagnosis using the four examinations. One must know the signs and symptoms, tongue and pulse signs of the main patterns of Chinese medicine and be able to discriminate one pattern from another. And one must have at least a rudimentary understanding of Chinese materia medica. By this, I mean that one should know the categorization[4], natures (*i.e.*, temperatures), flavors, channel-enterings, functions, indications, dosage parameters, combinations, and contraindications of the 150 most commonly used Chinese medicinals. In addition, one should at least know the categorization of the next 150 most commonly prescribed medicinals.

---

[4] By categorization, I mean in which chapter of the materia medica one finds the medicinal in question. Most Chinese materia medica divide medicinals in 22-28 chapters or categories, such as medicinals which resolve the exterior, medicinals which clear heat, medicinals which rectify the qi, medicinals which eliminate dampness, etc.

One should *never prescribe* any formula which contains any ingredient whose nature, flavors, functions, and indications are not known. One does not have to have memorized all of these, but one must know where and be able to look these up when necessary. The formulas in this book are made up of individual ingredients and the effects of a formula are nothing other than the cumulative effects and synergisms of these ingredients. Therefore, if one does not understand the nature, flavors, functions, and indications of individual medicinals, one cannot understand the functions and indications of a formula. Just as Western medical professionals would not prescribe Western pharmaceuticals whose ingredients they did not know or understand, one should not prescribe Chinese ready-made medicines whose ingredients they do not understand.

Further, professional training and licensure in some other health care profession besides Chinese medicine conveys no *a priori* knowledge or expertise when it comes to Chinese medicine. Chinese medicine is its own, very complicated and elaborate medical system which must be studied and learned on its own. Just as one should not dabble in the prescription of Western pharmaceuticals, one should also not dabble in the prescription of so-called Chinese herbal medicines. Chinese medicinals are only safe and effective when there are prescribed correctly according to the time-tested methodology of traditional Chinese medicine.

Translational terminology & medicinal identifications

The translational terminology used in this book is based on Nigel Wiseman's *English-Chinese Chinese-English Dictionary of Chinese Medicine*, Hunan Science & Technology Press, Changsha, 1995. When I have chosen to use a different term than that suggested by Wiseman, I have footnoted my reasons for doing so the first time I use the term. Definitions for the technical Chinese medical terms used in this book can be found in Wiseman and Feng's *A Practical Dictionary of Chinese Medicine*, Paradigm Publications, Brookline, MA, 1998.

Medicinals in this book have been identified similar to other Blue Poppy Press books. First the name is given in Latinate pharmacological nomenclature. This is then followed by the Pinyin name in parentheses. These pharmacological identifications primarily come from Bensky & Gamble's *Chinese Herbal Medicine: Materia Medica*, Eastland Press, Seattle, 1993. If a medicinal was not found in that standard English language reference, I next looked in Hong-yen Hsu's *Oriental Materia Medica: A Concise Guide*, Oriental Healing Arts, Long Beach, CA, 1986. If still the medicinal was not found, I next looked in Wiseman's *English-Chinese Chinese-English Dictionary of Chinese Medicine*, Hunan Science & Technology Press. And if still I could not find the pharmacological identification of a medicinal, I then looked it up in the *Zhong Yao Da Ci Dian (The Great Dictionary of Chinese Medicinals)*, Jiangsu New Medicine College, Shanghai Science & Technology Press, 1990. This order is predicated on the relative popularity, availability, and accessibility in the U.S. of these reference texts. The vast majority of medicinals in the formulas included in this book are found in Bensky & Gamble.

As for the names of the Chinese ready-made medicines themselves, I have first given their Chinese name spelled in Pinyin romanization. This is then followed in parentheses by my translation of the Chinese name. One can easily find any of these medicines in either the Mayway or Nuherbs catalog by using the Pinyin name. These are listed in alphabetical order in both those two catalogs. Sometimes my translation of the Chinese name is the same as that commonly used or appearing on the label of the medicine and sometimes it is different when I disagree with the former translation of the name in Chinese. Hopefully, my more literal English translations of these Chinese medicines will help clarify the logic of their use according to Chinese medical methodology.

2
Choosing a Chinese Patent Medicine

In professional Chinese medicine as practiced in the People's Republic of China, the basic prescriptive methodology is known as *bian zheng lun zhi*. This translates as basing treatment on pattern discrimination. Basing treatment on pattern discrimination is the single best and most important methodology for the safe and effective prescription of any Chinese medicinals, be they individually bulk-dispensed or ready-made. It is the basing of treatment on pattern discrimination that makes professional Chinese medicine the holistic, safe, and effective medicine it is.

Chinese medicine identifies two types of prescriptive methodologies. One is called *bian bing lun zhi* and the other is called *bian zheng lun zhi*. *Bian bing lun zhi* means the basing of treatment on a disease diagnosis. This is how most Western medicine is practiced no matter whether the practitioner is prescribing herbs, vitamins and minerals, or synthetic pharmaceuticals. Basing of treatment on disease diagnosis means that everyone with the same disease gets the same medicine. Using this methodology, there is headache medicine, ulcer medicine, constipation medicine, and diarrhea medicine. Certain medicines are known to treat certain diseases, and, using this methodology, the patient's disease is the main criterion for picking the medication. Therefore, everyone with headache gets certain headache medicines, while everyone with ulcers gets certain ulcer medications.

Professionally practiced Chinese medicine also uses this prescriptive methodology. However, in professional Chinese medicine, this method of selecting medicines and therapies is considered secondary. The most important thing in choosing the right medicine in professional Chinese medicine is to base treatment on the patient's pattern. Patterns and diseases are not the same thing. Let me explain the difference. One's ability to do high quality Chinese medicine hinges on one's careful understanding of the difference between a patient's pattern and their disease.

In Chinese medicine, headache is both a symptom and a disease in its own right. In order to be diagnosed as suffering from headache, you must have some kind of pain somewhere in your head. Pain in the head is the defining symptom of headache. If you do not have pain in the head, you cannot be diagnosed as having headache. That being said, a person can have many different kinds of pain in the head and that pain can be located in different areas of the head. In addition, people with headaches can and usually do have a number of other signs and symptoms besides the pain in their head. They may have constipation or loose stools. They may be restless or fatigued. They may be forgetful or irritable. They may have red eyes or cold hands and feet. They may sweat on slight exertion or never sweat at all. They may be dizzy when they stand up or get headaches when they see bright lights. Further, people with pain in the head may be of different sexes, different ages, and different body types. None of these other signs and symptoms are necessary to diagnose headache. However, these other signs and symptoms do make up the pattern of the entire person.

A Chinese medical pattern is the total of *all signs and symptoms gathered by the Chinese four examinations* (looking, smelling/hearing, questioning, and palpating). The signs and symptoms that go to make up a person's Chinese pattern discrimination are usually many more than the signs and symptoms which define their disease diagnosis. The disease is a tree, but the pattern is the forest within which this tree exists. The disease is the figure, but the pattern is the ground. And it is the pattern that professional Chinese medicine primarily seeks to treat.

Each Chinese medical pattern describes some imbalance in the bodymind.[1] For instance, if we say a patient exhibits the pattern of liver depression qi stagnation, this implies that the liver is not doing its duty of coursing and discharging the qi. Therefore, the qi has accumulated and become stagnant. It is not flowing freely as and where it should. Once the Chinese doctor knows that the patient's pattern is liver depression qi stagnation, then they also know that, in terms of reestablishing balance and harmony within the patient, they should course the liver and rectify the qi.

In professional Chinese medicine, we first and foremost rebalance or regulate the patient's pattern of disharmony and only secondarily make sure that our choice of treatment does also empirically address the patient's disease or major complaints. Thus it is said in Chinese medicine:

>   Different diseases, same treatment
>   Same diseases, different treatments

This saying means that two patients may have the same disease diagnosis. Yet, if their Chinese pattern discrimination is different, they will receive quite different treatments. Conversely, two patients may be diagnosed as suffering from two quite different diseases, yet they will receive essentially the same treatment if their Chinese pattern discrimination is the same. When doing professional Chinese medicine, we first choose and aim our treatment at the patient's pattern and only secondarily do we make sure that treatment, in fact, is clinically known through previous experience to address the patient's disease diagnosis.

---

[1] Chinese medicine does not recognize the Cartesian duality between the body and mind.

As stated above, it is treatment given on the basis of pattern discrimination which makes professional Chinese medicine the holistic, safe, and effective medicine it is. This is because it treats the entire person. When a medicine provokes unwanted side effects in some patients, it is because that medicine was not the right medicine for that person. It may address a specific symptom, but it did not take into account the ground in which that symptom exists. Medicines which cause side effects and unwanted, allergic, or toxic reactions are all *erroneously prescribed* medicines. They are neither good nor bad within themselves. They simply have been prescribed to the wrong person —the wrong pattern of that disease.

Therefore, if you are a professional practitioner of Chinese medicine and you begin by asking what Chinese ready-made medicine treats this or that disease, you are asking the wrong question and starting from the wrong place. On the other hand, you will never go wrong if you first do a Chinese pattern discrimination and primarily pick your remedy on that basis. Although I cannot stress this point too much, this book is also not designed to teach pattern discrimination. For that, I refer the reader to my and Daniel Finney's book, *A Compendium of TCM Patterns and Treatments*, also published by Blue Poppy Press.

The importance of treatment principles

Once you have gathered the patient's various signs and symptoms, including tongue and pulse signs, using the four examinations and you have made your initial pattern discrimination, then the next step is to formulate the treatment principles necessary to restore harmony and balance to a person with that pattern. This is an extremely important step. If you leave out this step, then the whole prescriptive methodology of professional Chinese medicine falls apart. In Chinese it is said that the treatment principles are the bridge which connects the pattern discrimination with the treatment plan. I like to say that the treatment principles are the neck of the magic funnel which funnels you from the welter of signs and symptoms and the pattern discrimination to the correct Chinese medicinal formula or medicine.

Above I said that the treatment principles for the pattern of liver depression qi stagnation are to course the liver and rectify the qi. Once we have said this, then we *must* pick our formula or remedy from the qi-rectifying chapter or category. There is a qi-rectifying chapter or category in every Chinese materia medica (*ben cao*) book and every Chinese formulas and strategies (*fang ji*) book. As soon as we've said that the first treatment principles are to course the liver and rectify the qi, then we know that we must pick a formula from the qi-rectification chapter. Secondly, we must then make sure that the formula does empirically address symptoms and diseases associated with liver depression (as opposed to stomach qi stagnation). If a patient's pattern is nothing other than liver depression qi stagnation, then, according to the standards of care of professional Chinese medicine, to pick a guiding formula from any other chapter is categorically wrong.

That being said, most Western patients' pattern discrimination is going to be more complex than simple liver depression qi stagnation. A more common, real-life scenario would be liver depression qi stagnation, spleen vacuity with damp accumulation, and a bit of blood vacuity. Now our treatment principles are to course the liver and rectify the qi and to fortify the spleen and eliminate dampness, assisted by nourishing or supplementing the blood. Hopefully the reader has studied enough Chinese medicine to know that, when you have a liver repletion/spleen vacuity, one should choose their guiding formula from the harmonizing category of formulas. Harmonizing formulas harmonize the constructive and defensive, but they also harmonize the liver and spleen, liver and stomach, spleen and stomach, and stomach and intestines.

It is also not uncommon to find a case where there is a combination of hot and cold. For instance, there may be a combination of spleen vacuity mixed with damp heat. In that case, one must prioritize which is more important. Is there more spleen vacuity or is there more damp heat? If there is more spleen vacuity, then one must choose a formula from the qi-supplementing category or chapter, insuring that the formula in question primarily fortifies the spleen and does treat the patient's disease or major complaint. Then one must also insure that the formula does include some heat-clearing, dampness-eliminating medicinals to deal with the damp heat. If there is more prominent damp heat and less prominent spleen vacuity, then one must pick a formula from the heat-clearing chapter, subcategory: heat-clearing and dampness-eliminating. If the chosen formula does not contain any medicinals to fortify the spleen and supplement the qi, then some must be added. If the relative balance between heat and cold, vacuity and repletion is pretty equal, then one may find one's remedy in the harmonizing category again, for instance, *Xiao Chai Hu Tang* (Minor Bupleurum Decoction) or *Ban Xia Xie Xin Tang* (Pinellia Drain the Heart Decoction).

The importance of the words you use

When stating your treatment principles, it is very important to A) be sure that you use professionally acceptable terminology. If you use the wrong words, you may not find the category of medicinals or formulas you want. B) Be sure to also state your treatment principles in the same order as you stated the patient's pattern discrimination. And C) be sure that every element of the pattern is addressed by one or more principles and that you also have not added any principles not warranted by the pattern discrimination.

Professional standards of care

Within professional Chinese medicine, there are definite standards of care when it comes to what treatment principles go with what patterns. Although there is some room for synonyms, there is remarkable consistency within the modern Chinese medical literature when it comes to what treatment principles go with what patterns. For instance, we use the principles of drying dampness when that dampness is encumbering the middle burner, but we use the principle of disinhibiting dampness when evil dampness is located primarily in the lower burner. A good sense of the appropriate treatment principles for different patterns using Wiseman's terminology can be seen in *A Compendium of TCM Patterns & Treatments*. Personally, I recommend sticking with the treatment principles which are correlated to the chapters or categories of Chinese materia medica and formula and strategy texts. It will help keep things simple.

Prioritizing patterns and, therefore, treatment

Secondly, if you say the patient is exhibiting a pattern of liver depression with spleen vacuity, by putting the words liver depression first, you are implying that liver depression is the most important thing and that the spleen vacuity is secondary. If your patient primarily exhibits spleen vacuity with a touch of liver depression, then it is important to say that their pattern discrimination is spleen vacuity with simultaneous liver depression. Then, whatever the order of your pattern discrimination, that should be the same order of your statement of treatment principles. If you stick with this protocol or methodology, then your guiding formula or prescription is typically going to be found in the chapter or category corresponding to the first treatment principle. If you say that the pattern is liver depression with spleen vacuity, then it is categorically wrong to pick a formula from the qi-supplementing chapter. Similarly, if you say that there is spleen vacuity complicated by some damp heat, it is categorically wrong to pick a formula from the heat-clearing, dampness-eliminating subcategory of the heat-clearing chapter. Rather, you should have first looked in the qi-supplementing chapter or at least in the harmonizing chapter.

Warranted & unwarranted treatment

And third, it is very important that you not gratuitously add any treatment principles not warranted by the pattern discrimination. Everything said in the pattern dis-crimination should be reflected in the treatment principles. And nothing should suddenly appear in the treatment principles not logically derived from the stated pattern. If one has not said that there is kidney yang vacuity in the pattern discrim-ination, one cannot suddenly say to supplement the kidneys and invigorate yang.

Here, the word warrant is extremely important. In legal terms, the word warrant gives officers of the law the legal right to do something which is otherwise illegal. To hold or take someone somewhere against their will is called kidnapping. However, police do this all the time. In order to do this, they must first get an arrest warrant from a judge. In order to get such a warrant, they must present the judge with evidence that the suspect is the person who has committed the crime. In Chinese medical terms, the signs and symptoms are our proof of a patient's pattern. If you say they have this or that pattern, then they have to have certain signs and symptoms. If they don't have those signs and symptoms, then, categorically, they do not exhibit that pattern. Your treat-ment principles are your warrant to use a certain group of medicinals, and you can only include those medicinals for which you have a warrant. Therefore, it is very important in the Chinese medical process of moving from signs and symptoms to pattern discrimination to treatment plan that one not add any treatment principles without A) substantiating evidence and B) those principles being derived from some element of the stated pattern discrimination.

Recapitulation of basic Chinese medical methodology

When presented with any new patient, first one gathers their signs and symptoms through the four examinations. Then one analyzes those signs and symptoms according to the logic of Chinese medical theory. Through this analysis, one discriminates one pattern from another, eventually stating on the patient's chart their pattern discrimination in appropriate, standard professional terminology. Based on this pattern discrimination, one next states the treatment methods necessary in principle to correct the disharmony implied by the name of the pattern. Having also written those principles on the patient's chart, one should first look in the chapter within this book corresponding to the first principle, *regardless of the disease diagnosis.*

Two patients may have a common cold. One patient has a fever, slight sweating, a severe sore throat, a stuffy nose, and a little dry cough. Their tongue is slightly red with white or slightly yellow fur, while their pulse is floating and rapid. Another patient also has a fever with slight sweating. They also have a sore throat and cough. However, they experience alternating fever and chills, they are fatigued, and they have no appetite. Their tongue is slightly red and the fur is yellow on one side while white on the other. In addition, their pulse is bowstring and rapid. In the first case, the pattern discrimination is a wind heat exterior pattern. In the second, it is a *shao yang* division condition. Therefore, the logical treatment principles (at least according to the logic of Chinese medicine) for treating the first case are to resolve the exterior and clear heat, while the treatment principles for the second case are to harmonize the constructive and defensive. This means that one must and will find their remedy for case #1 in the exterior-resolving chapter, subcategory: acrid, cool formulas which resolve the exterior and clear heat. The remedy for case #2 must and will be found in the harmonizing chapter under formulas which harmonize the constructive and defensive.

Treatment primarily based on pattern discrimination is the prescriptive methodology of professional Chinese medicine. It is a wonderfully wise prescriptive methodology because it takes into account the figure and the ground, the forest and the trees, the disease and the person who has the disease.

How to use this book

The arrangement and design of this book is based on the prescriptive methodology of professional Chinese medicine. To use this book, first do a pattern discrimination. Then state your treatment principles. Then begin your search for the right Chinese ready-made medicine in the chapter corresponding to the first stated set of treatment principles. When you think that you have found the right formula, check to make sure of two things: 1) that it is empirically known to treat your patient's major complaint or disease diagnosis, and 2) that it does not treat anything your patient does not have in the way of patterns. If the medicine in question addresses patterns and, therefore, disease mechanisms which your patient does not have, be very careful if you still choose to use that medicine.

No such thing as a medical panacea

Chinese medicine is about restoring harmony and balance. Taking an unwarranted Chinese medicinal is just as likely to cause unwanted side effects as taking any medicinal that is not right for that individual. If a medicine is strong enough to push a person back into balance when they are ill, it also must be strong enough to push a person out of balance if taken erroneously or unnecessarily. Remember, in the West, the legal arena in which we work, the first rule of medical ethics is, "First do no harm." It is better to treat only a part of a patient's pattern than to treat disease mechanisms a patient does not have. There is nothing inherently safe about Chinese medicinals.

Combining ready-made medicines

If a ready-made medicine only addresses a part of your patient's total pattern discrimination, then you may try to find another Chinese ready-made medicine based on the remaining treatment principles to combine with the first, deficient or incomplete medicine. For instance, your patient has constipation due to liver depression transforming heat, consuming blood and intestinal fluids. The treatment principles in this case are to course the liver and rectify the qi, clear heat and resolve depression, moisten dryness and free the flow of the stools. *Dan Zhi Xiao Yao Wan* (Moutan & Gardenia Rambling Pills) corresponds nicely to the first sets of principles but does not particularly moisten intestinal dryness and free the flow of the stools. Therefore, to make up this shortfall, one can combine *Dan Zhi Xiao Yao Wan* with either *Shou Wu Pian* (Polygonum Tablets) if constipation is not too severe or with *Ma Zi Ren Wan* (Cannabis Seed Pills) if the constipation is more severe.

Pattern discriminations & Chinese medicinal categories

As an aid to making this prescriptive methodology work, I have listed the main patterns for the main categories of Chinese medicinals. This should help readers get to the right chapter within this book.

For exterior patterns, look in the exterior-resolving chapter.
    For wind cold, look under acrid, warm exterior-resolving formulas.
    For wind heat, look under acrid, cool exterior-resolving formulas.

For interior repletion patterns with constipation or abdominal ascites, look in the draining and precipitating chapter.

For disharmonies of the constructive and defensive, liver and spleen, and stomach and intestines, look in the harmonizing chapter.

For heat patterns, look in the heat clearing chapter.
    For heat toxins, heat-clearing, toxin-resolving formulas.
    For liver heat, look under viscera & bowel heat-clearing formulas.

For interior cold patterns, look in the interior-warming chapter.

For dual exterior-interior conditions, look in the exterior-interior dual resolving chapter.

For qi stagnation patterns, look in the qi-rectifying chapter.

For blood stasis patterns, look in the blood-rectifying chapter, subcategory: quickening the blood and dispelling stasis.

For bleeding conditions, look in the blood-rectifying chapter, subcategory: stopping bleeding.

For damp patterns, look in the dampness-dispelling chapter.

For fluid dryness conditions, look in the moistening dryness chapter.

For phlegm patterns, look in the dispelling phlegm chapter.
    For phlegm cold, look under warming, phlegm-transforming formulas.
    For phlegm heat, look under clearing, phlegm-transforming formulas.

For coughing and panting, look in the qi-rectifying chapter, subcategory: qi-downbearing medicines.

For wind patterns, look in the wind-treating chapter.

For food stagnation, look in the food-dispersing, stagnation-abducting chapter.

For disquietude of the spirit, look in the spirit-quieting chapter.

For inhibited orifices, look in the orifice-opening chapter.

For vacuity patterns, look in the supplementing chapter.
    For qi vacuity, look under qi boosting and supplementing formulas.

For blood vacuity, look under blood nourishing and supplementing formulas.
For yin vacuity, look under yin enriching and supplementing formulas.
For yang vacuity, look under yang invigorating and supplementing formulas.

For lack of containing, restraining, astringing, and securing patterns, look in the astringing and securing chapter.

For parasites, look in the worm-dispelling chapter.

However, readers should be aware that there are not necessarily Chinese ready-made medicines covering all the same categories and indications as Chinese medicinal formulas in general. Not all problems are amenable to treatment with ready-made medicines. As the reader will see, there are far more Chinese ready-made supplementing medicines for chronic, enduring, or slow conditions than for acute, severe, rapidly progressing ones.

Dosages

Personally, I think the dosages listed on the packaging of the Chinese ready-made medicines described in this book tend to be on the low side. First of all, the average body weight of a Chinese person is probably less than the average body weight of a North American. Secondly, these dosages tend to be low in order to avoid unwanted effects when these medicines are taken inappropriately through self-medication by laypersons. If Chinese ready-made medicines have a relatively low capacity for iatrogenesis, it is not because of any inherent safety of Chinese medicinals themselves. Rather, these pills deliver relatively small doses of medicine compared to the much larger doses of medicinals currently the professional standard of care in the PRC when Chinese medicinals are administered in decoction.

For chronic conditions (which in Chinese also implies slow conditions) and for disease prevention, protracted administration of small, regular doses which are convenient to take is generally what is wanted. For acute conditions (in Chinese, read also rapid diseases), one may want a higher dose of medicine for more speedy remediation. In this case, depending on a combination of the patient's pattern, their disease, and the ingredients in the prescription, one may double, triple, or even quadruple the dosage suggested on the label. However, this should only be done based on professional judgement of all the factors involved. I am not making a blanket recommendation that all dosages on all labels should be adjusted upward. Rather, I am saying that the dosages on the labels are only standard dosages, and, in individual cases, one may have to adjust these either up *or* down.

Assessing treatment outcomes

The initial pattern discrimination is only a working hypothesis. Based on the signs and symptoms, this is what we think is going on and, therefore, this is what we think the patient should take. However, until the person takes the medicine, the initial diagnosis is only an educated supposition. By and large, Chinese medicine works by restoring balance to the organism and does not provoke healing crises. If a Chinese ready-made medicine is the correct one, it should result in improvement in all the patient's unwanted complaints without creating any side effects.

In Chinese medicine, every part of the body and every function is connected with every other part and every other function. The bodymind is a single, integrated organic whole. Side effects are symptoms that something is not right in the body. True health cannot be established by making one part of the body feel better at the expense of another. This is the same as robbing Peter to pay Paul. Therefore, when using Chinese medicinals, all one's signs and symptoms should move towards more healthy norms.

In particular, I tell my patients that they themselves can know whether a medicine or a treatment is really good for them. There are six areas of well-being that are good barometers of health. If any medicine negatively effects any of these six, then that medicine, be it Western or Chinese, is not entirely good for you. These six barometers of well-being are:

Mood
Energy
Sleep

Appetite
Digestion
Elimination

If our mood is good (*i.e.*, positive and stable), we have abundant energy, our sleep is sound and restful, we have a good appetite, our digestion is good, and our elimination is satisfying and regular, then we are basically in good health. If any of these six parameters is out of balance, then we cannot say that we are really healthy. Therefore, if we take any medication and all six of these parameters improve, it must be good for us; while if we take a medicine and one or more of these six are harmed, then that medicine is not unequivocally good for us. At best it is doing us some good at the same time as it is doing us some harm.

If you are a layperson or a student who is reading and trying to make use of this book and you have taken a medicine described herein, and if any of these six barometers of good health has been worsened after taking that medicine, I strongly advise that you stop that medication immediately and seek a consultation with a professional practitioner of Chinese herbal medicine.

3
Exterior-resolving Medicines

Generally speaking, exterior-resolving medicines include medicinals which can relieve or resolve exterior patterns. Typically, they expel external evils by promoting mild sweating. This diaphoresis out-thrusts and expels the pathogens. In addition, they resolve the muscles and promote the eruption of rashes or pox. They may also be used for the treatment of sores in the exterior and recent onset edema if either are accompanied by aversion to cold, fever, and other exterior pattern signs and symptoms. Exterior patterns are due to external invasion of the six environmental excesses. These include wind, cold, summerheat, dampness, dryness, and fire. The distinguishing characteristics of an exterior pattern are aversion to cold and wind, fever, headache, muscular aches and pains, and a floating pulse.

There are two main types of exterior patterns: hot and cold. Because the causative factors and the body's reaction to disease is different, these two types of exterior patterns require treatment with different medicinals. In exterior cold patterns, aversion to cold is pronounced, there is slight fever, no particular thirst, either no sore throat or just a tickle in the throat, a clear nasal discharge, a floating, tight pulse, and a thin, white tongue coating. In an exterior heat pattern, there is less aversion to cold and wind, more extreme fever, definite thirst, definite sore throat, yellow, sticky nasal mucus, a floating, rapid pulse, and a red tongue tip with a yellow coating. Based on these two main types of exterior patterns, exterior-resolving medicines are divided into two main subcategories: 1) acrid, warm, exterior-resolving formulas and 2) acrid, cool, exterior-resolving formulas. However, a third subcategory also exists, called formulas for exterior conditions with interior vacuity.

Cautions in using exterior-resolving medicines:

The right degree of perspiration induced by exterior-resolving medicinals is a mild perspiration over the entire body. If perspiration is too much, righteous qi will be damaged. This is especially so in children and the aged. Excessive perspiration will also damage fluids and humors.

Patients may exhibit both exterior and interior patterns. In such cases, first relieve the exterior and then treat the interior. However, if both exterior and interior are affected to the same degree, treat both simultaneously.

The five contraindications of exterior-resolving medicines:

1. Do not resolve the exterior once exterior patterns have transmuted into interior patterns.
2. Do not resolve the exterior once pox and rashes have erupted.
3. Do not resolve the exterior once sores have ulcerated.
4. Do not resolve the exterior for the treatment of edema due to vacuity.
5. Do not resolve the exterior if there is dehydration due to vomiting and diarrhea.

Acrid, warm, exterior-resolving medicines

Ge Gen Wan (Pueraria Pills)

Radix Puerariae (*Ge Gen*)
Radix Ephedrae (*Ma Huang*)
Ramulus Cinnamomi Cassiae (*Gui Zhi*)
Radix Albus Paeoniae Lactiflorae (*Bai Shao*)
uncooked Rhizoma Zingiberis (*Sheng Jiang*)
Radix Glycyrrhizae (*Gan Cao*)
Fructus Zizyphi Jujubae (*Da Zao*)

Functions: Dispels wind and resolves the exterior, resolves the muscles and engenders fluids

Indications: Stiffness and pain in the upper back, shoulders, nape of the neck, and occipital regions

Main signs & symptoms: Aversion to cold and effusion of heat, no sweating, neck and upper back stiffness and rigidity, thin, white tongue fur, and a floating, tight pulse

Dosage: 8 pills three times per day

Formula explanation: The sovereign medicinal in this formula, Pueraria, resolves the exterior and particularly the muscles of the upper back and neck. This is because this medicinal enters the *tai yang* channel. Ephedra and Cinnamon Twigs are the ministerial medicinals which resolve the exterior and scatter cold. Peony is an assistant medicinal which astringes yin and thus prevents the strong exterior-resolves from damaging the qi and fluids. Together with Cinnamon Twigs, it harmonizes the constructive and defensive. This harmonization of the constructive and defensive is further carried out by the other assistant medicinals, Ginger and Red Dates. In addition, they harmonize the stomach. Licorice is the messenger medicinal which harmonizes all the other ingredients. Together with Peony, Licorice also relaxes tension (*i.e.*, cramping) and is, therefore, useful in the treatment of upper back and neck stiffness and pain.

Comments: Some Chinese doctors use this basic formula to treat a wide variety of patterns and conditions. This is because it does supplement the spleen and, therefore, the qi and blood at the same time as it strongly upbears and effuses the qi. Upbearing and effusing can clear internal heat and upbearing and effusing can also disinhibit the qi mechanism, thus relieving depression. Therefore, when used skillfully, this formula can treat more than simple wind cold exterior patterns which are not that commonly met in Western patients. However, when used as a ready-made pill without modifying additions and subtractions, this formula's scope of use is not as great as when prescribed as an individually tailored, bulk-dispensed decoction.

Xiao Qing Long Wan (Minor Blue Dragon Pills)

Radix Ephedrae (*Ma Huang*)
Radix Albus Paeoniae Lactiflorae (*Bai Shao*)
Herba Asari Cum Radice (*Xi Xin*)
Ramulus Cinnamomi Cassiae (*Gui Zhi*)
Rhizoma Pinelliae Ternatae (*Ban Xia*)
Radix Glycyrrhizae (*Gan Cao*)
dry Rhizoma Zingiberis (*Gan Jiang*)
Fructus Schisandrae Chinensis (*Wu Wei Zi*)

Functions: Resolves the exterior and washes away rheum, stops cough and levels panting

Indications: Wind cold lodged in the exterior, water rheum collecting internally

Main signs & symptoms: Aversion to cold and emission of heat, no sweating, panting and coughing, profuse, thin phlegm, possible phlegm rheum coughing and panting, inability to lie down flat, possible generalized bodily aching and heaviness, puffy swelling of the face and four limbs, glossy, white tongue fur, and a floating pulse

Dosage: 8 pills three times per day

Formula explanation: In this formula, Ephedra and Cinnamon Twigs are the sovereign ingredients. They effuse the sweat and resolve the exterior, eliminating external cold and diffusing the lung qi. Dry Ginger and Asarum are the ministerial medicinals. They warm the lungs and transform rheum while simultaneously assisting Ephedra and Cinnamon Twigs in resolving the exterior. Schisandra and Peony are the assistant medicinals. Schisandra constrains the qi, while Peony nourishes the blood. Thus they prevent consumption and damage of the lung qi and drying and damage of the fluids and humors by the acrid, warm, scattering, and effusing main medicinals. Pinellia dispels phlegm, harmonizes the stomach, and scatters nodulation. It is also an assistant medicinal. Mix-fried Licorice boosts the qi and harmonizes the stomach. It is also able to regulate and harmonize the acrid and scattering with the sour and astringing. It is simultaneously an assistant and messenger medicinal. When these eight flavors are combined together, they promote the resolution of wind and cold, the dispelling of water and rheum, and the soothing of the lung qi. Diffusion and downbearing are restored to their duty and all the symptoms are automatically leveled or calmed.

Comments: This formula is especially good for treating acute episodes of cold asthma and cold-natured allergic rhinitis attacks in those whose constitutions are not very robust, such as children, and who have habitual, deep-lying phlegm rheum in their lungs. Because Schisandra and Peony restrain the draining and scattering effects of Ephedra, this formula is usually quite safe to use. During remission stages of asthma or before the seasonal occurrence of airborne allergies, one should use other formulas which primarily supplement the lungs, spleen, and/or kidneys and transform phlegm and eliminate dampness. This formula is not appropriate for long-term administration or during remission due to the presence of Ephedra.

Xin Yi Wan (Magnolia Flower Pills)

Flos Magnoliae Liliflorae (*Xin Yi Hua*)
Rhizoma Atractylodis (*Cang Zhu*)
Radix Ledebouriellae Divaricatae (*Fang Feng*)
Herba Asari Cum Radice (*Xi Xin*)
Radix Et Rhizoma Notopterygii (*Qiang Huo*)
Radix Et Rhizoma Ligustici Chinensis (*Gao Ben*)
Rhizoma Cimicifugae (*Sheng Ma*)
Caulis Akebiae (*Mu Tong*)
Radix Ligustici Wallichii (*Chuan Xiong*)
Radix Glycyrrhizae (*Gan Cao*)

Functions: Dispels wind and scatters cold, eliminates dampness and disinhibits the orifices of the nose

Indications: Wind cold exterior pattern runny nose and stuffy nose. Allergic rhinitis, common cold

Main signs & symptoms: Acute or recent onset of sneezing, runny nose, nasal congestion, profuse phlegm which is clear and white in color, white tongue fur, and a floating, bowstring pulse

Contraindications: Do not use this medicine if the nasal mucus is yellow or green due to wind heat, phlegm heat, or upward counterflow of depressive heat.

Dosage: 8 pills three times per day

Formula explanation: Magnolia Flowers are the sovereign medicinal in this formula. They dispel wind, scatter cold, and disinhibit the orifices of the nose. Ledebouriella, Notopterygium, Ligusticum Chinensis, Asarum, and Cimicifuga are all the minister medicinals which also dispel wind and resolves the exterior. Asarum also warms cold and transforms phlegm as well as strongly disinhibits the orifices of the nose. Atractylodes and Akebia are the assistant medicinals. The former aromatically dries dampness, while the latter percolates[1] dampness. Licorice and Ligusticum Wallichium are the messenger medicinals. Licorice harmonizes and regulates all the other medicinals in the formula. Ligusticum Wallichium leads the action of the other medicinals upward to the head and face region.

Comments: This is a very good Chinese ready-made medicine for treating the symptoms of stuffy nose and runny nose when these are characterized as a wind cold pattern. This medicine can be used alone, or it can be combined with other Chinese ready-made medicines when nasal congestion and runny nose are important symptoms in a more complex pattern. Since most allergic rhinitis displays a wind cold pattern, at least in its acute stage, this medicine is a very good one for hayfever and animal dander allergies, whereas *Xiao Qing Long Wan* (Minor Blue Dragon Pills) discussed above are better for allergic asthma due to their inclusion of the lung diffuser and counterflow downbearer Ephedra. This medicine should not be used during the remission stages of allergic rhinitis when the treatment principles should be to supplement the lung and spleen and transform deep-lying phlegm.

Acrid, cool, exterior-resolving medicines

Sang Ju Yin Wan (Morus & Chrysanthemum Drink Pills)

Folium Mori Albi (*Sang Ye*)
Flos Chrysanthemi Morifolii (*Ju Hua*)
Semen Pruni Armeniacae (*Xing Ren*)
Fructus Forsythiae Suspensae (*Lian Qiao*)
Herba Menthae Haplocalycis (*Bo He*)
Radix Platycodi Grandiflori (*Jie Geng*)
Radix Glycyrrhizae (*Gan Cao*)

---

[1] Previously, Wiseman had translated *shen* as seep. Now he suggests percolate.

Rhizoma Phragmitis Communis (*Lu Gen*)

Functions: To course wind and clear heat, diffuse the lungs and stop cough

Indications: Wind heat, initial stage. Common cold, flus, acute bronchitis, acute tonsillitis, epidemic conjunctivitis, headache, vertigo, acute tracheitis.

Main signs & symptoms: Cough, fever, a red, sore throat, slight fever, a thin, white or slightly yellow tongue coating with a red tongue proper, and a floating, rapid pulse

Dosage: 8 pills three times per day

Formula explanation: In this formula, Folium Mori and Chrysanthemum are the sovereign medicinals. Morus penetrates and clears heat from the network vessels of the lungs. Chrysanthemum clears and scatters wind heat in the upper burner. Mint, acrid and cool, is the minister medicinal. It assists Morus and Chrysanthemum scatter upper burner wind heat. Among Platycodon and Armeniaca, one upbears and one downbears, thus resolving the muscles, depurating the lungs, and, therefore, stopping cough. Forsythia clears heat above the diaphragm. Phragmites clears heat, engenders fluids, and stops thirst. These two are the assistant medicinals. Licorice regulates and harmonizes these medicinals and is the messenger medicinal. The combination of Licorice and Platycodon is called *Gan Cao Jie Geng Tang* (Licorice & Platycodon Decoction). This is especially for patients with cough and phlegm which is difficult to expectorate accompanied by a slight tickling sensation in the throat. Combined, these medicinals have the function of coursing wind and clearing heat, diffusing the lungs and stopping cough.

Comments: If fever is high and cough is severe, as in pneumonia, this formula may not be strong enough. In that case, one should definitely see a professional practitioner of Chinese herbal medicine to receive an individually written prescription for bulk-dispensed, decocted Chinese medicinals.

Yin Qiao Jie Du Wan (Lonicera & Forsythia Resolve Toxins Pills)

Fructus Forsythiae Suspensae (*Lian Qiao*)
Flos Lonicerae Japonicae (*Yin Hua*)
Radix Platycodi Grandiflori (*Jie Geng*)
Herba Menthae Haplocalycis (*Bo He*)
uncooked Radix Glycyrrhizae (*Gan Cao*)
Herba Seu Flos Schizonepetae Tenuifoliae (*Jing Jie Sui*)
Semen Praeparatus Sojae (*Dan Dou Chi*)
Fructus Arctii Lappae (*Niu Bang Zi*)
Herba Lophatheri Gracilis (*Dan Zhu Ye*)

Functions: Acridly and cooly penetrates the exterior, clears heat and resolves toxins

Indications: Warm disease, initial stage. Common cold, flus, acute tonsillitis, mumps, measles, scarlatina, epidemic meningitis, encephalitis B, acute suppurative infections, and early stage sores.

Main signs & symptoms: Fever, no sweating or possible perspiration which does not flow easily, slight aversion to wind cold, headache, thirst, cough, sore throat, a red tongue tip and a thin, white or thin, yellow coating, and a floating, rapid pulse

Dosage: 8 pills three times per day

Formula explanation: The medicinals in this formula can be divided into three groups. First, Schizonepeta, Soja, and Mint emit perspiration, relieve the exterior, and resolve the muscles. Secondly, Lonicera, Forsythia, and Lophatherum clear heat and resolve toxins. Thirdly, Arctium, Platycodon, and Licorice stop cough, expel phlegm, and secure yin. In this formula, Lonicera and Forsythia are the sovereigns, which, being acrid and cool, penetrate evils, clear heat, and resolve toxins. Schizonepeta and Soja are the ministers. Although they are acrid and warm, they assist the sovereign medicinals in opening the skin and hair and dispelling evils. Platycodon and Arctium diffuse the lungs and disinhibit the throat. Licorice clears heat and resolves toxins. Lophatherum clears heat from the upper burner. These are the assistant medicinals.

Comments: This formula is similar in many ways to the preceding one. The key to distinguishing these is that *Yin Qiao San* is for exterior wind heat with fever and sore throat, while *Sang Ju Yin* is for exterior wind heat with less fever and toxins but more serious cough.

Bi Tong Wan (Nose-freeing Pills)

Herba Centipedae (*Ou Bu Shi Cao*)
Flos Magnoliae Liliflorae (*Xin Yi Hua*)
Fructus Xanthii Sibirici (*Cang Er Zi*)
Radix Angelicae Dahuricae (*Bai Zhi*)
Radix Scutellariae Baicalensis (*Huang Qin*)
Herba Menthae Haplocalycis (*Bo He*)
Herba Ephedrae (*Ma Huang*)

Functions: Clears heat, resolves the exterior, and disinhibits the orifices of the nose

Indications: Wind heat exterior pattern nasal congestion and runny nose. Acute and chronic nasosinusitis, common cold

Main signs & symptoms: Nasal congestion, possible runny nose, yellow-colored phlegm, possible fever, headache, possible cough, yellow tongue fur, and a floating, bowstring, rapid pulse

Contraindications: Do not use this medicine if the nasal mucus is clear and white.

Dosage: 5 pills two times per day

Formula explanation: Ephedra is an acrid, warm exterior-resolving medicinal which strongly diffuses the lungs and frees the flow of the lung orifices, *i.e.*, the nose. It is assisted by Xanthium and Magnolia Flowers which are also exterior resolvers which specifically free the flow of the nose. Angelica Dahurica and Mentha are likewise exterior-resolvers. Angelica Dahurica is acrid and warm but is used for the treatment of damp hot nasal obstruction and discharge. Mentha is acrid and cool. It frees the flow of the nose at the same time as it clears depressive heat from the liver and stomach. Centipeda is an acrid, warm, phlegm-transformer and cough-stopper. It has a strong empirical function of freeing the flow of the nose. Scutellaria is bitter and cold and clears heat from the lungs, stomach, and liver. It is because of the inclusion of Scutellaria and Mentha that this formula is indicated for wind heat and damp heat obstructions of the nose and nasal discharge.

Comments: This medicine can be used alone or combined with other Chinese ready-made medicines. It primarily treats nasal congestion and runny nose due to wind evils with heat. However, it can also be used symptomatically and in combination to treat wind heat with simultaneous internal heat, phlegm heat, and a combination of repletion and vacuity patterns. For instance, if there is liver depression/depressive heat counterflowing upward to congest in the lungs complicated by spleen vacuity and dampness, thus resulting in phlegm heat deep source nasal congestion, this medicine can be combined with *Xiao Chai Hu Tang Wan* (Minor Bupleurum Decoction Pills) or *Jia Wei Xiao Yao Wan* (Added Flavors Rambling Pills).

Bi Min Gan Wan (Nasal Allergy Pills)

Flos Magnoliae Liliflorae (*Xin Yi Hua*)
Fructus Xanthii Sibirici (*Can Er Zi*)
Herba Agastachis Seu Pogostemi (*Huo Xiang*)
Herba Menthae Haplocalycis (*Bo He*)
Radix Angelicae Dahuricae (*Bai Zhi*)
Flos Lonicerae Japonicae (*Jin Yin Hua*)
Flos Chrysanthemi Morifolii (*Ju Hua*)

Functions: Dispels wind and clears heat, frees the flow of the nose

Indications: Wind heat or gallbladder damp heat nasal congestion. Infectious and allergic sinusitis

Main signs & symptoms: Profuse, thick, yellow and/or green nasal mucus, possible headache or head distention

Contraindications: Do not use for wind cold rhinitis.

Dosage: 2-3 pills three times per day

Formula explanation: Flos Magnoliae and Xanthium are the ruling medicinals in this formula and are one of Chinese medicine's most famous medicinal pairs for opening or freeing the flow of the nose. They are aided in this by the windy, aromatic medicinals Agastaches and Mentha which also free the flow of the nose. In addition, Mentha clears and dispels wind heat as well as clears depressive heat from the liver. Angelica Dahurica is acrid and warm but is excellent for damp, hot nasal mucus since it expels pus. In addition, it disperses swelling, stops pain, and opens the orifices of the nose. Lonicera clears heat and resolves toxins, while Chrysanthemum clears heat from the liver and the region of the eyes and head. Sinusitis is commonly a combination of wind heat evils and depressive heat in the liver and gallbladder channels.

Comments: This popular pill can be combined with numerous other Chinese ready-made medicines when there is wind heat and/or damp heat nasal obstruction and nasal discharge. Although this pill's name says it's for allergic rhinitis, most patients with allergic rhinitis exhibit a wind cold pattern, not a wind heat or damp heat pattern. Therefore, this formula should only be used when wind cold transforms and becomes a heat pattern.

Cang Er Zi Wan (Xanthium Pills)

Fructus Xanthii Sibirici (*Cang Er Zi*)
Radix Angelicae Dahuricae (*Bai Zhi*)
Flos Magnoliae Liliflorae (*Xin Yi Hua*)
Herba Menthae Haplocalycis (*Bo He*)

Functions: Dispels wind, stops pain, and frees the flow of the nose

Indications: Wind heat or wind cold pattern nasal obstruction. Acute and chronic rhinitis and sinusitis

Main signs & symptoms: Copious nasal mucus, nasal obstruction, dizziness, frontal headache, normal or yellow tongue fur, and a floating pulse

Dosage: 8 pills three times per day

Formula explanation: Xanthium and Flos Magnoliae are the ruling medicinals in this formula and have a strong empirical function of freeing the flow of the orifices of the nose. Magnolia is acrid and warm and Xanthium is bitter and warm. These two form the most commonly used combination for treating stuffed nose and profuse nasal mucus due to wind. The ministers in this formula are Angelica Dahurica and Mentha. Both of these medicinals also free the flow of the nasal orifices. Mentha is acrid and cool and specifically treats wind heat, while Angelica Dahurica is acrid and warm. However, even though Angelica Dahurica is acrid and warm, it is empirically very effective for a number of damp heat conditions.

Comments: Because it combines both warm and cool medicinals, this formula can be used for both cold and heat types of phlegm blocking and obstructing the nasal orifices. Therefore, these pills can be combined with a wide variety of other Chinese ready-made medicines whenever one wants symptomatically to increase the effect of freeing the flow of the orifices of the nose. Compared to the previous medicine, these pills do not clear heat as strongly, and thus have a wider range of application. If one is sure there is heat in the patient's pattern due to the presence of yellow-green mucus, I recommend using the preceding medicine instead.

Chai Ge Jie Ji Tang (Bupleurum & Pueraria Resolve the Muscles Decoction)

Radix Bupleuri (*Chai Hu*)
Radix Puerariae (*Ge Gen*)
Radix Glycyrrhizae (*Gan Cao*)
Radix Scutellariae Baicalensis (*Huang Qin*)
Radix Et Rhizoma Notopterygii (*Qiang Huo*)
Radix Angelicae Dahuricae (*Bai Zhi*)
Radix Albus Paeoniae Lactiflorae (*Bai Shao*)
Radix Platycodi Grandiflori (*Jie Geng*)

Functions: Resolves the muscles and clears heat

Indications: Common cold wind cold, depression transforming heat

Main signs & symptoms: Aversion to cold which gradually lessens, bodily heat which steadily increases, no sweating, headache, eye aching, dry nose, heart vexation and insomnia, a floating, slightly surging pulse

Dosage: 5 pills three times per day

Formula explanation: Within this formula, Bupleurum and Pueraria are the sovereign medicinals which resolve the muscles and clear heat. Notopterygium and Angelica Dahurica assist Bupleurum and Pueraria to resolve the muscular exterior, thus altogether eliminating pain. Scutellaria clears evils which have become depressed and transformed into heat. Platycodon diffuses the lung qi in order to assist the coursing and discharging of evils externally. Peony and Licorice together harmonize the constructive and discharge heat. These are all assistant medicinals.

Comments: This formula is especially good for treating muscular stiffness and pain in the back of the neck and occipital region with headache and eye pain due to cold evils lodged in the exterior which are in the process of undergoing transformation into heat. Therefore, aversion to cold is getting less and less, and fever is getting more and more. This formula might also be used for liver depression headache when combined with another appropriate formula, such as *Xiao Chai Hu Tang Wan* (Minor Bupleurum Decoction Pills) or *Xiao Yao Wan* (Rambling Pills). However, it should not be used for ascendant hyperactivity of liver yang headache nor for liver blood vacuity headache.

Medicines for exterior conditions with interior vacuity

Ren Shen Bai Du Wan (Ginseng Vanquish Toxins Pills)

Radix Et Rhizoma Notopterygii (*Qiang Huo*)
Radix Angelicae Pubescentis (*Du Huo*)
Radix Ligustici Wallichii (*Chuan Xiong*)
Radix Bupleuri (*Chai Hu*)
Radix Peucedani (*Qian Hu*)
Sclerotium Poriae Cocos (*Fu Ling*)
Fructus Citri Aurantii (*Zhi Ke*)
Radix Platycodi Grandiflori (*Jie Geng*)
Herba Menthae Haplocalycis (*Bo He*)
Radix Panacis Ginseng (*Ren Shen*)
Radix Glycyrrhizae (*Gan Cao*)
uncooked Rhizoma Zingiberis (*Sheng Jiang*)

Functions: Resolves the exterior, dispels wind and eliminates dampness, and supplements the qi

Indications: Externally contracted wind cold dampness with simultaneous righteous qi vacuity which is unable to expel the disease evils. Upper respiratory tract infections, influenza, initial stage dysentery, initial stage measles, and post-surgical infections

Main signs & symptoms: High fever, severe chills, shivering, no sweating, pain and stiffness of the head and neck, pain and soreness of the four limbs, chest and venter fullness and glomus, nasal congestion, cough with profuse phlegm, slimy, white tongue fur, and a soggy pulse

Contraindications: This formula is contraindicated if there is any heat.

Dosage: 8 pills three times per day

Formula explanation: Notopterygium and Angelica Pubescens dispel wind cold from the exterior, dispel dampness and stop pain. Ligusticum upbears and out-thrusts yang qi and moves the blood, thus assisting the previous two medicinals in out-thrusting evils at the same time as guiding the other medicinals upwards to the head and face region and moving the blood to stop pain. Bupleurum and Mentha likewise resolve the exterior and out-thrust evils. In particular, this combination is especially effective for resolving evils from the muscles. Platycodon upbears while Aurantium downbears, thus regulating and rectifying the qi in the chest and epigastrium. In addition, the combination of Platycodon and Peucedanum transforms phlegm, diffuses the lungs, and stops coughing. Poria and uncooked Ginger transform and eliminate dampness, thus eliminating the root of phlegm engenderment. Further, Ginseng, Poria, and Licorice fortify the spleen and supplement the qi. Thus the righteous qi is supplemented and restored so that it can expel evils from the exterior.

Comments: This formula was originally designed to expel wind cold damp evils from children who are, by nature, inherently spleen qi vacuous and weak. Now, however, it can be used to treat wind cold damp external invasions in anyone with a vacuous and weak bodily condition.

Jing Fang Bai Du Wan (Schizonepeta & Ledebouriella Vanquish Toxins Pills)

Herba Seu Flos Schizonepetae Tenuifoliae (*Jing Jie*)
Radix Ledebouriellae Divaricatae (*Fang Feng*)
Radix Bupleuri (*Chai Hu*)
Radix Peucedani (*Qian Hu*)
Radix Ligustici Wallichii (*Chuan Xiong*)
Radix Et Rhizoma Notopterygii (*Qiang Huo*)
Radix Angelicae Pubescentis (*Du Huo*)
Sclerotium Poriae Cocos (*Fu Ling*)
Radix Platycodi Grandiflori (*Jie Geng*)
Fructus Citri Aurantii (*Zhi Ke*)
Radix Glycyrrhizae (*Gan Cao*)

uncooked Rhizoma Zingiberis (*Sheng Jiang*)

Functions: Resolves the exterior, dispels wind, stops pain and only mildly supplements the spleen

Indications: Externally contracted wind cold damp conditions with minor qi vacuity. Redness and swelling of the eyes, epidemic parotitis, the initial stages of abscesses and sores

Main signs & symptoms: Emission of heat and aversion to wind, pain and stiffness of the head and neck, generalized body pain, possible cough with profuse, white phlegm, a fat, enlarged tongue with possible teeth marks on its edges and thin, white tongue fur, and a floating pulse

Dosage: 8 pills three times per day

Formula explanation: This formula is very similar in ingredients and rationale to the one above. Schizonepeta has been added to more forcefully resolve the exterior and dispel wind cold evils, while Ginseng has been removed since the qi vacuity is not so pronounced. Therefore, some authors might place this formula under acrid, warm exterior-resolving prescriptions.

4
Draining & Precipitating Medicines

Draining and precipitating medicines are used to treat interior repletion patterns when turbid qi is unable to descend due to internal accumulation of evil qi. In this case, typically there will be epigastric and/or lower abdominal distention, loss of appetite, constipation, and abdominal pain aggravated by pressure. Precipitating medicinals free the flow of and conduct the large intestine and eliminate accumulations and stagnation from the stomach and intestines. These can consist of replete heat, water rheum, or accumulation of cold. Thus there are three subcategories of draining and precipitating formulas which purge replete evils through the bowels. These are 1) cold precipitating formulas, 2) warm precipitating formulas, and 3) water-dispelling precipitating formulas. Cold precipitating formulas use cold-natured medicinals to drain and precipitate replete heat. Warm precipitating formulas use warm medicinals combined with draining and precipitating medicinals. They are for the treatment of cold binding interior repletion patterns causing constipation and abdominal fullness and distention. Water-dispelling precipitating formulas use harsh cathartics to drain, via the bowels and urination, water rheum gathering and accumulating in the interior causing repletion patterns.

However, all three of these types of conditions are relatively serious conditions which typically require professional diagnosis and the prescription of individually modified, bulk-dispensed, decocted formulas. Therefore, there are only two Chinese ready-made medicines available from the suppliers included in this which are representative of these classes of Chinese medicinal formulas. In addition, these strongly attacking and precipitating formulas easily consume and damage the righteous qi. Because lay people do not have the specialized knowledge and experience to use such formulas safely, they are also not typically made into ready-made medicines.

That being said, under this category of draining and precipitating formulas, there is the subcategory of moistening precipitating formulas for the treatment of fluid dryness constipation. This type of constipation tends to be chronic and enduring and is due more to vacuity than repletion. Therefore, there are several formulas from this subcategory of draining and precipitating formulas which are available as ready-made medicines.

Cautions & Contraindications When Using Draining & Precipitating Medicines

1. Do not drain and precipitate when exterior patterns have not yet been relieved nor when interior symptoms are not serious.
2. Do not drain and precipitate pregnant women nor postpartum except with great care.
3. Do not drain during prolonged illness with bodily weakness nor in the elderly except with great care.
4. When the evil is eliminated, draining and precipitation must stop. Do not overdose.

Cold precipitating medicines

Liang Ge Wan (Cool the Diaphragm Pills)

Herba Lophatheri Gracilis (*Dan Zhu Ye*)
Fructus Forsythiae Suspensae (*Lian Qiao*)
Radix Et Rhizoma Rhei (*Da Huang*)
Mirabilitum (*Mang Xiao*)
Radix Glycyrrhizae (*Gan Cao*)
Fructus Gardeniae Jasminoidis (*Shan Zhi Zi*)
Radix Scutellariae Baicalensis (*Huang Qin*)
Herba Menthae Haplocalycis (*Bo He*)

Functions: Drains fire and frees the flow of the stools, clears the upper burner and drains the middle burner

Indications: Accumulated heat in the middle burner or blazing heat in the upper burner. Upper respiratory tract infections, tonsillitis, meningitis, encephalitis B, hypertension, cholecystitis, cholelithiasis, welling abscesses, acute conjunctivitis, pediatric pneumonia, various gynecological diseases, and dark, macular rashes and poxes

Main signs & symptoms: Vexatious heat in the chest, irritability, delirious speech, oral thirst, a flushed red facial complexion, red lips, mouth and tongue sores, a swollen tongue, red eyes, spontaneous ejection of blood, *i.e.,* epistaxis, constipation, dark, scanty urination, a red tongue or tongue edges with dry, yellow or white fur, and a rapid, possibly slippery pulse

Contraindications: Use cautiously during pregnancy or in patients with bodily vacuity since it easily damages the spleen and stomach. As soon as the bowels are freely flowing, its use should be suspended.

Dosage: 8 pills three times per day

Formula explanation: Rhubarb and Mirabilitum drain and precipitate heat accumulated in the *yang ming* as well as free the flow of the stools. Lophatherum clears heat from the lungs and heart, while Scutellaria clears heat from the lungs, stomach, and liver. Gardenia clears heat from all three burners and disinhibits urination. Forsythia clears heat and resolves toxins, while Mentha out-thrusts heat from the upper burner and alleviates symptoms in the head and throat. Licorice harmonizes all the other medicinals in the formula and also relaxes the cramps that may be caused by harsh precipitating medicinals.

Comments: This formula is typically used alone and is not combined with other formulas.

Da Huang Mu Dan Pi Tang (Rhubarb & Moutan Decoction)

Radix Et Rhizoma Rhei (*Da Huang*)
Mirabilitum (*Mang Xiao*)
Cortex Radicis Moutan (*Dan Pi*)
Semen Pruni Persicae (*Tao Ren*)
Semen Benincasae Hispidae (*Dong Gua Ren*)

Functions: Clears heat and drains downward, quickens the blood and disperses swelling

Indications: The initial stage of intestinal abscesses

Main signs & symptoms: Right-sided lower abdominal aching and pain which refuses pressure, flexure of right leg (*i.e.*, hip) without wanting to extend it, effusion of heat, and a slippery, rapid pulse

Dosage: 4 tablets three times per day

Formula explanation: Rhubarb and Moutan are the sovereign medicinals in the formula. Rhubarb not only clears heat and frees the flow of the stools but also quickens the blood and dispels stasis. Moutan also quickens the blood and dispels stasis. However, it also cools the blood. Together, these two medicinals combine acrid and bitter flavors to free the flow, downbear, precipitate, and move, thus draining stasis and heat. Mirabilitum softens the hard and scatters nodulations. It assists Rhubarb's draining and precipitating function. Persica's nature tends to break the blood. It assists Moutan's quickening of the blood. Benincasa scatters nodulations and disperses welling abscesses which have not yet produced pus. It is also able to expel pus once it has formed. When all these medicinals are used together, stasis and heat are cleared and discharged. Thus pain is automatically diminished and swelling is dispersed. Hence the condition is automatically cured.

Comments: This formula is traditionally for the initial stage of appendicitis. Although it is not a bad idea to try this formula (along with emergency acupuncture) at the first sign of any right-sided pain, fever, and rebound or pressure pain over McBurney's point, if this does not quickly relieve the pain and other symptoms, one should see a professional practitioner without delay. Chinese medicine does treat appendicitis quite well. I have prevented a number of patients from having to have surgery. However, I typically use decocted medicinals in high doses accompanied by two or more acupuncture treatments per day, each of which may last for up to one hour.

This formula can also be used to treat endometriosis with abdominal pain and other signs of stasis and heat as long as the heat is replete heat. The patient should have constipation, and there may be hemafecia.

Da Huang Jiang Zhi Wan (Rhubarb Reduce Fat Pills)

Radix Et Rhizoma Rhei (*Da Huang*)

Functions: Clears heat, precipitates and discharges, frees the flow of the stools

Indications: Internal heat binding constipation

Main signs & symptoms: Dry, bound stools, a red tongue with thick, yellow fur

Dosage: 3 pills three times per day

Formula explanation: Rhubarb, the single ingredient in these pills, drains heat and precipitates accumulations.

Comments: The Chinese name of this medicine says that it reduces fat. This means that this pill can be used for loss of weight. However, purging the bowels is a very dangerous way of losing weight unless the person truly does display a replete internal heat pattern. Nevertheless, these pills can be used in combination with other appropriate Chinese ready-made medicines whenever there are dry, bound, constipated stools due to internal heat complicating other patterns. For instance, if there is liver depression/depressive heat and constipation, these pills can be combined with *Jia Wei Xiao Yao Wan* (Added Flavors Rambling Pills).

Moistening & precipitating medicines

Ma Zi Ren Wan (Cannabis Seed Pills)

Semen Cannabis Sativae (*Huo Ma Ren*)
Radix Albus Paeoniae Lactiflorae (*Shao Yao*)
Fructus Immaturus Citri Aurantii (*Zhi Shi*)
Radix Et Rhizoma Rhei (*Da Huang*)
Cortex Magnoliae Officinalis (*Hou Po*)
Semen Pruni Armeniacae (*Xing Ren*)
Mel (*Feng Mi*)

Functions: Moistens the intestines and discharges heat, moves the qi and frees the flow of the stools

Indications: Stomach and intestinal dry heat, fluid and humor insufficiency. Constipation in those who are either aged or bodily weak and vacuous, postpartum or post-surgical constipation, habitual constipation, chronic colitis, or hemorrhoids.

Main signs & symptoms: Dry, bound stools, short, frequent urination, dry, yellow tongue fur, and a floating, rapid pulse

Contraindications: 1. Do not use during pregnancy unless warranted by the pattern discrimination.

Dosage: 8 pills three times per day

Formula explanation: Cannabis Seeds are the sovereign medicinal in this formula. They moisten the intestines and open the bowels. Rhubarb opens the bowels and discharges heat. Armeniaca downbears the qi and moistens the intestines. White Peony nourishes yin and harmonizes the interior. These are the minister medicinals. Aurantium Immaturus and Magnolia precipitate the qi and break binding. Additionally, they have a strong power to downbear, discharge, and free the flow of the stools. Honey is able to moisten dryness and lubricate the intestines. These are the assistant medicinals.

Comments: Once constipation has been relieved, the use of these pills should be stopped since it is not good to take Rhubarb habitually.

Tao Ren Wan (Persica Pills)

Semen Pruni Persicae (*Tao Ren*)
Semen Cannabis Sativae (*Huo Ma Ren*)

Radix Peucedani (*Qian Hu*)
Radix Angelicae Sinensis (*Dang Gui*)
Radix Et Rhizoma Rhei (*Da Huang*)

Functions: Moistens the intestines and frees the flow of the stools

Indications: Habitual constipation due to fluid dryness in the elderly or those with a vacuous body

Main signs & symptoms: Dry, bound stools, dry skin, pale nails, pale lips, pallor on the undersides of the eyelids, possible signs and symptoms of blood stasis, such as varicose veins, spider nevi, and small hemangiomas, a pale tongue, and a fine, bowstring, possibly choppy pulse

Dosage: 4 pills three times per day

Formula explanation: Like the preceding medicine, this formula also treats chronic constipation. However, it does not address qi stagnation, but rather emphasizes blood vacuity. Because blood vacuity goes hand in hand with blood stasis, there may also be signs and symptoms of blood stasis as well. Persica is the sovereign medicinal which both moistens the intestines and frees the flow of the stools as well as quickens the blood and dispels stasis. Cannabis is the ministerial medicinal which assists Persica's moistening of the intestines and freeing the flow of the stools. Peucedanum downbears the lung qi, and the lungs and large intestine have a mutual interior/exterior relationship. In addition, Peucedanum does clear heat in the lungs. Many Chinese doctors believe that many people have deep-lying heat in the lungs due to the lungs being the florid canopy and heat's nature being yang and, therefore, tending to rise. Deep-lying or hidden heat in the lungs can consume and damage fluids. Therefore, Peucedanum's inclusion in the formula is quite sophisticated. Dang Gui and Rhubarb are also assistant medicinals. Dang Gui nourishes the blood and frees the flow of the stools, while Rhubarb frees the flow of the stools and also quickens the blood.

Comments: This medicine can be combined with other ready-made medicines whenever there is the complication of blood vacuity/fluid dryness constipation. In general, I would say that it is safer to use than the preceding formula which is more attacking to the qi and less nourishing to the blood.

Tong Shun Wan (Freeing the Flow & Normalizing Pills)

Semen Pruni Persicae (*Tao Ren*)
Semen Cannabis Sativae (*Huo Ma Ren*)
Radix Peucedani (*Qian Hu*)

Radix Angelicae Sinensis (*Dang Gui*)
Radix Et Rhizoma Rhei (*Da Huang*)
Folium Sennae (*Fan Xie Ye*)

Dosage: 6 pills once per day

Comments: This medicine's functions, indications, and main symptoms are the same as *Tao Ren Wan*'s above. Likewise, its formula explanation is the same. The only difference is that this medicine also includes Senna. Therefore, its stool-freeing and precipitating power is stronger. Long-term use of Senna, however, can be irritating to the bowels and cause intestinal cramping.

Wu Ren Wan (Five Seeds Pills)

Semen Pruni Armeniacae (*Xing Ren*)
Pericarpium Citri Reticulatae (*Chen Pi*)
Semen Pruni Persicae (*Tao Ren*)
Semen Biotae Orientalis (*Bai Zi Ren*)
Semen Pruni (*Yu Li Ren*)
Semen Pini (*Song Zi Ren*)

Functions: Moistens the intestines and frees the flow of the stools

Indications: Habitual constipation due to fluid dryness in the elderly or those with a vacuous body

Main signs & symptoms: Dry, bound stools, dry skin, dry, astringent eyes, scanty urination, a possibly red tongue with scanty fur, fine, bowstring, possibly rapid pulse

Dosage: 6 pills three times per day

Formula explanation: The five main ingredients in this formula, Armeniaca, Persica, Prune Seeds, Biota, and Pinenuts, are all fatty, slimy ones which moisten dryness and free the flow of the stools. Orange Peel rectifies the qi and harmonizes the stomach, assisting descending and downbearing.

Comments: This formula does not rectify the qi strongly, nor does it drain and precipitate. Its five main ingredients all moisten dryness and gloss the intestines. However, this formula does not nourish the blood as does the preceding medicine. This medicine can be combined with other medicines where there is yin vacuity/fluid insufficiency complicated by constipation.

5
Harmonizing & Resolving Medicines

Harmonizing and resolving (or relieving) formulas are those which regulate and harmonize. Typically, they support the righteous while simultaneously attacking evil. There are three subcategories of harmonizing and resolving formulas: 1) formulas which harmonize and resolve the *shao yang*, 2) formulas which regulate and harmonize the liver and spleen, and 3) formulas which regulate and harmonize the stomach and intestines. The first subcategory of harmonizing formulas is used in order to relieve and eliminate *shao yang* half exterior/half interior evils. The second subcategory is used when the functions of the liver and spleen have lost their regularity. The third subcategory is used when cold and heat above and below are mutually binding.

Medicines which harmonize & resolve the *shao yang*

Xiao Chai Hu Tang Wan (Minor Bupleurum Decoction Pills)

Radix Bupleuri (*Chai Hu*)
Radix Scutellariae Baicalensis (*Huang Qin*)
Radix Panacis Ginseng (*Ren Shen*)
Rhizoma Pinelliae Ternatae (*Ban Xia*)
Radix Glycyrrhizae (*Gan Cao*)
dry Rhizoma Zingiberis (*Gan Jiang*)
Fructus Zizyphi Jujubae (*Da Zao*)

Functions: Harmonizes and resolves the *shao yang*

Indications: 1) Cold damage *shao yang* patterns and 2) women's damage by cold. Common cold with lingering fever after several days, acute and chronic bronchitis, pleuritis, pneumonia, pulmonary tuberculosis, sinusitis, malaria, hepatitis, both acute viral and chronic, cholecystitis, gallstones, jaundice, gastritis, gastric ulcer, stomachache, lymphadenitis, tonsillitis, otitis media, mumps, mastitis, intercostal neuralgia, torticollis, pyelonephritis, puerperal fever, severe chills and fever due to uterine disease, stuttering, epilepsy, impotence in young men, neurosis, alopecia, and mental instability in children

Main signs & symptoms: Alternating fever and chills, chest and rib-side region bitterness (*i.e.*, pain) and fullness, diminished intake of food and drink, heart vexation, a desire to vomit, acid eructations, possible jaundice, a bitter taste in the mouth, a dry throat, vertigo, a thin, white tongue coating, and a bowstring pulse

Contraindications:

1. Do not use in patients with repletion above and vacuity below.
2. Do not use in case of liver fire and bleeding gums.
3. Use cautiously with patients with ascendant hyperactivity of liver yang, hypertension, or vomiting of blood due to yin vacuity.
4. Use cautiously with patients with headache and dizziness.
5. Do not use in combination with Interferon therapy. The combination of this formula with Interferon has caused several deaths due to liver failure in Japanese patients.

Dosage: 8 pills three times per day

Formula explanation: Within this formula, Bupleurum is the particular medicinal which enters the *shao yang*. It gently clears, upbears, and scatters. It also courses evils and penetrates the exterior. Thus it is the sovereign medicinal in this formula. Scutellaria is bitter and cold. It clears *shao yang* ministerial fire. It is the minister medicinal. Combined with Bupleurum, one scatters and the other clears, thus resolving *shao yang* evils. Pinellia harmonizes the stomach and downbears counterflow, scatters nodulation and disperses glomus. It is the assistant medicinal. It assists both the sovereign and minister medicinals attack evils. Ginseng and Licorice are also assistants, while Ginger and Red Dates are the messengers. They boost stomach qi, engender fluids and humors, harmonize the constructive and defensive, and support the righteous in order to help dispel evils. They also replenish the interior so that evils cannot enter it.

Comments: This is the single most commonly prescribed Chinese medicinal formula in the world. It is very useful that this formula is now available in pill form. Although this formula is traditionally described as resolving the *shao yang* division, it can also be used, and more commonly is, for harmonizing the liver and spleen. In this case, there is liver depression with spleen vacuity, either phlegm or dampness, and heat in the lungs, stomach, liver, and/or intestines. This is a very common pattern, and, therefore, this formula can be used in a wide variety of cases. Likewise, it can be combined with a wide range of other formulas when other patterns complicate the case. For instance, if there is accompanying lung-stomach yin vacuity, *Xiao Chai Hu Tang Wan* can be combined with *Sheng Mai San* (Engender the Pulse Powder). If there is accompanying blood vacuity, it can be combined with *Si Wu Tang Wan* (Four Materials Decoction Pills). If there is accompanying blood stasis, it can be combined with *Tao Hong Si Wu Tang Wan* (Persica & Carthamus Four Materials Decoction Pills). And if there is more pronounced accompanied phlegm dampness, it may be combined with *Er Chen Wan* (Two Aged [Ingredients] Pills) to name just a few representative combinations.

Regulating & harmonizing the liver & spleen medicines

Si Ni San Wan (Four Counterflows Powder Pills)

Radix Albus Paeoniae Lactiflorae (*Bai Shao*)
Radix Bupleuri (*Chai Hu*)
Fructus Immaturus Citri Aurantii (*Zhi Shi*)
mix-fried Radix Glycyrrhizae (*Gan Cao*)

Functions: Out-thrusts evils and resolves depression, courses the liver and rectifies the spleen

Indications: Liver-spleen disharmony with internal heat but cold extremities; gastritis, peptic ulcers, cholecystitis, cholelithiasis, hepatitis, intestinal obstruction, mastitis, fibrocystic breasts

Main signs & symptoms: Irritability, vexatious heat, chest and venter oppression and fullness, a red tongue with yellow fur, and a bowstring pulse

Dosage: 8 pills three times per day

Formula explanation: Bupleurum courses the liver and rectifies the qi at the same time as it resolves the exterior and out-thrusts internal heat. Immature Aurantium rectifies the stomach and intestinal qi, dispersing accumulations in the middle burner, and thereby promoting the spleen's movement and transformation. Peony emolliates and harmonizes the liver which thereby promotes the liver's function of coursing and discharge. Mix-fried Licorice harmonizes the middle and relaxes tension. When Peony and Licorice are combined together, they are especially effective for relaxing cramps and spasms resulting in pain.

Comments: The cold extremities in this case primarily refer to cold hands. These become chilled in response to stress. When the patient relaxes, the hands warm back up. In this case, the cold hands are a type of false cold. In actuality, there is heat depressed internally. That is why there is a red tongue and often a rapid pulse. Practitioners must, therefore, be sure to clarify whether a patient *always* has cold hands or only has cold hands under stress. They should also be careful to reevaluate their diagnosis of spleen and/or kidney vacuity cold if there is a dark red tongue with bowstring pulse.

This formula can be combined with others, such as *Xiao Chai Hu Tang Wan* (Minor Bupleurum Decoction Pills) and *Xiao Yao Wan* (Rambling Pills), when there is more pronounced qi stagnation leading to abdominal cramping.

Xiao Yao Wan (Rambling Pills)

Radix Bupleuri (*Chai Hu*)
Radix Angelicae Sinensis (*Dang Gui*)
Radix Albus Paeoniae Lactiflorae (*Bai Shao*)
Rhizoma Atractylodis Macrocephalae (*Bai Zhu*)
Sclerotium Poriae Cocos (*Fu Ling*)
Radix Glycyrrhizae (*Gan Cao*)
Herba Menthae Haplocalycis (*Bo He*)
dry Rhizoma Zingiberis (*Gan Jiang*)

Functions: Courses the liver and resolves depression, fortifies the spleen and harmonizes the constructive

Indications: Liver depression, blood vacuity. Irregular menstruation, uterine bleeding, abnormal vaginal discharge, breast distention, premenstrual tension, climacteric disorders, chronic hepatitis, pleurisy, chronic gastritis, peptic ulcer, neurosis, anemia, insomnia, optic nerve atrophy, central retinitis, and neurasthenia

Main signs & symptoms: Rib-side pain, headache, dizziness, a dry mouth and throat, fatigue, lack of strength of the four limbs, lassitude of the spirit, cold hands due to stress but which tend to get warmer on relaxation, irritability, reduced appetite, menstrual irregularity, breast distention, a pale red tongue, and a bowstring, fine, vacuous pulse

Dosage: 8 pills three times per day

Formula explanation: In this formula, Bupleurum courses the liver and resolves depression. The combination of Dang Gui and Peony nourishes the blood and softens the liver. Because Dang Gui is somewhat aromatic, it moves the qi, but, because it is sweet, it also relaxes tension. Therefore, it is an essential medicinal for treating liver depression with blood vacuity. Atractylodes and Poria fortify the spleen and remove dampness, thus promoting transportation and transformation and, ultimately, the origin of qi and blood. Licorice boosts the qi and supplements the center as well as relaxes the liver's tension. It is the assistant medicinal in this formula. The two messengers in this formula are Ginger and Mint. Ginger warms and harmonizes the center. Mint, when used in small amounts, assists Bupleurum's scattering of liver depression. Thus this formula as a whole regulates and harmonizes the liver and spleen.

Comments: This is one of the most commonly used formulas in Chinese medicine. It is especially useful in the treatment of various gynecological complaints. It can be combined with other medicines when one needs to supplement either the qi and blood more, transform and eliminate phlegm and dampness, quicken the blood and dispel stasis, etc.

Jia Wei Xiao Yao Wan (Added Flavors Rambling Pills)

Radix Albus Paeoniae Lactiflorae (*Bai Shao*)
Sclerotium Poriae Cocos (*Fu Ling*)
Rhizoma Atractylodis Macrocephalae (*Bai Zhu*)
Radix Angelicae Sinensis (*Dang Gui*)
dry Rhizoma Zingiberis (*Gan Jiang*)
Radix Glycyrrhizae (*Gan Cao*)
Cortex Radicis Moutan (*Dan Pi*)
Fructus Gardeniae Jasminoidis (*Shan Zhi Zi*)
Radix Bupleuri (*Chai Hu*)
Herba Menthae Haplocalycis (*Bo He*)

Functions: Courses the liver and fortifies the spleen, clears heat and resolves depression

Indications: Same as above plus early menstruation, profuse menstruation, flooding and leaking, spontaneous ejection of blood, female acne

Main signs & symptoms: Same as above but irascibility, a bitter taste in the mouth, a red tongue with yellow fur, and a bowstring, rapid pulse

Dosage: 8 pills three times per day

Formula explanation: This formula's explanation is the same as the above. However, in addition, Moutan quickens and clears heat from the blood, while Gardenia clears heat from all three burners and eliminates vexation. Because of Moutan and Gardenia's effect on the blood division, this formula is especially good for all sorts of bleeding due to depressive heat.

Comments: Although this medicine might be categorized as a heat-clearing formula, most Chinese sources place it in the harmonizing chapter since it is a modification of *Xiao Yao San*. This formula is also frequently referred to as *Dan Zhi Xiao Yao Wan* (Moutan & Gardenia Rambling Powder).

Tong Xie Yao Fang Wan (Essential Formula for Painful Diarrhea Pills)

stir-fried Radix Albus Paeoniae Lactiflorae (*Bai Shao*)
Rhizoma Atractylodis Macrocephalae (*Bai Zhu*)
stir-fried Pericarpium Citri Reticulatae (*Chen Pi*)
Radix Ledebouriellae Divaricatae (*Fang Feng*)

Functions: Soothes the liver, fortifies the spleen, and stops pain

Indications: Liver assailing the spleen diarrhea and lower abdominal cramping. Acute gastroenteritis, bacterial dysentery, hyperthyroidism, irritable bowel syndrome, colitis, and Crohn's disease

Main signs & symptoms: Recurrent diarrhea with pain which is aggravated by emotional upsetment, abdominal pain, borborygmus, thin, white tongue fur, and a bowstring pulse

Dosage: 8 pills three times per day

Formula explanation: Peony harmonizes the liver and relaxes tension. Atractylodes fortifies the spleen and dries dampness. Thus these two ingredients are the sovereign medicinals in this formula. Orange Peel harmonizes the middle and also transforms dampness. Ledebouriella enters both the liver and spleen and harmonizes these two viscera.

Comments: This formula is an extremely useful one in clinical practice and I am extremely happy it is now available in pill form. It can be used alone, but is more commonly combined with other formulas. For instance, when there is liver assailing the spleen and damp heat in the stomach and intestines, it can be combined with *Ban Xia Xie Xin Tang Wan* (Pinellia Drain the Heart Decoction Pills). It can also be combined with *Xiao Yao Wan* (Rambling Pills), *Jia Wei Xiao Yao Wan* (Added Flavors Rambling Pills), or *Xiao Chai Hu Tang Wan* (Minor Bupleurum Decoction Pills). Liver assailing the spleen is the most common cause of irritable bowel syndrome.

Therefore, these pills almost always play a part in the treatment of that disease. When combined with other formulas to fit the patient's total pattern discrimination, it can be a very effective treatment.

Regulating & harmonizing the stomach & intestines medicines

Ban Xia Xie Xin Tang Wan (Pinellia Drain the Heart Decoction Pills)

Rhizoma Pinelliae Ternatae (*Ban Xia*)
Radix Scutellariae Baicalensis (*Huang Qin*)
dry Rhizoma Zingiberis (*Gan Jiang*)
Radix Panacis Ginseng (*Ren Shen*)
Radix Glycyrrhizae (*Gan Cao*)

Rhizoma Coptidis Chinensis (*Huang Lian*)
Fructus Zizyphi Jujubae (*Da Zao*)

Functions: Harmonizes the stomach and downbears counterflow, opens binding and eliminates glomus

Indications: Lack of harmony of the stomach. Acute and chronic gastritis, enteritis, indigestion, pediatric vomiting and diarrhea, chronic hepatitis, early-stage cirrhosis, and gastric ulcers due to hyperacidity

Main signs & symptoms: Glomus and fullness below the heart but no pain, vomiting or dry heaves, borborygmus, diarrhea, a thin, yellow or slimy tongue coating, and a wiry, rapid pulse

Dosage: 5 tablets three times per day

Formula explanation: This formula is a modification of *Xiao Chai Hu Tang*. It is used when there is diarrhea and detriment damage of the central yang with possible external evils inhibiting qi dynamic. In this case, cold and heat are mutually binding, producing glomus underneath the heart since the qi is not upbearing and downbearing, is full and not freely flowing. Coptis and Scutellaria are bitter and cold, downbearing and discharging. Thus they eliminate heat. Dry Ginger and Pinellia are acrid, warm, and open nodulation, thus scattering cold. Ginseng, Licorice, and Red Dates are sweet and warm and boost the qi, thus supplementing vacuity. When these seven flavors (*i.e.*, ingredients) are combined, cold and hot medicinals are used together as are bitter, downbearing and acrid, opening ingredients. In addition, the qi is supplemented and the center is harmonized. Therefore, evils are removed at the same time as the righteous is augmented.

Comments: This formula is a very useful one in clinical practice, since few Westerners exhibit pure patterns of spleen-stomach vacuity weakness. Although many, if not most, Western patients suffer from spleen vacuity, typically, our stomachs and/or intestines are hot or hot and damp. This formula treats this real-life, complex pattern. In this case, heat can be replete heat, damp heat, or depressive heat, and cold may simply be due to exuberant yin and insufficient yang. Like the other two harmonizing formulas discussed above, this Chinese ready-made medicine can be combined with other ready-made medicines in order to treat even more complex patterns.

6
Heat-clearing Medicines

Formulas in this category are mainly composed of heat-clearing medicinals. They clear heat, drain fire, cool the blood, resolve toxins, and enrich yin. Heat-clearing formulas are used to clear internal heat where there is neither an external pattern nor internal accumulation and binding. When prescribing heat-clearing formulas, one must clearly distinguish whether the heat is replete or vacuous and also where the heat is located. Location in this context means either a) the *fen* or division *vis á vis* warm disease theory or b) the viscera and bowels.

Within Chinese medicine, there are six subcategories of heat-clearing formulas. These are: 1) formulas which cleat heat from the qi division, 2) formulas which clear the constructive and cool the blood, 3) formulas which clear heat and resolve toxins, 4) formulas which clear heat and dispel summerheat, 5) formulas which clear heat from the viscera and bowels, and 6) formulas which clear vacuity heat. However, there are only Chinese ready-made medicines available from the suppliers included in this book for clearing heat from the qi division, clearing heat and resolving toxins, clearing heat from the viscera and bowels, and clearing vacuity heat. Heat patterns usually describe acute conditions which do not lend themselves as well to treatment with such ready-made pills.

Cautions & contraindications when using heat-clearing medicines:

Because these medicines are mostly composed of bitter, cold medicinals, their exces-sive or prolonged use can damage the spleen/stomach. Therefore, they should be used only when necessary and their use should be discontinued as soon as the evil heat is cleared.

Medicines for clearing heat from the qi division

Bai Hu Tang (White Tiger Decoction)

Gypsum Fibrosum (*Shi Gao*)
Radix Dioscoreae Oppositae (*Shan Yao*)
Rhizoma Anemarrhenae Aspheloidis (*Zhi Mu*)
mix-fried Radix Glycyrrhizae (*Gan Cao*)

Functions: Clears heat from the qi division and drains stomach fire, engenders fluids and stops thirst

Indications: Blazing heat in the *yang ming* damage due to cold disease, or heat in the qi division four divisions warm heat disease. Encephalitis, meningitis, lobar pneumonia, heat stroke, diabetes mellitus, periodontitis

Main signs & symptoms: High fever with profuse sweating, aversion to heat, a red facial complexion, severe oral thirst, irritability, possible headache, toothache, and/or bleeding gums, and a surging, forceful or slippery, rapid pulse

Contraindications: This formula is contraindicated for fever due to spleen vacuity and cases of false heat and true cold. Its use should be suspended immediately if signs of headache, stiff neck, counterflow chilling of the extremities, or clouding or dimming of the spirit occur.

Dosage: 8 pills three times per day

Formula explanation: Gypsum is the sovereign medicinal in this formula which greatly clears heat and drains fire. Its minister is Anemarrhena which clears heat and drains fire but also enriches yin and engenders fluids. Mix-fried Licorice and Dioscorea harmonize the stomach and protect the spleen from damage by such greatly cold medicinals. Both of these assistants fortify the spleen and boost the stomach at the same time as engendering fluids. Therefore, they help Anemarrhena repair any damage to yin fluids which may have been consumed by great heat.

Comments: For great heat in the *yang ming* or qi division, I think one should preferably use a freshly brewed decoction made from bulk-dispensed medicinals. Such conditions are deemed emergency conditions which typically require large doses. However, if such bulk-dispensed medicinals were unavailable, for instance when traveling, these pills might be a good stop-gap measure. They can also be combined with other formulas when there is a combination of vigorous replete heat in the stomach and spleen and/or fluid vacuities. This formula differs from the standard prescription of the same name in that Dioscorea has been substituted for Semen Oryzae Sativae (*Geng Mi*). This latter ingredient does not lend itself for inclusion in pill formulas.

Medicines for clearing heat & resolving toxins

Huang Lian Jie Du Wan (Coptis Resolve Toxins Pills)

Rhizoma Coptidis (*Huang Lian*)
Radix Scutellariae Baicalensis (*Huang Qin*)

Cortex Phellodendri (*Huang Bai*)
Fructus Gardeniae Jasminoidis (*Zhi Zi*)

Functions: Drains fire and resolves toxins

Indications: Replete heat and fire toxins, exuberant heat in the three burners patterns. Septicemia, dysentery, pneumonia, acute urinary tract infections, ulcers, carbuncles, furuncles, boils, acute enteritis, acute icteric hepatitis, acute cholecystitis, encephalitis, acute conjunctivitis, acute pelvic inflammation, erysipelas, cellulitis, hemoptysis, epistaxis, urticaria, pruritus, cerebral hemorrhage, hypertension, anxiety, palpitations, insomnia, neurasthenia, and hysteria

Main signs & symptoms: Great heat, vexation and agitation, a dry mouth and throat, delirious speech, insomnia, possible hot diseases with hemoptysis and/or epistaxis, possible high fever with macular eruptions, generalized heat with dysentery, damp heat jaundice, a red tongue with yellow fur, and a rapid, forceful pulse

Contraindications:

1. Do not use this medicine in patients with bodily vacuity or weakness of the spleen and stomach.
2. Do not administer for prolonged periods of time.
3. Do not use for heat in the constructive or blood divisions.

Dosage: 3 pills three times per day

Formula explanation: In this formula, Coptis is the sovereign. It drains heart fire as well as draining fire from the middle burner. Scutellaria clears lung heat and drains upper burner fire. It acts as the minister. Phellodendron and Gardenia are the assistants. Phellodendron drains fire from the lower burner and Gardenia opens and drains fire from all three burners. It leads heat downward and moves it. Therefore, as a whole, this formula has the functions of draining fire, clearing heat, and resolving toxins.

Comments: This formula is composed of Chinese medicine's most often used antimycotic, antibacterial ingredients. For serious conditions, one needs to either combine with other ready-made medicines or increase its dosages. This formula can be used simultaneously with antibiotics administered either orally or intravenously. For use against sores and boils, such sores should be treated locally with external applications as well as internally (*i.e.*, systemically).

Pu Ji Xiao Du San (Universal Relief Disperse Toxins Powder)

Radix Scutellariae Baicalensis (*Huang Qin*)
Rhizoma Coptidis Chinensis (*Huang Lian*)
Pericarpium Citri Reticulatae (*Chen Pi*)
Radix Glycyrrhizae (*Gan Cao*)
Radix Scrophulariae Ningpoensis (*Xuan Shen*)
Radix Bupleuri (*Chai Hu*)
Radix Platycodi Grandiflori (*Jie Geng*)
Fructus Forsythiae Suspensae (*Lian Qiao*)
Radix Isatidis Seu Baphicacanthi (*Ban Lan Gen*)
Fructificatio Lasiosphaerae Seu Calvatiae (*Ma Bo*)
Fructus Arctii Lappae (*Niu Bang Zi*)
Herba Menthae Haplocalycis (*Bo He*)
Bombyx Batryticatus (*Jiang Can*)
Rhizoma Cimicifugae (*Sheng Ma*)

Functions: Courses wind and scatters evils, clears heat and resolves toxins

Indications: Great head scourge, wind heat epidemic toxins congesting in the upper burner. Mumps, tonsillitis, sore throat

Main signs & symptoms: Aversion to cold and effusion of heat, redness, swelling, and burning pain of the face and head, inability to open the eyes, inhibited throat, a dry tongue and oral thirst, a red tongue with yellow fur, and a rapid, forceful pulse

Contraindications: Because most of the medicinals in this formula are bitter and acrid, dispersing and scattering, it should be used with caution in those with yin vacuity.

Dosage: 8 pills three times per day

Formula explanation: Within this formula, Scutellaria and Coptis are the sovereign medicinals which clear, downbear, and out-thrust heat toxins from the head and face. Arctium, Forsythia, Mint, and Batryticated Silkworms are acrid and cooling and course and scatter wind heat from the head and face. They are the minister medicinals. Scrophularia, Lasiosphaera, and Isatis have the function of increasing and strengthening the clearing of heat and resolving of toxins. When combined with Licorice and Platycodon, they clear and disinhibit the throat. In addition, Scrophularia prevents damage to yin. Orange Peel rectifies the qi and courses blockage, thus helping scatter evil heat which has become depressed and bound. Cimicifuga and Bupleurum have the function within this formula of coursing and scattering wind heat and are based on the idea of "emitting fire depression." Cimicifuga and Bupleurum also lead Scutellaria and Coptis to move upward, thus clearing toxic heat in the head and face. Conversely,

Scutellaria and Coptis prevent Bupleurum and Cimicifuga from upbearing and emitting or effusing too much.

Comments: This Chinese ready-made medicine is especially effective for severe sore throat due to heat toxins. It is not usually combined with other medicines. However, when it is combined with bleeding *Shao Shang* (Lu 11), its effects are even more immediate. Likewise, one can spray *Xi Gua Shuang* (Watermelon Frost) directly onto the swollen, inflamed areas of the throat.

Wu Wei Xiao Du Yin Wan (Five Flavors Disperse Toxins Drink Pills)

Flos Lonicerae Japonicae (*Jin Yin Hua*)
Flos Chrysanthemi Indici (*Ye Ju Hua*)
Herba Taraxaci Mongolici Cum Radice (*Pu Gong Ying*)
Herba Violae Yedoensis Cum Radice (*Zi Hua Di Ding*)
Fructus Forsythiae Suspensae (*Lian Qiao*)[1]

Functions: Clears heat and resolves toxins, cools the blood and disperses swelling

Indications: Clove sore toxins, welling and flat abscesses. Carbuncles, furuncles, erysipelas, mastitis, appendicitis, conjunctivitis, urinary tract infection, and acute pyelonephritis

Main signs & symptoms: The affected area is red, swollen, hot, and painful. The sores are fine and small in form but are hard and are like a nail or clove in shape. The tongue is red and the pulse is rapid.

Contraindications: This formula is not for use with yin-type sores. Use with caution in those with spleen vacuity.

Dosage: 8 pills three times per day

Formula explanation: Lonicera is the sovereign medicinal in this medicine. It clears heat and resolves toxins, disperses and scatters welling abscesses and sores. Chrysanthemum Indicum, Dandelion, Viola, and Forsythia also clear heat and resolve toxins and are essential medicinals for treating clove sores.

---

[1] When described as a water-based decoction, the fifth ingredient is usually given as Herba Begoniae Fimbristipulae (*Zi Bei Tian Kuei*).

Comments: This medicine can be used in conjunction with other ready-made medicines when there are complicated patterns resulting in heat toxin sores. Such sores should be treated externally for best results.

Chuan Xin Lian (Andrograhis [Pills])

Herba Taraxaci Mongolici Cum Radice (*Ru Gong Ying*)
Radix Isatidis Seu Baphicacanthi (*Ban Lan Gen*)
Herba Andrographitis Paniculatae (*Chuan Xin Lian*)

Functions: Clears heat and resolves toxins, clears heat and eliminates dampness

Indications: Heat toxins and/or damp heat evils. Pharyngitis, laryngitis, tonsillitis, various types of dermatoses

Main signs & symptoms: A wide variety of heat toxin and damp heat conditions mostly associated with the lungs, throat, and skin but possibly also including the biliary and urinary tracts.

Dosage: 2 pills as needed

Formula explanation: Dandelion clears heat and resolves toxins, clears heat and eliminates dampness, disperses welling abscesses and scatters nodulations. Some Chinese authors also feel this medicinal has the ability to course the liver and rectify the qi as well as promote lactation and, therefore, even supplement yin. Isatis clears heat and resolves toxins, cools the blood and disinhibits the throat. It is used for a variety of epidemic or pestilential warm diseases, such as viral flus and mumps and also for damp heat hepatitis. Andrographis also clears heat and resolves toxins and clears heat and eliminates dampness. It is mostly used for diseases in the lungs, throat, and urinary tract. Some Chinese use this medicinal as a cheap substitute for Rhizoma Coptidis Chinensis (*Huang Lian*).

Comments: These pills are a very useful ready-made medicine which I always try to keep on hand. In China, many people take Isatis preventively for epidemic conditions, such as viral flus, measles, mumps, and even viral hepatitis. I typically take these pills at the first sign of a sore throat. Isatis is known to have some anti-viral capabilities. In my experience, Dandelion and Isatis have a low capability for causing side effects. So these medicinals can be taken preventively by many patients without too much worry. This medicine can also be combined with other Chinese ready-made medicine when one wants to add or increase the treatment principles of clearing heat and resolving toxins.

Medicines for clearing heat from the viscera & bowels

Long Dan Xie Gan Wan (Gentiana Scabra Drain the Liver Pills)

Radix Gentianae Scabrae (*Long Dan Cao*)
Radix Scutellariae Baicalensis (*Huang Qin*)
Fructus Gardeniae Jasminoidis (*Shan Zhi Zi*)
Rhizoma Alismatis (*Ze Xie*)
Caulis Akebiae Mutong (*Mu Tong*)
Semen Plantaginis (*Che Qian Zi*)
Radix Angelicae Sinensis (*Dang Gui*)
uncooked Radix Rehmanniae (*Sheng Di*)
Radix Bupleuri (*Chai Hu*)
Radix Glycyrrhizae (*Gan Cao*)

Functions: Drains liver-gallbladder replete heat, clears lower burner damp heat

Indications: 1) Liver-gallbladder replete heat harassing above or 2) damp heat pouring below. Acute conjunctivitis, uveitis, corneal ulcers, acute glaucoma, central retinitis, acute otitis media, boils and carbuncles in the vestibular and external auditory canal, nasal furuncles, hypertension, acute icteric hepatitis, acute cholecystitis, herpes zoster, herpes genitalia, cold sores, acute pyelonephritis, acute cystitis, urethritis, acute pelvic inflammation, acute prostatitis, orchitis, epididymitis, vaginitis, abnormal vaginal discharge, vaginal itching, lymphadenitis of the groin, hyperthyroidism, migraine headache, eczema in general and scrotal eczema in particular, and intercostal neuralgia

Main signs & symptoms: 1) Headache, red eyes, rib-side pain, a bitter taste in the mouth, loss of hearing, swelling of the ears; 2) genital swelling, genital itching, impotence, genital sweating, urinary strangury, turbid urine, damp heat abnormal vaginal discharge in women, a red tongue with yellow fur, and a rapid, forceful pulse

Contraindications:

1. Do not use this medicine in large doses or for prolonged periods of time in patients with spleen-stomach vacuity.
2. Do not use in large doses or for prolonged periods of time in patients with damaged body fluids.
3. Do not use in cases with a red tongue but scanty fur.

Dosage: 8 pills three times per day

Formula explanation: Within this formula, Gentiana Scabra, greatly bitter and greatly cold, is the sovereign for both draining fire and eliminating dampness. It drains replete liver-gallbladder fire from the upper body. It also precipitates and clears damp heat from the lower body. Scutellaria and Gardenia are the ministers. They also have the functions of draining fire with bitterness and cold and are combined with Gentian Scabra for that purpose. Alisma, Akebia, and Plantago clear heat and disinhibit dampness. They, therefore, assist in eliminating damp heat via the urinary tract. Because the liver stores the blood and heat within the liver channel can easily damage yin and blood, at the same time as using bitter cold ingredients to dry dampness, uncooked Rehmannia and Dang Gui are used as assistants to enrich yin and nourish the blood. Licorice regulates and harmonizes all the other medicinals. Therefore, within this formula there is supplementation within drainage and enrichment within disinhibition. This assists the downbearing of fire and the clearing of heat and the separation of clear from damp turbidity.

Comments: This formula can also be used effectively in combination with Western antibiotics. However, it is one of the most widely misapplied formulas in Chinese medicine in the West. This formula should really not be used unless there is simple replete damp heat or liver fire. Most Western patients have an element of vacuity, especially spleen vacuity, in their pattern discrimination. Although many practitioners assume that it is alright to use this formula for a short period of time to clear heat and eliminate dampness in those with a mixed repletion-vacuity pattern, when damp heat is due to spleen vacuity as it so commonly is, this formula is not a good choice. In that case, one should use *Bi Xie Shen Shi Wan* (Dioscorea Hypoglauca Overcome Dampness Pills).

Li Dan Wan (Disinhibit the Gallbladder Pills)

Radix Scutellariae Baicalensis (*Huang Qin*)
Radix Auklandiae Lappae (*Mu Xiang*)
Herba Lysimachiae Seu Desmodii (*Jin Qian Cao*)
Flos Lonicerae Japonicae (*Jin Yin Hua*)
Folium Artemisiae Capillaris (*Yin Chen Hao*)
Radix Bupleuri (*Chai Hu*)
Folium Daqingye (*Da Qing Ye*)
Radix Et Rhizoma Rhei (*Da Huang*)

Functions: Clears heat and eliminates dampness, disinhibits the gallbladder and expels stones

Indications: Liver-gallbladder damp heat, yang jaundice. Acute jaundice, acute and chronic cholecystitis, cholelithiasis if stones less than 1 cm in diameter

Main signs & symptoms: Nausea, vomiting, acute abdominal pain, worse after eating greasy, fried, fatty foods, constipation, irritability, vexation and agitation, a bitter taste in the mouth, possible dark urine and white-colored stools, red tongue with slimy, yellow fur, and a slippery, bowstring, rapid pulse

Dosage: 6 pills three times per day

Formula explanation: Scutellaria, Lonicera, and Daqingye clear heat and resolve toxins. Auklandia moves the qi and stops pain. Lysimachia clears heat and recedes yellowing, disinhibits urination and expels stones. Capillaris clears heat and eliminates dampness, recedes yellowing. Bupleurum courses the liver and disinhibits the gallbladder, Rhubarb drains heat from the intestines and frees the flow of the stool.

Comments: For acute cholecystitis and acute jaundice, this medicine is commonly used alone. For chronic cholecystitis, it may be combined with other Chinese ready-made medicines, such as *Xiao Chai Hu Tang Wan* (Minor Bupleurum Decoction Pills) and *Xue Fu Zhu Yu Tang Wan* (Blood Mansion Dispel Stasis Decoction Pills). This latter medicine is used based on the fact that blood stasis typically complicates cases of enduring cholecystitis and cholelithiasis.

Qing Wei San Wan (Clear the Stomach Powder Pills)

Rhizoma Cimicifugae (*Sheng Ma*)
Rhizoma Coptidis Chinensis (*Huang Lian*)
Cortex Radicis Moutan (*Dan Pi*)
uncooked Radix Rehmanniae (*Sheng Di*)
Radix Angelicae Sinensis (*Dang Gui*)

Functions: Clears the stomach and drains fire, cools the blood and enriches yin

Indications: Stomach heat damaging yin fluids stomatitis, trigeminal neuralgia, gingivitis, periodontal disease, glossitis, and halitosis

Main signs & symptoms: Toothache, swelling of the face, emission of heat, bad breath, a dry mouth, a red tongue with scanty fur, and a slippery, large, rapid pulse

Dosage: 8 pills three times per day

Formula explanation: The bitter and cold of Coptis clear heat from the stomach and drain fire. This is assisted by Cimicifuga which clears heat both due to its cold nature and also by upbearing and out-thrusting depressive heat. Moutan and uncooked

Rehmannia clear heat and cool the blood, while Dang Gui disperses swelling and stops pain by harmonizing the blood.

Comments: This formula can be combined with others when stomach heat is more pronounced. For instance, it can be combined with *Xiao Chai Hu Tang Wan*, *Jia Wei Xiao Yao Wan*, or *Bu Zhong Yi Qi Wan* in order to clear stomach heat or fire.

Xiang Lian Wan (Auklandia & Coptis Pills)

Rhizoma Coptidis Chinensis (*Huang Lian*)
Radix Auklandiae Lappae (*Mu Xiang*)

Functions: Clears heat and transforms dampness, moves the qi and stops dysentery

Indications: Large intestine damp heat diarrhea and dysentery. Bacterial and amebic dysentery, acute gastroenteritis, ulcerative colitis

Main signs & symptoms: Red and white dysentery, chest and diaphragm glomus and oppression, tenesmus, a red tongue with slimy, yellow fur, and a slippery bowstring, rapid pulse

Dosage: 8 pills three times per day

Formula explanation: Coptis clears heat and eliminates dampness, draining heat from the *yang ming*. Auklandia moves and rectifies the qi, stops pain.

Comments: This simple two ingredient medicine is for damp heat in the large intestine causing diarrhea and dysentery. Auklandia has a specific ability to relieve tenesmus. This medicine can either be taken alone or combined with other Chinese ready-made medicines depending on the case at hand. This medicine is considered a variation or derivative of *Zuo Jin Wan* (Left Gold Pills) since the Coptis is supposed to be prepared with Fructus Evodiae Rutecarpae (*Wu Zhu Yu*).

Bai Xing Shi Gan Wan (Cynanchum, Armeniaca, Gypsum & Licorice Pills)

Gypsum Fibrosum (*Shi Gao*)
Semen Pruni Armeniacae (*Xing Ren*)
Radix Cynanchi Stautoni (*Bai Qian*)
Radix Glycyrrhizae (*Gan Cao*)

Functions: Diffuses the lungs and clears heat, downbears counterflow and levels panting

Indications: Heat lodged in the lungs obstructing the flow of qi causing coughing and panting. Upper respiratory tract infections, lobar pneumonia, bronchial pneumonia, bronchial asthma, pneumonitis as a complication of measles, bronchiolitis, pertussis, and diphtheria

Main signs & symptoms: Emission of heat with or without sweating, coughing, panting and wheezing, flaring of the wings of the nostrils when breathing, possible chest pain, yellow tongue fur, and a slippery, rapid pulse

Contraindications: Do not use this formula for coughing and panting due to cold or when complicated by righteous qi vacuity.

Dosage: 8 pills three times per day

Formula explanation: Gypsum strongly clears heat and drains fire. Cynanchum and Armeniaca diffuse the lungs and downbear counterflow, transform phlegm and stop coughing. Licorice engenders fluids to moisten the lungs, protects the stomach and harmonizes all the other medicinals.

Comments: This is a modification of the famous formula, *Ma Xing Shi Gan Tang* (Ephedra, Armeniaca, Gypsum & Licorice Decoction). In this case, Cynanchum Stautonum has been substituted for Ephedra. This formula is the single most commonly prescribed Chinese medicinal formula for replete pattern pneumonia. It is usually prescribed alone. These pills can be used in first aid situations where bulk-dispensed Chinese medicinals are unavailable.

Dao Chi Wan (Abduct the Red Pills)

uncooked Radix Rehmanniae (*Sheng Di*)
Caulis Akebiae (*Mu Tong*)
Herba Lophatheri Gracilis (*Dan Zhu Ye*)
Extremitas Radicis Glycyrrhizae (*Gan Cao Shao*)

Functions: Clears the heart and disinhibits urination

Indications: Heat in the heart being transferred to the bladder via the small intestine. Stomatitis, night-crying in children, urethritis, cystitis, and glomerulonephritis

Main signs & symptoms: Irritability, vexatious heat in the chest, oral thirst with a desire for chilled drinks, a red facial complexion, possible tongue and mouth sores, possible dark, scanty, painful, astringent urination, in severe cases, hematuria, and a slippery, rapid pulse

Contraindications: Do not use alone in case of concomitant spleen vacuity.

Dosage: 8 pills three times per day

Formula explanation: Uncooked Rehmannia is the sovereign medicinal in this formula. It cools the blood, and it is the heart which controls the blood. Thus uncooked Rehmannia clears heat from the heart. It is also explained that, since uncooked Rehmannia enriches kidney water, kidney water can control blazing of heart fire. Akebia clears heat from the heart by leading yang downward. It does this by disinhibiting urination. Lophatherum clears heat from the heart and resolves vexation, while Licorice Tips clear heat and resolve toxins as well as harmonize all the other medicinals in this prescription.

Comments: Pronounced redness and sores on the tip of the tongue are one of the main diagnostic characteristics of this pattern. In addition, there may or may not be urinary disturbances. This pattern occurs with spleen qi vacuity, in which case, this medicine can be combined with other Chinese ready-made medicines in order to fortify the spleen and supplement the qi. Patients with this pattern are strongly advised to stick to a clear bland, hypoallergenic, yeast-free diet as much as possible.

Medicines for clearing vacuity heat

Qing Gu Wan (Clearing the Bones Pills)

Radix Stellariae Dichotomae (*Yin Chai Hu*)
Rhizoma Anemarrhenae Aspheloidis (*Zhi Mu*)
Rhizoma Picrorrhizae (*Hu Huang Lian*)
Cortex Radicis Lycii Chinensis (*Di Gu Pi*)
Herba Artemisiae Apiaceae (*Qing Hao*)
Radix Gentianae Macrophyllae (*Qin Jiao*)
mix-fried Carapax Amydae Sinensis (*Bie Jia*)
Radix Glycyrrhizae (*Gan Cao*)

Functions: Clears vacuity heat and eliminates bone-steaming

Indications: Yin vacuity-vacuity heat tidal fever and steaming bones

Main signs & symptoms: Afternoon tidal fever, enduring low-grade fever, steaming heat in the bones, irritability, insomnia, emaciation, taxation fatigue, red lips, malar flushing, night sweats, oral thirst, dry throat, a red tongue with scanty fur, and a fine, rapid pulse

Dosage: 8 pills three times per day

Formula explanation: Stellaria is the ruling medicinal in this formula. It clears heat without damaging yin. It is assisted by Anemarrhena which enriches yin and clears heat, Picrorrhiza which clears heat from the blood division, and Cortex Lycii which also clears heat from the blood division as well as deep-lying heat from the lungs. Artemisia Apiacea also clears heat due to vacuity but without damaging the qi or blood. Along with Gentiana Macrophylla, it out-thrusts heat from the bones to muscles and skin. Amyda enriches yin and subdues yang, thus guiding the other medicinals to the yin portion of the body. Licorice harmonizes all the other medicinals and protects the spleen and stomach from damage.

Comments: This formula can be combined with other yin supplements when there is the symptom of yin vacuity bone-steaming. It can also be combined with other appropriate formulas to treat wind damp heat impediment in cases with concomitant yin and qi vacuity. In addition, this formula should not be overlooked in the treatment of *lao nue*, taxation malaria. For instance, if there is qi and yin vacuity with tidal heat, this formula may be combined with *Bu Zhong Yi Qi Wan* (Supplement the Center & Boost the Qi Pills).

7
Interior-warming Medicines

The formulas in this chapter are composed mainly of warm and hot medicinals. Interior cold may be due to either external invasion of cold having reached the interior or from internal generation of cold due to yang vacuity. In addition, improper use of cool and cold medicinals may result in damage to the yang qi, as can overeating uncooked and chilled foods and drinking chilled liquids. Within Chinese medicine, there are three subcategories of interior-warming formulas. These are 1) formulas which warm the center and dispel cold, 2) formulas which secure yang and save counterflow, and 3) formulas which warm the channels and scatter cold. For relatively superficial conditions, formulas which warm the channels and scatter cold are used. For cold affecting the middle burner, formulas which warm the center and dispel cold are used. For extreme conditions associated with cold which has devastated yang, formulas which secure yang and save counterflow are used. However, only three interior-warming ready-made Chinese medicines are available from the suppliers included in this book. Two are for cold affecting the middle burner and one is for warming the channels.

Cautions & contraindications:

1. These medicines must be used with care in patients with yin vacuity or blood loss.
2. Do not use these medicines with true heat/false cold.

Center-warming medicines

Xiao Jian Zhong Wan (Minor Fortify the Center Pills)

Radix Albus Paeoniae Lactiflorae (*Bai Shao*)
Fructus Zizyphi Jujubae (*Da Zao*)
dry Rhizoma Zingiberis (*Gan Jiang*)
Ramulus Cinnamomi Cassiae (*Gui Zhi*)
Radix Glycyrrhizae (*Gan Cao*)

Functions: Warms the center and supplements vacuity, harmonizes the interior and relaxes urgency (*i.e.*, cramping)

Indications: Vacuity taxation, interior urgency, *i.e.*, abdominal cramps. Gastritis, gastric ulcers, duodenal ulcers, inflammatory bowel disease, neurasthenia, chronic hepatitis, chronic nephritis, pernicious anemia, hypoglycemia, fever of unknown origin, leukemia

Main signs & symptoms: Occasional abdominal pain which gets better with obtaint of warmth, a pale tongue with white fur, and a fine, bowstring, moderate (*i.e.*, slightly slow) pulse, possible heart palpitations, vacuity vexation, restlessness, a lusterless facial complexion, aching and discomfort in the four extremities, possible vexatious heat in the hands and feet, a dry throat and parched mouth

Contraindications: This medicine is contraindicated in case of vacuity heat due to yin vacuity. It should not be used alone for vomiting or roundworms or for abdominal distention.

Dosage: 8 pills three times per day

Formula explanation: Cinnamon Twigs and Peony are the two sovereign medicinals in this formula. Cinnamon Twigs warm yang qi, while Peony boosts yin blood. Licorice warms and boosts the qi, thus assisting Cinnamon Twigs to boost the qi and warm the center. When Licorice is combined with Peony, sour and sweet transform yin, boost the liver, and enrich the spleen. Therefore, Licorice is an assistant medicinal. Ginger and Red Dates are also assistant medicinals in this formula. Ginger warms the stomach and Red Dates supplement the spleen. Together they promote the middle burner's production of the qi and movement of fluids and humors as well as harmonize the constructive and defensive.

Comments: Although Western patients do not, in my experience, suffer from simple center cold as often as do Chinese patients, this formula is a useful one for gently supplementing the middle burner qi in children or when children experience a stomachache after eating chilled, frozen foods.

Fu Zi Li Zhong Wan (Aconite Rectify the Center Pills)[1]

Radix Codonopsitis Pilosulae (*Dang Shen*)
dry Rhizoma Zingiberis (*Gan Jiang*)
Radix Glycyrrhizae (*Gan Cao*)
Rhizoma Atractylodis Macrocephalae (*Bai Zhu*)

---

[1] The Mayway catalog has this formula's Chinese and Pinyin names misspelled written as *Xiang Fu Li Zhong Wan*. No such standard formula exists.

Radix Lateralis Praeparatus Aconiti Carmichaeli (*Fu Zi*)

Functions: Warms the center and dispels cold, supplements the qi and fortifies the spleen

Indications: 1) Middle burner vacuity cold, 2) yang vacuity, loss of blood, and 3) pediatric chronic fright (*i.e.*, convulsions). Acute and chronic gastritis, gastric or duodenal ulcers, gastroptosis, gastrectasis, irritable bowel syndrome, chronic colitis, cholera-like disorders, chronic bronchitis, oral herpes, functional uterine bleeding, bloody stools due to gastroduodenal ulcer, angina pectoris, and anemia

Main signs & symptoms: Diarrhea but no thirst, nausea and vomiting, abdominal pain, no desire for food or drink, possible sudden turmoil, *i.e.*, cholera-like conditions, a pale tongue with a white coating, and a deep, fine pulse

Contraindications:

1. Do not use for externally contracted diseases with fever even though accompanied by chills.
2. Do not use in cases with yin vacuity.
3. When used with cholera-like conditions, discontinue use after vomiting and diarrhea have stopped.

Dosage: 8 pills three times per day

Formula explanation: Within this formula, acrid, hot Aconite and dry Ginger are the sovereign medicinals in this medicine. They warm the middle burner spleen and stomach and dispel interior cold. Codonopsis supplements the source qi. It assists transportation and transformation and rectifies upbearing and downbearing. It is the minister medicinal. Atractylodes fortifies the spleen and dries dampness. Licorice boosts the qi and harmonizes the center. It is used as both assistant and messenger. When these four medicinals are combined, cold in the middle burner obtains acrid heat and is eliminated, while middle burner vacuity obtains sweet warmth and is augmented. Thus the clear yang is upborne and the turbid yin is downborne, transportation and transformation are fortified and the middle burner is cured.

Medicines which warm the channels & scatter cold

Dang Gui Si Ni Wan (Dang Gui Four Counterflows Pills)

Radix Angelicae Sinensis (*Dang Gui*)

Radix Albus Paeoniae Lactiflorae (*Bai Shao*)
Ramulus Cinnamomi Cassiae (*Gui Zhi*)
Herba Asari Cum Radice (*Xi Xin*)
mix-fried Radix Glycyrrhizae (*Gan Cao*)
Caulis Akebiae (*Mu Tong*)
Fructus Zizyphi Jujubae (*Da Zao*)

Functions: Warms the channels and scatters cold, nourishes the blood and frees the flow of the network vessels

Indications: Enduring cold evils congealing the blood and obstructing the free flow of qi complicated by possible blood vacuity. Reynaud's disease, rheumatoid arthritis, fibromyalgia, sciatica, peptic ulcers, chronic urticaria, frostbite, and thromboangiitis obliterans

Main signs & symptoms: Enduring cold hands and/or feet which are also cold to the touch, a pale tongue with white fur, and a deep, fine, possibly faint pulse

Dosage: 8 pills three times per day

Contraindications: Use cautiously in warm weather or in warm climates. Contraindicated in cases of heat or fire from yin vacuity.

Formula explanation: Dang Gui and Peony nourish the blood, while Dang Gui also quickens the blood and transforms stasis. Cinnamon Twigs warm the channels and scatter cold. Asarum is very hot, acrid, penetrating, and moving and frees the flow of the network vessels. Mix-fried Licorice and Red Dates fortify the spleen and supplement the qi. Since the qi transforms the blood, they assist Dang Gui and Peony to transform and engender the blood. Akebia also frees the flow of the network vessels while also preventing the acrid, hot ingredients from giving rise to heat ascending upward. This is because Akebia disinhibits urination, and urination helps lead yang back down to its lower source.

Comments: This formula can be combined with others whenever there are cold evils lodged in the channels and network vessels causing congelation and stagnation.

8
Exterior-Interior Dual Resolving Medicines

Formulas which combine resolving the exterior medicinals with draining and precipitating and heat-clearing medicinals or with warming the interior medicinals are designed to treat simultaneous exterior-interior patterns. In this case, there is an exterior pattern superimposed on an interior pattern, and both of these patterns must be treated at the same time. If only one of these patterns were treated, it would result in worsening of the other. Formulas which resolve both the exterior and interior at the same time are called exterior-interior dual resolving formulas. These are subdivided into three categories: 1) resolving the exterior and attacking the interior formulas, 2) resolving the exterior and clearing the interior formulas, and 3) resolving the exterior and warming the interior formulas. In terms of Chinese ready-made medicines, only two formulas are available from the suppliers included in this book. Both are from the resolving the exterior and attacking the interior subcategory.

Medicines which resolve the exterior & attack the interior

Da Chai Hu Wan (Major Bupleurum Pills)

dry Rhizoma Zingiberis (*Gan Jiang*)
Radix Bupleuri (*Chai Hu*)
Rhizoma Pinelliae Ternatae (*Ban Xia*)
Radix Scutellariae Baicalensis (*Huan Qin*)
Fructus Immaturus Citri Aurantii (*Zhi Shi*)
Radix Albus Paeoniae Lactiflorae (*Bai Shao*)
Fructus Zizyphi Jujubae (*Da Zao*)
Radix Et Rhizoma Rhei (*Da Huang*)

Functions: Harmonizes and resolves the *shao yang*, drains internal heat binding

Indications: Combined *shao yang-yang ming* diseases. Acute cholecystitis, acute pancreatitis, intestinal obstruction, hypertension, headache, tinnitus, and acute conjunctivitis

Main signs & symptoms: Alternating cold and heat, upper abdominal distention and pain, vomiting, constipation or diarrhea, yellow tongue fur, and a bowstring, forceful pulse

Dosage: 8 pills three times per day

Formula explanation: This formula is made up from the main medicinals from *Xiao Chai Hu Tang* (Minor Bupleurum Decoction) and *Xiao Cheng Qi Tang* (Minor Order the Qi Decoction). In this case, evils exist in both the *shao yang* and *yang ming* divisions and there are replete heat symptoms in the *yang ming*, such as constipation, abdominal pain, and yellow tongue fur. Therefore, Radix Panacis Ginseng (*Ren Shen*) and Radix Glycyrrhizae (*Gan Cao*) are removed, since they would otherwise result in stagnation of the evils, while Cortex Magnoliae Officinalis (*Hou Po*) is removed because there is not severe fullness and glomus. Peony is added to assist Bupleurum and Immature Aurantium to course the liver and stop pain.

Comments: While I would probably not try to treat acute cholecystitis or acute pancreatitis with a ready-made pill such as this, this pill might be a good therapeutic choice for patients with hypertension, headache, and tinnitus due to liver fire harassing above accompanied by replete pattern chronic constipation. In that case, treatment would be ongoing and might benefit from coming in pill form.

Fang Feng Tong Sheng San (Ledebouriella Communicate with the Divine Powder)

Fructus Forsythiae Suspensae (*Lian Qiao*)
Radix Angelicae Sinensis (*Dang Gui*)
Flos Seu Herba Schizonepetae Tenuifoliae (*Jing Jie Sui*)
Radix Albus Paeoniae Lactiflorae (*Bai Shao*)
Radix Scutellariae Baicalensis (*Huang Qin*)
Radix Ligustici Wallichii (*Chuan Xiong*)
Radix Platycodi Grandiflori (*Jie Geng*)
Rhizoma Atractylodis Macrocephalae (*Bai Zhu*)
dry Rhizoma Zingiberis (*Gan Jiang*)
Radix Et Rhizoma Rhei (*Da Huang*)
Herba Menthae Haplocalycis (*Bo He*)
Radix Glycyrrhizae (*Gan Cao*)

Functions: Courses wind and resolves the exterior, drains heat and frees the flow of the stools

Indications: Wind and heat congestion and exuberance, exterior and interior both replete. Influenza, erysipelas, food poisoning, carbuncles, urticaria, dermatitis, acne, obesity

Main signs & symptoms: Increased cold and strong heat, dizziness and vertigo, red eyes, eye pain, a bitter taste in and a dry mouth, inhibited throat, chest and diaphragm glomus and oppression, cough, vomiting, panting, and fullness, constipation, red, astringent urination, possible sore and welling abscess swelling and toxins, possible intestinal wind and hemorrhoidal leakage, possible cinnabar macules and rashes, slimy, yellow tongue fur, and a surging, rapid or bowstring, slippery pulse

Dosage: 8 pills three times per day

Formula explanation: The ingredients in this formula accomplish three main functions simultaneously. They resolve the exterior, clear heat, and attack and precipitate. Within it, Ledebouriella, Schizonepeta, and Mint course wind and resolve the exterior, thus promoting the resolution of wind evils via sweating. Rhubarb and Mirabilitum discharge heat and free the flow of the stools. These are combined with Scutellaria, Forsythia, and Platycodon which clear and resolve lung and stomach heat. Dang Gui, Ligusticum Wallichium, and Peony nourish and quicken the blood, while Atractylodes fortifies the spleen and dries dampness. Finally, Licorice harmonizes the center and relaxes urgency. Hence sweating does not damage the exterior, nor does clearing and precipitating damage the interior.

Comments: According to the ingredients listed in Mayway's catalog, the following ingredients have been omitted from this formula's standard composition: Herba Ephedrae (*Ma Huang*), Gypsum Fibrosum (*Shi Gao*), Talcum (*Hua Shi*), and Fructus Gardeniae Jasminoidis (*Shan Zhi Zi*). Therefore, this version of this formula is not going to be so effective for red, astringent or rough urination.

9
Qi-rectifying Medicines

Qi-rectifying medicines address either of two anomalies of the qi. In the first case, there may be qi stagnation. This means the qi does not move freely as it should. Usually this is due to the liver losing its control over coursing and discharge. However, because the qi transports and transforms the blood, dampness, phlegm, and food, qi stagnation may be complicated by depression of any of these yin substances. In addition, if qi becomes depressed, it may transform into depressive heat or fire. Therefore, the subcategory of qi-rectifying formulas known as qi-moving formulas commonly include medicinals which treat one or more of these complicating depressions. This subcategory is itself divided into two groups of formulas: 1) those formulas which treat stagnation of the spleen and stomach qi with upper abdominal distention, belching, nausea, and possible vomiting and 2) those formulas which treat liver depression, qi stagnation with distention and pain in the rib-side region with possible distention and pain more prominent in the lower abdomen.

Secondly, if qi accumulates, because it is yang, it will eventually counterflow upward. This may affect the downward flow of the qi of the stomach and lungs. In such cases, the qi of this viscus and bowel may counterflow upward. Therefore, the second subcategory of qi-rectifying formulas is known as qi-downbearing formulas. These formulas downbear upwardly counterflowing qi, thus insuring the regular and harmonious arising of clear yang and the downbearing of turbid yin. The medicines in this chapter which specifically downbear lung, as opposed to stomach, qi might also be described as cough-stopping, panting-leveling medicines.

Qi-rectifying ingredients have many similarities to exterior-resolving medicinals. Both groups can be referred to as windy medicinals. This is because both groups tend to be acrid, drying, ascending, and out-thrusting. Even within the downbearing group of qi-rectifying formulas, downbearing medicinals are usually used in tandem with dry, acrid medicinals to upbear yang and thrust outward. Due to their dry, windy nature, qi-rectifying ingredients can consume yin and blood if improperly used and damage the righteous qi.

Cautions & contraindications:

1. Use with care in patients with blood vacuity, yin vacuity, or insufficient body fluids.
2. Do not use indefinitely once the condition improves.

Qi-moving medicines which treat stagnation of the spleen & stomach

Ban Xia Hou Po Wan (Pinellia & Magnolia Pills)

Rhizoma Pinelliae Ternatae (*Ban Xia*)
Cortex Magnoliae Officinalis (*Hou Po*)
Sclerotium Poriae Cocos (*Fu Ling*)
dry Rhizoma Zingiberis (*Gan Jiang*)
Folium Perillae Frutescentis (*Su Ye*)

Functions: Moves the qi and scatters nodulations, downbears counterflow and transforms phlegm

Indications: Plum pit qi. Neurotic esophageal stenosis, globus hystericus, gastrointestinal neurosis, chronic laryngitis, tracheitis, neurasthenia, morning sickness, bronchitis, hysteria, neurosis, recurrent palpitations, asthma, pertussis, toxemia during pregnancy, and edema

Main signs & symptoms: The sensation of something stuck in the throat which cannot be spit up or swallowed down, chest and rib-side fullness and oppression, possible cough with copious phlegm, possible vomiting, a white, moist or slimy, glossy tongue coating, and a bowstring or bowstring, slippery pulse

Contraindications: Do not use this medicine in patients with a flushed face, a bitter taste in the mouth, and a red tongue with scanty fur. This means those with yin vacuity or heat due to liver depression, stagnant qi transforming into internal heat.

Dosage: 8 pills three times per day

Formula explanation: This medicine uses Pinellia to transform phlegm and scatter nodulation, downbear counterflow and harmonize the stomach. It is the sovereign medicinal in this prescription. Magnolia lowers the qi and eliminates fullness. It assists Pinellia in scattering nodulation and downbearing counterflow. Poria, sweet and bland, percolates dampness. It assists Pinellia in transforming phlegm. Magnolia and Poria are this formula's minister medicinals. Fresh Ginger, acrid and warm, scatters nodulation, harmonizes the stomach, and stops vomiting, while Folium Perillae aromatically moves the qi, rectifies the lungs, and soothes the liver. These are the assistant and messenger medicinals.

Qi-moving medicines which treat liver depression qi stagnation

Chai Hu Shu Gan Wan (Bupleurum Soothe the Liver Pills)[1]

Radix Bupleuri (*Chai Hu*)
Radix Albus Paeoniae Lactiflorae (*Bai Shao*)
Rhizoma Cyperi Rotundi (*Xiang Fu*)
Fructus Citri Aurantii (*Zhi Ke*)
Radix Ligustici Wallichii (*Chuan Xiong*)
Radix Glycyrrhizae (*Gan Cao*)

Functions: Courses the liver and rectifies the qi, quickens the blood and stops pain

Indications: Liver depression qi stagnation breast distention, rib-side pain, painful menstruation, or stomach pain

Main signs & symptoms: Abdominal and rib-side distention and pain, breast distention and pain, or lower abdominal distention which are worse before the menstrual movement or due to emotional stress, possible alternating fever and chills, possible cold hands due to stress, a normal or darkish tongue with thin, white fur, and a bowstring pulse

Dosage: 8 pills three times per day

Formula explanation: Within this formula, Bupleurum and Ligusticum Wallichium course and free the flow of the blood in the liver channel. Cyperus and Aurantium open and smooth the flow of the qi within the liver channel. Peony and Licorice emolliate the liver and relax urgency (or cramping). They also prevent the preceding medicinals' acrid, drying natures from damaging yin. When used together, these medicinals course and soften the liver and smooth and free the flow of both the qi and blood.

Comments: Although many Western adults suffer from liver depression qi stagnation, this medicine is not so useful all by itself. This is because this pattern rarely presents in its simple, textbook form. Because of the relationships between the six depressions and between the liver, spleen, stomach, and intestines, when the liver is depressed and the qi is stagnant, there is usually something else going on as well. However, this formula is a good one for combining with other Chinese ready-made medicines. For instance, if liver

---

[1] This formula is very similar but not exactly the same as the standard formula, *Chai Hu Shu Gan San* (Bupleurum Course the Liver Powder). This latter formula contains Pericarpium Citri Reticulatae (*Chen Pi*) in addition to the ingredients listed in this formula.

depression qi stagnation and spleen vacuity symptoms are both more pronounced than appropriate for *Xiao Yao Wan* (Rambling Pills), then *Chai Hu Shu Gan Wan* can be combined with *Si Jun Zi Wan* (Four Gentlemen Pills). Or if there is spleen vacuity and depressive heat affecting the stomach and/or lungs, this medicine might be combined with *Xiao Chai Hu Tang Wan* (Minor Bupleurum Decoction Pills).

Shu Gan Wan (Soothe the Liver Pills)

Rhizoma Cyperi Rotundi (*Xiang Fu*)
Radix Albus Paeoniae Lactiflorae (*Bai Shao*)
Fructus Citri Aurantii (*Zhi Ke*)
Fructus Amomi (*Sha Ren*)
Pericarpium Citri Reticulatae Viride (*Qing Pi*)
Rhizoma Corydalis Yanhusuo (*Yan Hu Suo*)
Radix Bupleuri (*Chai Hu*)
Pericarpium Citri Reticulatae (*Chen Pi*)
Cortex Radicis Moutan (*Dan Pi*)
Flos Inulae Racemosae (*Xuan Fu Hua*)
Fructus Citri Medicae Seu Wilsoni (*Xiang Yuan*)
Radix Glycyrrhizae (*Gan Cao*)
Tuber Curcumae (*Yu Jin*)
Lignum Aquilariae Agallochae (*Chen Xiang*)
Fructus Cardamomi (*Dou Kou*)
Lignum Santali Albi (*Tan Xiang*)

Functions: Courses the liver and rectifies the qi, disperses accumulation and stops pain

Indications: Liver depression qi stagnation with food stagnation, abdominal distention and pain. Chronic hepatitis, chronic cholecystitis, cholelithiasis, acute or chronic gastritis, idiopathic, functional, or stress-related digestive disorders

Main signs & symptoms: Indigestion, stomach duct glomus and fullness, abdominal distention, rib-side distention and pain, nausea, eructation, vomiting, possible acid regurgitation, a normal or slightly dark tongue with slimy fur, and a bowstring pulse

Contraindications: This medicine is contraindicated during pregnancy unless warranted.

Dosage: 8 pills three times per day

Formula explanation: Cyperus moves the qi and disperses distention, while Peony softens and harmonizes the liver. Aurantium, Orange Peel, Green Orange Peel,

Amomum, Cardamon, Citrus Medica, Aquilaria, Sandalwood, and Bupleurum all rectify and move the qi. Inula downbears counterflow and stops vomiting, while Moutan, Curcuma, and Corydalis quicken the blood and stop pain.

Comments: This medicine strongly moves and even breaks the qi and it is quite effective for stopping abdominal, rib-side, and even chest pain due to liver depression. As explained above, since liver depression typically is complicated by other disease mechanisms and patterns, this medicine is usually used in combination with other ready-made medicines which address elements of those other mechanisms and patterns.

Mu Xiang Shun Qi Wan (Auklandia Normalize the Flow of Qi Pills)

Radix Auklandiae Lappae (*Mu Xiang*)
Cortex Magnoliae Officinalis (*Hou Po*)
Fructus Cardamomi (*Dou Kou*)
Rhizoma Atractylodis (*Cang Zhu*)
Fructus Citri Aurantii (*Zhi Ke*)
Pericarpium Citri Reticulatae (*Chen Pi*)
Pericarpium Citri Reticulatae Viride (*Qing Pi*)
Sclerotium Poriae Cocos (*Fu Ling*)
dry Rhizoma Zingiberis (*Gan Jiang*)
Semen Arecae Catechu (*Bing Lang*)
Radix Linderae Strychnifoliae (*Wu Yao*)
Semen Raphani Sativi (*Lai Fu Zi*)
Fructus Crataegi (*Shan Zha*)
Massa Medica Fermentata (*Shen Qu*)
Fructus Germinatus Hordei Vulgaris (*Mai Ya*)
Radix Bupleuri (*Chai Hu*)
Radix Glycyrrhizae (*Gan Cao*)

Functions: Courses the liver and rectifies the qi, disperses accumulation and abducts stagnation

Indications: Liver depression qi stagnation complicated by food stagnation, indigestion, and abdominal distention. Chronic hepatitis, early stage cirrhosis of the liver, chronic gastritis, and intestinal spasm

Main signs & symptoms: Chest and diaphragm glomus and fullness, bad breath, burping and eructation, a normal or slightly dark tongue with slimy fur, and a bowstring, slippery pulse

Dosage: 8 pills two times per day

Formula explanation: Auklandia, Orange Peel, Green Orange Peel, Aurantium, Areca, Lindera, Bupleurum, and Magnolia all move the qi and disperse distention. Cardamon, Atractylodes, and Ginger acridly and warmly transform dampness, while Poria assists the elimination of turbid dampness through percolation. Crataegus, Massa Medica, Malted Barley, and Radish Seeds all disperse food and abduct stagnation, while Licorice harmonizes the functions of all the other medicinals in this formula.

Comments: In comparison to the preceding medicine, this medicine is stronger at dispersing food and abducting stagnation. The previous medicine is stronger at stopping pain.

Ji Sheng Ju He Wan (*Aid the Living* Orange Seed Pills)

Semen Citri Reticulatae (*Ju He*)
Fructus Meliae Toosendan (*Chuan Lian Zi*)
Radix Auklandiae Lappae (*Mu Xiang*)
Semen Pruni Persicae (*Tao Ren*)
Rhizoma Corydalis Yanhusuo (*Yan Hu Suo*)
Cortex Cinnamomi Cassiae (*Rou Gui*)
Caulis Akebiae (*Mu Tong*)
Cortex Magnoliae Officinalis (*Hou Po*)
Fructus Immaturus Citri Aurantii (*Zhi Shi*)
Herba Sargassii (*Hai Zao*)
Thallus Algae (*Kun Bu*)
Herba Laminariae Japonicae (*Hai Dai*)

Functions: Moves the qi and stops pain, softens the hard and scatters nodulations

Indications: Cold damp mounting qi. Hydrocele, orchitis, epididymitis

Main signs & symptoms: Testicular swelling, distention, and one-sided sagging, testicles as hard as a rock, possible pain leading to the navel

Dosage: 8 pills three times per day

Formula explanation: Within this formula, Orange Seeds are the sovereign medicinal. They move the qi and scatter nodulation and are particularly effective for treating mounting pain. Melia and Auklandia assist Orange Seeds in moving the qi and stopping pain. Persica and Corydalis quicken the blood and scatter nodulation. Corydalis also has the propensity to move the qi and stop pain. These are the minister medicinals. This combination of sovereign and minister ingredients scatters *jue yin* liver channel qi and blood depression. Cortex Cinnamomi warms the kidneys, warms the liver, and scatters cold. Akebia frees the flow of and disinhibits the blood vessels and eliminates dampness. Magnolia descends the qi and dries dampness. Immature Aurantium moves the qi and breaks hardness. Sargassum, Algae, and Laminaria soften the hard and scatter nodulation. These are all the assistant and messenger medicinals.

Comments: This formula can also be used for fibrocystic breast condition and benign breast lumps due to a combination of liver depression, phlegm nodulation, and blood stasis. Since the incidence of these conditions increases in women over 35 years of age, this medicine is often combined with others which also supplement the qi and/or blood, the spleen and/or the kidneys.

Tian Tai Wu Yao San Wan (Tian Tai Lindera Powder Pills)

Radix Linderae Strychnifoliae (*Wu Yao*)
Fructus Foeniculi Vulgaris (*Xiao Hui Xiang*)
Rhizoma Alpiniae Officinari (*Gao Liang Jiang*)
Radix Auklandiae Lappae (*Mu Xiang*)
Pericarpium Citri Reticulatae Viride (*Qing Pi*)
Fructus Meliae Toosendan (*Chuan Lian Zi*)
Semen Arecae Catechu (*Bing Lang*)
Fructus Evodiae Rutecarpae (*Wu Zhu Yu*)

Functions: Moves the qi and soothes the liver, scatters cold and stops pain

Indications: Cold stagnating in the liver channel causing mounting conditions. Hypochondral pain, lower abdominal pain, and menstrual pain

Main signs & symptoms: Lower abdominal pain, possibly radiating to the testicles, a pale tongue with white fur, and a deep, slow, bowstring pulse

Dosage: 8 pills three times per day

Formula explanation: Lindera, which is acrid and warm, is the sovereign medicinal in this formula. It enters the liver channel and rectifies the qi, scatters cold and stops pain. It is assisted by Fennel which essentially does the same things and by several other medicinals from the qi-rectifying category. Alpinia Officinarum scatters cold and stops pain. Green Orange Peel rectifies the qi and disperses accumulations. Auklandia moves the qi and stops pain. Areca leads the qi to move downward as well as disperses accumulations in the lower burner, while Melia also rectifies the qi and stops pain. Evodia enters the liver channel, scatters cold, and stops pain.

Comments: This formula is a modification of the standard prescription of the same name. It substitutes Evodia for Semen Crotonis Tiglii (*Ba Dou*). It is mainly indicated for mounting. Mounting includes hernias but also encompasses other types of qi stagnation pain and accumulation conditions in the lower burner, including some gynecological conditions. These pills can be combined with other Chinese ready-made formulas when one wants to increase their ability to treat lower abdominal qi stagnation pain.

Qi-downbearing medicines

Chen Xiang Hua Qi Wan (Aquilaria Transforming Qi Pills)

Lignum Aquilariae Agallochae (*Chen Xiang*)
Semen Arecae Catechu (*Bing Lang*)
Semen Alpiniae Katsumadai (*Cao Dou Kou*)
Fructus Amomi (*Sha Ren*)
Rhizoma Cyperi Rotundi (*Xiang Fu*)
Cortex Magnoliae Officinalis (*Hou Po*)
Sclerotium Poriae Cocos (*Fu Ling*)
Pericarpium Citri Reticulatae (*Chen Pi*)
Semen Raphani Sativi (*Lai Fu Zi*)
Radix Glycyrrhizae (*Gan Cao*)

Functions: Rectifies the qi, downbears counterflow, and disperses accumulation

Indications: Spleen-stomach qi stagnation and upward counterflow complicated by food stagnation. Lack of appetite, belching, and acid regurgitation. Chronic hepatitis, gastritis, stomach ulcers, duodenal ulcers, intestinal obstruction, and chronic cholecystitis

Main signs & symptoms: No thought for food or drink, burping and belching, possible acid regurgitation, bad breath, stomach duct and abdominal fullness and distention, a normal tongue with possible slimy fur, and a bowstring, slippery pulse

Contraindications: This medicine is contraindicated in cases of yin depletion due to its inclusion of warm, acrid, windy medicinals which easily damage and consume fluids and humors.

Dosage: 8 pills three times per day

Formula explanation: Aquilaria and Areca are the sovereign medicinals in this formula. They disperse stagnation and descend the qi. Alpinia Katsumadai, Amomum, and Magnolia are the ministers which rectify the qi and dry dampness. The assistants in this formula are Cyperus which rectifies the qi and disperses distention, Poria which percolates dampness, Radish Seeds which transform food and disperse accumulation, and Orange Peel which dries dampness and harmonizes the stomach. And finally, Licorice is the messenger medicinal which harmonizes all the rest.

Comments: This formula differs from the preceding one in that it is stronger at downbearing upward counterflow. Therefore, it is particularly indicated when there is burping, belching, hiccup, and eructation.

Ding Chuan Wan (Stabilize Panting Pills)

Semen Ginkgonis Bilobae (*Bai Guo*)
Cortex Radicis Mori Albi (*Sang Bai Pi*)
Radix Platycodi Grandiflori (*Jie Geng*)
Fructus Perillae Frutescentis (*Zi Su Zi*)
Semen Pruni Armeniacae (*Xing Ren*)
Radix Scutellariae Baicalensis (*Huang Qin*)
Rhizoma Pinelliae Ternatae (*Ban Xia*)
Radix Glycyrrhizae (*Gan Cao*)
Radix Stemonae (*Bai Bu*)
Radix Asteris Tatarici (*Zi Wan*)[2]

Functions: Diffuses the lungs and downbears the qi, dispels phlegm and levels panting

Indications: Wind cold externally fettering, phlegm heat brewing internally, coughing and panting. Chronic bronchitis, bronchial asthma, and bronchiolitis

Main signs & symptoms: Profuse phlegm, hasty breathing, thick, yellow-colored phlegm, wheezing and panting, cough, slimy, yellow tongue fur, and a slippery, rapid pulse

Contraindications: This formula is not for wind cold acute asthma without phlegm nor for enduring asthma due to qi vacuity.

Dosage: 8 pills three times per day

---

[2] The textbook composition of this formula includes Herba Ephedrae (*Ma Huang*) and Flos Tussilaginis Farfarae (*Kuan Dong Hua*) and does not include Aster or Stemona.

Formula explanation: Within this formula, Ginkgo constrains the lungs, stabilizes panting, and dispels phlegm. It is the sovereign medicinal. Perilla Seeds, Armeniaca, Pinellia, Aster, and Stemona downbear the qi and level panting, stop coughing and dispel phlegm. They are the minister medicinals. Cortex Mori and Scutellaria clear and discharge lung heat, stop coughing and level panting. They are the assistant medicinals, while Licorice is the messenger medicinal which harmonizes and regulates all the rest. Taken as a whole, this formula promotes the lungs' obtaint of diffusion, phlegm heat's obtaint of clearing, and wind cold's obtaint of resolution. Thus the symptoms of panting, coughing, and profuse phlegm are all spontaneously eliminated.

Comments: In Chinese medicine, the pattern discrimination and treatment of asthma is divided into two stages. The acute stage is divided into wind heat and wind cold, while the remission stage is divided into lung, spleen, and/or kidney qi vacuity with deep-lying phlegm. However, it is also possible, and in fact quite common clinically, to have wind cold fettering the exterior with enduring phlegm heat brewing internally. This formula is appropriate for that more complex pattern of acute asthma. This formula is not for treatment of chronic asthma during the remission stage.

Ning Sou Wan (Calming Cough Pills)

Radix Platycodi Grandiflori (*Jie Geng*)
Herba Dendrobii (*Shi Hu*)
Rhizoma Pinelliae Ternatae (*Ban Xia*)
Bulbus Fritillariae Cirrhosae (*Chuan Bei Mu*)
Fructus Perillae Frutescentis (*Zi Su Zi*)
Sclerotium Poriae Cocos (*Fu Ling*)
Herba Menthae Haplocalycis (*Bo He*)
Cortex Radicis Mori Albi (*Sang Bai Pi*)
Semen Pruni Armeniacae (*Xing Ren*)
Pericarpium Citri Reticulatae (*Chen Pi*)
Radix Glycyrrhizae (*Gan Cao*)

Functions: Diffuses the lungs and downbears the qi, dispels phlegm and stops coughing

Indications: Depressive heat accumulating in the lungs resulting in the engenderment of phlegm and upward counterflow of the lung qi with coughing and panting. Chronic bronchitis, bronchial asthma

Main signs & symptoms: Coughing and panting with scanty, dry or thick, yellow phlegm, a red tongue with scant, dry, yellow fur, and a bowstring, fine, rapid pulse

Dosage: 8 pills three times per day

Formula explanation: Perilla and Pinellia are the sovereign ingredients in this formula. The first downbears the qi and transforms phlegm, while the second transforms phlegm and downbears the qi. The minister medicinals in this formula are Platycodon, Cortex Mori, Sichuan Fritillaria, Semen Armeniaca, and Dendrobium which clear heat and transform phlegm, stop coughing and level panting. In addition, Fritillaria and Dendrobium also moisten the lungs and engender fluids. The assistant medicinals in this formula are Poria, which percolates dampness and fortifies the spleen, and Mint, which clears heat and resolves depression. Licorice is then the messenger which harmonizes the actions of all the other medicinals.

Comments: In this case, there is liver depression transforming heat. This heat counterflows upward and accumulates in the lungs. Thus the lungs lose their diffusion and downbearing and accumulate evil phlegm and heat. Because this heat tends to be lingering and enduring, it damages lung yin. Therefore, the phlegm is not only yellow in color but also tends to be scanty in amount and thick in consistency. This formula is more for chronic cough than for acute episodes of asthma and wheezing, although it might be used during remission stages of asthma.

10
Blood-rectifying Medicines

Formulas which rectify the blood are divided into two subcategories: 1) formulas which quicken the blood and dispel stasis, and 2) formulas which stop bleeding. Blood stasis may be due to prolonged qi depression, cold, heat, or trauma. It may also be categorized as replete or vacuous, mild or severe, acute or chronic. In addition, treatment typically takes into account the location of the stasis. Blood-quickening, stasis-dispelling formulas are commonly used in internal medicine, gynecology, traumatology, and in external medicine.

Stop-bleeding formulas are used in all sorts of hemorrhagic disorders. Bleeding may be due to only four disease mechanisms in Chinese medicine. First, heat may cause the blood to flow recklessly outside its pathways. Evil heat causing bleeding may be further divided between replete heat, vacuity heat, depressive heat, and damp or phlegm heat. Secondly, stasis may force the blood outside its pathways. Third, qi may be too vacuous to restrain the blood within its channels. Fourth, traumatic injury may rupture the channels and vessels, so the blood cannot be canalized and flow freely. Under the stop-bleeding category of formulas, most formulas stop bleeding by either clearing heat or supplementing vacuity.

Cautions & contraindications:

1. Hemostatic medicinals may cause stasis if used in too large doses, for too long a time, or unwarrantedly.
2. Blood-quickening, stasis-dispelling medicinals are attacking in nature. Therefore, if they are used in too large a dose or for too long a time, they can consume blood and yin.
3. In case of blood desertion, first supplement the qi greatly before using hemostatic medicinals.
4. If blood stasis complicates or is causing bleeding, one must use blood-quickening medicinals *in order* to help stop bleeding.

Blood-quickening, stasis-dispelling medicines

Xue Fu Zhu Yu Tang Wan (Blood Mansion Dispel Stasis Decoction Pills) —

Semen Pruni Persicae (*Tao Ren*)
Flos Carthami Tinctorii (*Hong Hua*)

Radix Angelicae Sinensis (*Dang Gui*)
uncooked Radix Rehmanniae (*Sheng Di*)
Radix Ligustici Wallichii (*Chuan Xiong*)
Radix Rubrus Paeoniae Lactiflorae (*Chi Shao*)
Radix Achyranthis Bidentatae (*Niu Xi*)
Radix Platycodi Grandiflori (*Jie Geng*)
Radix Bupleuri (*Chai Hu*)
Fructus Citri Aurantii (*Zhi Ke*)
Radix Glycyrrhizae (*Gan Cao*)

Functions: Quickens the blood and dispels stasis, moves the qi and stops pain

Indications: Blood stasis in the chest, blood not moving smoothly. Coronary heart disease, angina pectoris, rheumatic heart disease, intercostal neuralgia, costochondritis, functional neurosis, post-concussion syndrome, migraine, trigeminal neuralgia, external injury to the chest, irregular menstruation, dysmenorrhea, menopausal syndrome, cerebral hemorrhage, hypertension, cor pulmonale, and urticaria

Main signs & symptoms: Chest pain, headache which does not heal for many days, pain like a needle prick, possible hiccup for many days which will not stop, a choking sensation when drinking water, dry heaves, internal heat and oppression, possible heart palpitations, possible inability to sleep at night or one's sleep is not quiet, tension, agitation, easy anger, tidal fever, a dark red tongue, possible static patches or spots on the tongue, dark lips or dark around the eyes, and a choppy[3] or bowstring, tight pulse

Contraindications:

1. Do not use unwarrantedly during pregnancy.
2. Do not use for uterine bleeding or other hemorrhagic disorders.

Dosage: 5 pills three times per day

Formula explanation: Within this formula, *Tao Hong Si Wu Tang* (Persica & Carthamus Four Materials Decoction, *i.e.*, Dang Gui, Ligusticum Wallichium, Peony, Rehmannia, Persica, and Carthamus) quickens the blood, transforms stasis, and also nourishes the blood, while *Si Ni San* (Four Counterflows Powder, *i.e.*, Bupleurum, Aurantium, Peony, and Licorice) moves the qi, harmonizes the blood, and soothes the liver. Platycodon opens the lung qi and guides the other medicinals upward. Combined with Aurantium, these two upbear and downbear the qi of the upper burner and loosen

---

[3] Wiseman has changed his translation of *se mai* to rough pulse. We are sticking with choppy in order to remain consistent with our other Blue Poppy books which use this term.

the chest. Achyranthes frees the flow of and disinhibits the blood vessels and leads the qi to move downward. Taken as a whole, this formula quickens the blood and moves the qi, transforms phlegm and disperses heat while it also resolves depression of the liver.

Ge Xia Zhu Yu Wan (Below the Diaphragm Dispel Stasis Pills)

Feces Trogopterori Seu Pteromi (*Wu Ling Zhi*)
Radix Angelicae Sinensis (*Dang Gui*)
Semen Pruni Persicae (*Tao Ren*)
Flos Carthami Tinctorii (*Hong Hua*)
Radix Linderae Strychnifoliae (*Wu Yao*)
Radix Ligustici Wallichii (*Chuan Xiong*)
Cortex Radicis Moutan (*Dan Pi*)
Radix Rubrus Paeoniae Lactiflorae (*Bai Shao*)
Rhizoma Cyperi Rotundi (*Xiang Fu*)
Fructus Citri Aurantii (*Zhi Ke*)
Rhizoma Corydalis Yanhusuo (*Yan Hu Suo*)
Radix Glycyrrhizae (*Gan Cao*)

Functions: Quickens the blood and dispels stasis, moves the qi and stops pain

Indications: Qi stagnation and blood stasis below the diaphragm. Endometriosis, dysmenorrhea, and abdominal masses, including hepato- and splenomegaly and various types of tumors

Main signs & symptoms: Pain and palpable lumps below the diaphragm, painful menstruation which is better after discharge of clots, dark menses, a dark, possibly purple tongue or possible static spots and macules, and a bowstring, deep, and/or choppy pulse

Contraindications: Use cautiously during pregnancy and only when warranted by definite signs and symptoms of blood stasis.

Dosage: 8 pills three times per day

Formula explanation: Within this formula, Trogopterorus, Dang Gui, Persica, Carthamus, Red Peony, Ligusticum Wallichium, and Corydalis all quicken the blood and dispel stasis. Cyperus, Lindera, and Aurantium course the liver and move the qi. Licorice harmonizes all the other medicinals.

Comments: This formula is especially for blood stasis located below the diaphragm.

Shao Fu Zhu Yu Wan (Lower Abdomen Dispel Stasis Pills)

Radix Angelicae Sinensis (*Dang Gui*)
Pollen Typhae (*Pu Huang*)
Radix Rubrus Paeoniae Lactiflorae (*Chi Shao*)
Feces Trogopterori Seu Pteromi (*Wu Ling Zhi*)
Rhizoma Corydalis Yanhusuo (*Yan Hun Suo*)
Radix Ligustici Wallichii (*Chuan Xiong*)
Resina Myrrhae (*Mo Yao*)
Cortex Tubiformis Cinnamomi Cassiae (*Guan Gui*)
Fructus Foeniculi Vulgaris (*Xiao Hui Xiang*)
dry Rhizoma Zingiberis (*Gan Jiang*)

Functions: Quickens the blood and dispels stasis, warms the channels (or menses) and stops pain

Indications: Qi stagnation and blood stasis mixed with cold causing lower abdominal pain. Dysmenorrhea, endometriosis, cirrhosis of the liver, lower abdominal masses

Main signs & symptoms: Chilly lower abdominal pain with or without palpable masses, painful menstruation which is alleviated by warmth, dark-colored menses containing clots, a bluish purplish tongue, and a bowstring, deep, and/or choppy pulse

Contraindications: Use cautiously during pregnancy and only when warranted by definite signs and symptoms of blood stasis.

Dosage: 8 pills three times per day

Formula explanation: Pollen Typhae and Trogopterorus when used together as a pair are referred to as *Shi Xiao San* (Loose a Smile Powder) and are especially effective for relieving pain due to blood stasis. Dang Gui, Ligusticum Wallichium, Red Peony, Corydalis, and Myrrha all also quicken the blood, dispel stasis, and stop pain. Cinnamon and dry Ginger warm the uterus and scatter cold, while Fennel moves the qi and stops pain in the liver channel.

Comments: While both this formula and the one above can be used for lower abdominal qi stagnation and blood stasis pain, because of the inclusion of warming ingredients, this formula is better suited for conditions complicated by cold congelation.

Shen Tong Zhu Yu Wan (Body Pain Dispel Stasis Pills)

Semen Pruni Persicae (*Tao Ren*)
Flos Carthami Tinctorii (*Hong Hua*)

Radix Angelicae Sinensis (*Dang Gui*)
Radix Cyathulae (*Chuan Niu Xi*)
Radix Ligustici Wallichii (*Chuan Xiong*)
Radix Glycyrrhizae (*Gan Cao*)
Resina Myrrhae (*Mo Yao*)
Feces Trogopterori Sei Pteromi (*Wu Ling Zhi*)
Lumbricus (*Di Long*)
Radix Gentianae Macrophyllae (*Qin Jiao*)
Radix Et Rhizoma Notopterygii (*Qiang Huo*)
Rhizoma Cyperi Rotundi (*Xiang Fu*)

Functions: Quickens the blood and dispels stasis, frees the flow of the network vessels and stops pain

Indications: Qi stagnation and blood stasis body pain. Endometriosis, lochioschesis, coronary artery disease

Main signs & symptoms: Irregular menstruation, painful menstruation, non-descension of the lochia, postpartum abdominal pain, lower abdominal pain, severe venter and abdominal pain, possible varicosities, a possible dark, sooty facial complexion, a dark, possibly purple tongue or possible static spots or macules, engorged, tortuous sublingual veins, a bowstring, deep, bound, and/or choppy pulse

Contraindications: Use cautiously during pregnancy and only when warranted by definite signs and symptoms of blood stasis.

Dosage: 8 pills three times per day

Formula explanation: Persica and Carthamus quicken the blood and dispel stasis. Dang Gui both quickens and nourishes the blood. Ligusticum Wallichium moves the qi within the blood and stops pain. Cyathula quickens the blood, dispels stasis, and leads the blood to move downward. Trogopterorus quickens the blood, dispels stasis, and stops pain. Lumbricus and Myrrha both quicken the blood and dispel stasis from the network vessels. Lumbricus extinguishes wind and thus settles tetany (*i.e.*, relaxes spasms), while Myrrh also greatly stops pain. Gentiana Macrophylla and Notopterygium both dispel wind dampness and stop pain. Licorice harmonizes all the other medicinals in the formula and also relaxes tension.

Comments: This formula is a good one for treating enduring wind damp impediment pain which has resulted in qi stagnation and blood stasis which has entered the network vessels. It is usually used by itself, although it could be combined with other ready-made medicines when the condition is complicated by other patterns. Such other patterns might include spleen vacuity or kidney yin and/or yang vacuity.

Tao Hong Si Wu Tang Wan (Persica & Carthamus Four Materials Decoction Pills)

Radix Angelicae Sinensis (*Dang Gui*)
Radix Albus Paeoniae Lactiflorae (*Bai Shao*)
cooked Radix Rehmanniae (*Shu Di*)
Semen Pruni Persicae (*Tao Ren*)
Radix Ligustici Wallichii (*Chuan Xiong*)
Flos Carthami Tinctorii (*Hong Hua*)

Functions: Supplements and quickens the blood, regulates menstruation

Indications: Blood vacuity and blood stasis, painful menstruation, early menstruation, profuse menstruation

Main signs & symptoms: Early menstruation, profuse menstruation, painful menstruation, dark, purple menstrual blood possibly containing clots, a pale, possibly purple tongue with dry, white coating, and a fine, bowstring, possibly choppy pulse

Dosage: 8 pills three times per day

Formula explanation: Within this formula, Dang Gui both supplements and quickens the blood while cooked Rehmannia only supplements the blood. These are the main medicinals in this formula. Ligusticum Wallichium enters the blood division and rectifies the qi within the blood. Peony constrains yin and nourishes the blood. Persica and Carthamus quicken the blood and dispel stasis.

Comments: In Chinese, another name for static blood is dead blood. If static blood is not dispelled, fresh or new blood cannot be engendered. Conversely, if blood is insufficient to nourish the vessels, the vessels cannot fulfill their duty of promoting the circulation of the blood. Therefore, blood stasis and blood vacuity are mutually engendering. Either can lead to the other, and this medicine treats this common combination of blood stasis and blood vacuity.

Tong Qiao Huo Xue Wan (Free the Flow of the Orifices & Quicken the Blood Pills)

Semen Pruni Persicae (*Tao Ren*)
Flos Carthami Tinctorii (*Hong Hua*)
Radix Rubrus Paeoniae Lactiflorae (*Chi Shao*)
Radix Ligustici Wallichii (*Chuan Xiong*)
Radix Angelicae Dahuricae (*Bai Zhi*)

Fructus Zizyphi Jujubae (*Da Zao*)
uncooked Rhizoma Zingiberis (*Sheng Jiang*)
Rhizoma Acori Graminei (*Shi Chang Pu*)

Functions: Quickens the blood, dispels stasis, and frees the flow of the orifices

Indications: Blood stasis blocking the clear portals in the upper body. Headache, vertigo, chronic tinnitus, balding, acne rosacea, chronic nasal obstruction

Main signs & symptoms: Headache, dizziness and vertigo, nasal blockage, dimming of vision, loss of auditory acuity, falling hair, a sooty, dark facial complexion, various types of varicosities and hemangiomas, liver or age spots, a dark, purplish tongue or possible static spots or macules, and a bowstring, deep, possibly choppy pulse

Dosage: 8 pills three times per day

Formula explanation: The sovereign ingredients in this formula are Persica and Carthamus which quicken the blood and dispel stasis. They are assisted in this by Red Peony and Ligusticum Wallichium. Ligusticum Wallichium also acts as a messenger medicinal, guiding the other medicinals in this formula to the head and upper part of the body. Angelica Dahurica frees the flow of the clear orifices in the head, while Acorus transforms phlegm and also frees the flow of the orifices. Red Dates and uncooked Ginger harmonize and protect the center. In addition, Ginger helps Acorus transform any complicating phlegm. It also moves the qi to help move blood and body fluids.

Comments: This formula is not the same as the standard prescription of the same name. Angelica Dahurica and Acorus have been substituted for Secretio Moschi Moschiferi (*She Xiang*) and Bulbus Allii Fistulosi (*Cong Bai*). Although Musk is a very effective Chinese medicinal, when "wild-crafted", it does come from an endangered species. In general, I think these modifications are good ones and make this formula especially effective for nasal obstruction or any obstruction of the orifices where phlegm is complicating blood stasis.

Jin Gu Die Shang Wan (Sinew & Bone Fall & Injury Pills)

Radix Pseudoginseng (*San Qi*)
Radix Angelicae Sinensis (*Dang Gui*)
Radix Albus Paeoniae Lactiflorae (*Bai Shao*)
Radix Rubrus Paeoniae Lactiflorae (*Chi Shao*)
Semen Pruni Persicae (*Tao Ren*)
Flos Carthamus Tinctorii (*Hong Hua*)
Sanguis Draconis (*Xue Jie*)

Folium Artemisiae Anomalae (*Liu Ji Nu*)
Rhizoma Drynariae (*Gu Sui Bu*)
Lignum Sappan (*Su Mu*)
Cortex Radicis Moutan (*Dan Pi*)
Radix Dipsaci (*Xu Duan*)
Resina Olibani (*Ru Xiang*)
Resina Myrrhae (*Mo Yao*)
Rhizoma Curcumae Longae (*Jiang Huang*)
Rhizoma Sparganii (*San Leng*)
Radix Ledebouriellae Divaricatae (*Fang Feng*)
Semen Cucumidis Melonis (*Tian Kui Zi*)
Fructus Immaturus Citri Aurantii (*Zhi Shi*)
Radix Platycodi Grandiflori (*Jie Geng*)
Radix Glycyrrhizae (*Gan Cao*)
Caulis Akebiae (*Mu Tong*)
Pyritum (*Zi Ran Tong*)
Eupolyphaga Seu Ophistoplatia (*Tu Bie Chong*)

Functions: Quickens the blood and transforms stasis, disperses swelling and stops pain

Indications: Blood stasis, swelling, and pain due to traumatic injury

Main signs & symptoms: Ecchymosis, swelling, and pain due to traumatic injury. There may not be other generalized signs and symptoms. In some cases, the pulse may be bowstring or tight.

Contraindications: This medicine is contraindicated during pregnancy unless warranted by traumatic injury.

Dosage: 8 pills three times per day

Formula explanation: Most of the ingredients in this rather large formula quicken the blood and transform or dispel stasis. These include: Dang Gui, White Peony, Red Peony, Persica, Carthamus, Dragon's Blood, Artemisia Anomala, Sappan, Moutan, Frankincense, Myrrh, Turmeric, Sparganium, Pyritum, and Eupolyphaga. Amongst these, Dragon's Blood, Artemisia Anomala, Sappan, Frankincense, Myrrh, and Pyritum are commonly used for blood stasis due to traumatic injury. These blood-rectifying medicinals are then combined with qi-rectifying medicinals, dampness-percolating medicinals, bleeding-stopping medicinals, and yang supplementing medicinals. The exterior-resolving, qi-rectifying, upbearing and moving medicinals in this formula are Ledebouriella, Immature Aurantium, and Platycodon. These are to help stop pain. The dampness-percolating medicinals consist of Akebia and Melon Seeds. These help disperse swelling. The bleeding-stopping medicinal is Pseudoginseng. This stops bleeding at the same time as it quickens the blood and transforms stasis. And the yang-supplementing medicinals are Dipsacus and Drynaria. These are not included in order to supplement the kidneys and invigorate yang so much as to strengthen the sinews and bones as well as quicken the blood and transform stasis. And finally, Licorice is included to harmonize the rest of the ingredients in this formula.

Comments: For best effect, these pills should be taken either with alcohol or half water and half alcohol. This increases these medicinals' effects of moving the qi and quickening the blood and also makes them act faster.

Tong Jing Wan (Painful Menstruation Pills)

Semen Pruni Persicae (*Tao Ren*)
Radix Albus Paeoniae Lactiflorae (*Bai Shao*)
Radix Salviae Miltiorrhizae (*Dan Shen*)
Pollen Typhae (*Pu Huang*)
Radix Linderae Strychnifoliae (*Wu Yao*)
Rhizoma Corydalis Yanhusuo (*Yan Hu Suo*)
Radix Angelicae Sinensis (*Dang Gui*)
Rhizoma Cyperi Rotundi (*Xiang Fu*)
Radix Ligustici Wallichii (*Chuan Xiong*)
Flos Carthami Tinctorii (*Hong Hua*)
Radix Pseudoginseng (*San Qi*)

Functions: Quickens the blood and transforms stasis, regulates the menses and stops pain

Indications: Lower abdominal and menstrual pain due to blood stasis. Dysmenorrhea, endometriosis, chronic pelvic inflammatory disease, painful ovarian cysts

Main signs & symptoms: Premenstrual or menstrual lower abdominal pain which is severe in intensity, sharp or stabbing in nature, and fixed in location possibly accompanied by varicosities, large and small hemangiomas, a dark, purplish tongue or static spots or macules on the tongue, and a fine, bowstring, possibly choppy pulse

Contraindications: Use with care and only when warranted during pregnancy.

Dosage: 8 pills three times per day

Formula explanation: Persica, Carthamus, Salvia, and Corydalis all quicken the blood and transform stasis. Corydalis also is particularly good at stopping pain. Dang Gui nourishes as well as quickens the blood, while Peony nourishes the blood and emolliates the liver. Ligusticum Wallichium moves the qi within the blood, while Cyperus and Lindera move the qi in order to move the blood. This is based on the saying:

> The qi moves the blood. If the qi moves, the blood moves. If the qi stops, the blood stops.

Pollen Typhae and Pseudoginseng both stop bleeding and quicken the blood. Pollen Typhae and Corydalis together are known to be an empirically effective combination for addressing specifically menstrual or gynecological pain.

Comments: This medicine can either be used alone or combined with other medicines in order to address more complicated patterns. For instance, if there is chronic menstrual pain associated with a combination of spleen vacuity, blood stasis, and some liver depression, then this medicine can be combined with *Bu Zhong Yi Qi Wan* (Supplement the Center & Boost the Qi Pills). If there is a combination of liver depression, blood stasis, and spleen vacuity, then it can be combined with *Xiao Yao Wan* (Rambling Pills). If there is blood stasis with phlegm nodulation and heat, it can be combined with *Nei Xiao Luo Li Wan* (Internally Dispersing Scrofula Pills), etc.

Blood stasis is one of the four causes for pathological bleeding according to Chinese medical theory. Because this formula contains two medicinals which both quicken the blood and stop bleeding, this is a good medicine for any type of pathological gynecological bleeding due to, at least in part, blood stasis. Usually, such pathological bleeding is complicated by other disease mechanisms and patterns necessitating the combination of this medicine with one or more others.

Gui Zhi Fu Ling Wan (Cinnamon Twigs & Poria Pills)

Ramulus Cinnamomi Cassiae (*Gui Zhi*)
Sclerotium Poriae Cocos (*Fu Ling*)
Cortex Radicis Moutan (*Dan Pi*)
Radix Rubrus Paeoniae Lactiflorae (*Chi Shao*)
Semen Pruni Persicae (*Tao Ren*)
Mel (*Feng Mi*)

Functions: Quickens the blood and transforms stasis, relaxes and disperses concretions and lumps

Indications: Static blood retained and binding in the uterus, menstrual pain, fetal stirring restlessness, leaking precipitation which does not stop. Dysmenorrhea, uterine myomas, cervical erosion, ovarian cysts, chronic salpingitis, chronic pelvic inflammatory disease, endometriosis, lochioschesis

Main signs & symptoms: Lower abdominal or menstrual pain which refuses pressure, dark, purplish, black menstrual blood, possible blood clots, palpable lumps within the abdomen, a dark or purplish tongue, possible static spots or macules, and a fine, bowstring, possibly choppy pulse

Contraindications: Use with care and only when warranted during pregnancy.

Dosage: 8 pills three times per day

Formula explanation: Within this formula, Cinnamon Twigs and Poria are the sovereign ingredients. Cinnamon Twigs warm and free the flow of the blood vessels, while Poria percolates, disinhibits, and moves downward at the same time as boosting the qi of the heart and spleen. Hence they assist each other to move static blood and also disinhibit and quiet the fetal source. Because concretion lumps, an enduring depression, are often able to transform heat, Red Peony and Moutan are combined with Persica in order to transform static blood at the same time as clear stasis heat. These are the minister and assistant medicinals in this formula. By making these pills with honey, this also moderates and harmonizes the power of the blood-dispelling medicinals, thus moderating their dispersing effect. Therefore, honey is the messenger medicinal. When all these medicinals are used together, their effect is to quicken the blood and transform stasis and moderately disperse concretions and lumps.

Comments: This formula is quite sophisticated even though it is not a large one. It recognizes that there can be lower burner cold at the same time as stasis heat. It also recognizes that blood and fluids travel together, concretions are often associated with phlegm dampness, and the spleen is the root of phlegm engenderment. That being said, this formula should usually be combined with other formulas, and especially if there are actual abdominal masses. For instance, the clinical symptoms of uterine myomas are often only fatigue, lower abdominal heaviness, persistent vaginal discharge, and low back pain. In that case, this medicine would need to be combined with *Bu Zhong Yi Qi Wan* (Supplement the Center & Boost the Qi Pills) and *Ba Ji Yin Yang Wan* (Morinda & Epimedium Pills).

In China, concretions and conglomerations tend to be treated with very large doses of water-decocted, bulk-dispensed Chinese medicinals. However, abdominal masses typically only shrink very slowly. Therefore, the Chinese medical treatment of conditions such as uterine fibroids may take 12-36 months! In such cases, it may make more sense to use ready-made medicines in the form of pills. Since physical results in such cases only come slowly and grudgingly, persistence in treatment may be more important than large doses. Nevertheless, it is probable that the standard dose on the bottle will have to be increased.

Wen Jing Tang Wan (Warm the Menses Decoction Pills)

cooked Radix Rehmanniae (*Shu Di*)
Fructus Evodiae Rutecarpae (*Wu Zhu Yu*)
Radix Angelicae Sinensis (*Dang Gui*)
Radix Albus Paeoniae Lactiflorae (*Bai Shao*)
Radix Panacis Ginseng (*Ren Shen*)
Rhizoma Pinelliae Ternatae (*Ban Xia*)
Ramulus Cinnamomi Cassiae (*Gui Zhi*)
Cortex Radicis Moutan (*Dan Pi*)
Radix Glycyrrhizae (*Gan Cao*)
Radix Ligustici Wallichii (*Chuan Xiong*)
Tuber Ophiopogonis Japonici (*Mai Dong*)
uncooked Rhizoma Zingiberis (*Sheng Jiang*)
Gelatinum Corii Asini (*E Jiao*)

Functions: Warms the channels (or menses) and scatters cold, dispels stasis and nourishes the blood

Indications: *Chong* and *ren* vacuity cold, static blood obstruction and stagnation, menstrual irregularities, leaking precipitating which will not stop. Functional uterine bleeding, primary dysmenorrhea, infertility, polycystic ovarian disease, chronic pelvic inflammatory disease, menopausal syndrome

Main signs & symptoms: Early, late, or intermenstrual bleeding, leaking precipitation which will not stop, ceased menstruation which does not arrive, afternoon effusion of heat, vexatious heat in the hands and feet, dry lips and mouth, lower abdominal tenesmus, abdominal fullness

Contraindications: This medicine is contraindicated in cases of abdominal masses exhibiting repletion patterns.

Dosage: 8 pills three times per day

Formula explanation: Within this formula, Evodia and Cinnamon Twigs are the sovereign medicinals. They warm the channels and/or menses and scatter cold, free the flow of and disinhibit the blood vessels. Dang Gui, Ligusticum Wallichium, and Peony quicken the blood and dispel stasis, nourish the blood and regulate menstruation. Moutan dispels stasis and frees the flow of the channels and/or menses at the same time as receding or abating vacuity heat. These are the minister medicinals. Donkey Skin Glue and Ophiopogon nourish yin and moisten dryness at the same time as clearing vacuity heat. Donkey Skin Glue is also able to stop bleeding. Ginseng and Licorice boost the qi and fortify the spleen. They insure that the blood has a source from which it can be engendered and which can contain and restrain the blood within its vessels. The two vessels of the *chong* and *ren* connect with the foot *yang ming* stomach channel. Pinellia is able to free the flow of and downbear the stomach qi as well as scatter nodulation. This assists in the dispelling of stasis and regulation of menstruation. Uncooked Ginger warms the stomach qi in order to assist engenderment and transformation. These are all the assistant medicinals. Licorice is simultaneously a messenger medicinal since it also is able to regulate and harmonize all the other medicinals. When all these medicinals are used together, they warm the channels (or menses) and free the flow of the vessels, nourish the blood and dispel stasis. Hence static blood is removed, new blood is engendered, vacuity heat is dispersed, the menstruation is regulated, and the disease is automatically resolved.

Comments: This is another complex and sophisticated formula. It treats blood stasis in the lower burner accompanied by vacuity cold, vacuity heat, spleen and blood vacuity, and phlegm nodulation. Originally it was created to treat menopausal uterine bleeding. It takes into account that women's spleens typically get vacuous and weak from their mid-30s to menopause. After menopause, if the change has gone correctly and is entirely complete, the spleen and kidneys can recuperate themselves. Because menopausal conditions often include signs and symptoms of kidney yang vacuity and not just spleen vacuity, one may choose to combine this medicine with *Bai Ji Yin Yang Wan* (Morinda & Epimedium Pills). If there are more prominent symptoms of yin vacuity/vacuity heat, then it may be combined with *Da Bu Yin Wan* (Greatly Supplementing Yin Pills).

Huo Luo Xiao Ling Wan (Quicken the Network Vessels Miraculously Effective Pills)

Radix Angelicae Sinensis (*Dang Gui*)
Radix Salviae Miltiorrhizae (*Dan Shen*)
Resina Olibani (*Ru Xiang*)
Resina Myrrhae (*Mo Yao*)

Functions: Quickens the blood and frees the flow of the network vessels

Indications: Enduring blood stasis which has entered the network vessels

Main signs & symptoms: A dark, sooty facial complexion, varicosities, including small, mole-like hemangiomas and spider nevi, age or liver spots, chronic pain conditions which tend to be worse at night, static spots or macules on the tongue, and a possibly choppy pulse

Dosage: 8 pills three times per day

Formula explanation: Dang Gui and Salvia both nourish and quicken the blood, while Frankincense and Myrrh both free the flow of the network vessels and stop pain.

Comments: These pills can be combined with many other pills when enduring disease has entered the blood vessels. They may also be combined with decoctions when one wants to administer Frankincense and Myrrh. These two medicinals can cause stomach upset when taken in decoction but are less likely to when taken in pill form.

Dan Shen Yin Wan (Salvia Drink Pills)

Radix Salviae Miltiorrhizae (*Dan Shen*)
Lignum Santali Albi (*Tan Xiang*)
Fructus Amomi (*Sha Ren*)

Functions: Quickens the blood and dispels stasis, moves the qi and stops pain

Indications: Chest impediment due to blood stasis and qi stagnation. Angina pectoris, coronary artery disease

Main signs & symptoms: Chest pain which is fixed in location and severe or stabbing and, if severe, the pain may radiate down the left arm, a purple tongue or possible static spots or macules on the tongue or distended, tortuous veins under the tongue, and a bowstring, fine, deep, and/or choppy pulse

Dosage: 8 pills three times per day

Formula explanation: Salvia is the sovereign medicinal in this formula. It quickens the blood and dispels stasis, entering the heart, pericardium, and liver channels. Sandalwood is the minister medicinal. It moves the qi and stops pain, especially chest pain. Amomum also moves the qi. However, it additionally transforms dampness and downbears counterflow.

Comments: This medicine can be used for the symptomatic relief of chest pain due to qi stagnation and blood stasis. However, it can also be combined with other Chinese ready-made medicines whenever chest pain is a part of a more complicated scenario. Although Salvia mainly quickens the blood, it does also have some ability to supplement the heart. Likewise, although Amomum mainly moves and rectifies the qi, it does also fortify the spleen.

Yan Hu Suo Wan (Corydalis Pills)

Rhizoma Corydalis Yanhusuo (*Yan Hu Suo*)
Radix Angelicae Dahuricae (*Bai Zhi*)

Functions: Quickens the blood, moves the qi, and stops pain

Indications: All types of pain

Main signs & symptoms: Pain

Dosage: 8 pills three times per day

Formula explanation: This medicine only has two ingredients. Corydalis quickens the blood and stops pain, while Angelica Dahurica moves the qi and stops pain. Actually, Angelica Dahurica is an exterior-resolving medicinal. However, because it strongly upbears and effuses, it also strongly moves the qi. Both of these medicinals have a marked ability to stop pain.

Comments: This medicine can be used alone for the symptomatic relief of most kinds of pain. However, it is even more useful when combined with other Chinese ready-made medicines which address the root causes of the pain. For instance, when liver depression and blood vacuity cause migraine headaches before or at the onset of menstruation, this medicine can be combined with *Xiao Yao Wan* (Rambling Pills). Or if sinusitis is causing a severe headache, this medicine can be combined with *Bi Tong Wan* (Nose-freeing Pills).

Bu Yang Huan Wu Wan (Supplement Yang & Restore the Five [Tenths] Pills)

Radix Astragali Membranacei (*Huang Qi*)
Radix Angelicae Sinensis (*Dang Gui*)
Radix Rubrus Paeoniae Lactiflorae (*Chi Shao*)
Radix Ligustici Wallichii (*Chuan Xiong*)
Semen Pruni Persicae (*Tao Ren*)
Flos Carthami Tinctorii (*Hong Hua*)
Lumbricus (*Di Long*)

Functions: Supplements the qi, quickens the blood, and frees the flow of the network vessels

Indications: The sequellae of wind stroke. The sequellae of a cerebrovascular accident, the sequellae of poliomyelitis, acute myelitis, sciatica, thromboangiitis obliterans

Main signs & symptoms: Hemiplegia, deviation of the mouth and eyes, difficult, slurred speech, drooling from the corners of the mouth, lower limb wilting and atrophy, numerous, repeated urination or urinary incontinence, white tongue fur, and a moderate (*i.e.*, relaxed, slightly slow) pulse

Contraindications: Some Chinese medical authorities say not to use this formula too soon after a cerebral hemorrhage as it might cause more bleeding. It is contraindicated in wind stroke patients who have a large, forceful, bowstring pulse or in cases of yin vacuity and blood heat. It is also contraindicated unless truly warranted during pregnancy.

Dosage: 8 pills three times per day

Formula explanation: Within this formula, a heavy dose of Astragalus greatly supplements the source qi of the spleen and stomach, thus making the qi effulgent in order to promote the movement of the blood. Therefore, stasis is dispelled but there is damage to the righteous. Astragalus is the sovereign medicinal in this formula. Dang Gui quickens the blood. Its ability to dispel stasis without causing damage is wondrous. Dang Gui is the minister medicinal in this formula. Ligusticum Wallichium, Red Peony, Persica, and Carthamus assist Dang Gui in quickening the blood and dispelling stasis. Earthworms free the flow of the channels and quicken the network vessels. All these are the assistant medicinals. When used together, these ingredients make the qi effulgent and the blood move, stasis is dispelled and the network vessels' flow is freed. Therefore, all the symptoms are automatically progressively cured.

Stop-bleeding medicines

Shi Hui San (Ten Ashes Powder)

Herba Cirsii Japonici (*Da Ji*)
Herba Cephalanoploris Segeti (*Xiao Ji*)
Folium Nelumbinis Nuciferae (*He Ye*)
Cacumen Biotae Orientalis (*Ce Bai Ye*)
Rhizoma Imperatae Cylindricae (*Mao Gen*)
Radix Rubiae Cordifoliae (*Qian Cao*)
Fructus Gardeniae Jasminoidis (*Shan Zhi*)
Radix Et Rhizoma Rhei (*Da Huang*)
Cortex Radicis Moutan (*Dan Pi*)
Fibra Stipulae Trachycarpi (*Zong Lu Pi*)

Blood-rectifying Medicines

Functions: Cools the blood and stops bleeding

Indications: Blood heat reckless movement, replete fire in the liver and stomach. Hematemesis, hemoptysis, epistaxis, pulmonary tuberculosis, bronchiectasis, acute hemorrhagic esophagitis or gastritis, peptic ulcer bleeding, hemorrhagic febrile diseases, and functional uterine bleeding

Main signs & symptoms: Acute onset vomiting, coughing or spitting up blood, nosebleed, a red tongue, and a replete, rapid pulse

Contraindications:

1. Do not use for vacuity bleeding patterns.
2. Do not use for cold bleeding patterns.

Formula explanation: Within this formula, Cirsium, Cephalanoplos, Lotus Leaf, Rubia, Cacumen Biotae, and Imperata all cool the blood and stop bleeding. Trachycarpus restrains and astringes and stops bleeding. Gardenia clears heat and drains fire, while Rhubarb leads away heat and moves it downward. Thus these two ingredients help the others by downbearing fire. Moutan combined with Rhubarb cools the blood and dispels stasis, thus this combination helps cool the blood and stop bleeding without retaining stasis. The ingredients in this formula are preferably used carbonized since this strengthens their ability to restrain, astringe, and stop bleeding. Lotus Root or Radish Root Juice mixed with ink also helps strengthen the heat-clearing, blood-cooling, and stop-bleeding functions of the above medicinals.

Comments: This formula combines bleeding-stopping medicinals from all the subcategories of bleeding-stopping medicinals. There are bleeding-stopping medicinals which clear heat, those that quicken the blood, and those that astringe and secure. Thus this formula can be used for the first aid treatment of any type of pathological bleeding. This is based on Ye Tian-shi's first principles of treating hemorrhagic conditions, "First, stop bleeding." After the bleeding has been brought under control, one can then prescribe the right medicine to treat the underlying cause of the bleeding, whether qi vacuity, blood heat, or blood stasis. After that, Ye Tian-shi's third principle is to "Treat the root." By this, various Chinese doctors understand either to treat the spleen (the latter heaven root) or the kidneys (the former heaven root). Either viscus may be damaged by bleeding and either viscus may play a major role in the disease mechanisms of bleeding.

If one knows right from the beginning what the disease mechanism is, then this medicine can be given in combination with the appropriate other medicine(s). For instance, if there is bleeding due to liver depression transforming heat, then this medicine can be combined with *Jia Wei Xiao Yao Wan* (Added Flavors Rambling Pills). If the bleeding is due to yin vacuity/vacuity heat, then it can be combined with *Zhi Bai Di Huang Wan*

(Anemarrhena & Phellodendron Rehmannia Pills). And if it is due to spleen qi vacuity, it can be combined with *Gui Pi Wan* (Restore the Spleen Pills).

Jiao Ai Tang (Donkey Skin Glue & Mugwort Decoction)

Radix Ligustici Wallichii (*Chuan Xiong*)
Gelatinum Corii Asini (*E Jiao*)
Folium Artemisiae Argyii (*Ai Ye*)
Radix Glycyrrhizae (*Gan Cao*)
Radix Angelicae Sinensis (*Dang Gui*)
Radix Albus Paeoniae Lactiflorae (*Bai Shao*)
dry Radix Rehmanniae (*Gan Di Huang*)

Functions: Supplements the blood and stops bleeding, regulates menstruation and quiets the fetus

Indications: Women's *chong* and *ren* vacuity detriment, flooding and leaking, excessively profuse menstruation, vaginal bleeding during pregnancy. Functional uterine bleeding, threatened miscarriage, post-partum uterine bleeding, bleeding peptic ulcers, bleeding hemorrhoids

Main signs & symptoms: Excessive menstruation, flooding and leaking, dribbling and dripping which will not stop, post-partum precipitation of blood which will not stop, precipitation of blood during pregnancy, aching and pain within the abdomen, pale-colored, thin consistency blood without clots, low back soreness and weakness, a dull, lusterless complexion, a pale tongue with thin, white fur, and a fine, weak pulse

Dosage: 4 tablets three times per day

Formula explanation: Within this formula, Donkey Skin Glue supplements the blood and stops bleeding, while Mugwort warms the channels and stops bleeding. These two medicinals are also essential medicinals for regulating menstruation and quieting the fetus, treating flooding and stopping leaking. They are the sovereign medicinals in this formula. Cooked Rehmannia, Dang Gui, Peony, and Ligusticum Wallichium (the so-called Four Materials) supplement the blood and regulate menstruation. They are also able to quicken the blood and regulate the blood. They are in order to prevent discharge of the blood enduring for days resulting in retained blood. They are both minister and assistant medicinals. Licorice regulates and harmonizes all the other ingredients in this formula. When combined with Donkey Skin Glue, it also has a tendency to stop bleeding. When combined with Peony, it is able to relax urgency (*i.e.*, cramping) and stop pain. When all these medicinals are used together, they mainly supplement the blood and stop bleeding. However, they simultaneously regulate menstruation and quiet the fetus.

Therefore, they are a commonly used prescription for the treatment of blood vacuity flooding and leaking and for quieting the fetus.

Huai Jiao Wan (Fructus Sophorae Pills)

Fructus Immaturus Sophorae Japonicae (*Huai Hua Mi*)
Radix Sanguisorbae (*Di Yu*)
Radix Scutellariae Baicalensis (*Huang Qin*)
Fructus Citri Aurantii (*Zhi Ke*)
Radix Ledebouriellae Divaricatae (*Fang Feng*)
Radix Angelicae Sinensis (*Dang Gui*)

Functions: Clears heat and stops bleeding, dispels wind and rectifies the qi

Indications: Intestinal wind hemafecia, *i.e.*, anal bleeding due to damp and depressive heat in the intestines. Bleeding hemorrhoids

Main signs & symptoms: Bright red anal bleeding, a red tongue with yellow or slimy, yellow fur, and a slippery, bowstring, rapid pulse

Contraindications: This formula is for acute hemorrhoidal bleeding. It is not appropriate for long-term use in case of chronic hemorrhoids.

Dosage: 8 pills three times per day

Formula explanation: Fructus Sophorae clears heat and eliminates dampness from the intestines and has a pronounced empirical effect of stopping hemorrhoidal bleeding. Scutellaria clears heat and eliminates dampness from the stomach and intestines, while Sanguisorba clears heat and stops bleeding. Ledebouriella and Aurantium rectify the intestinal qi. Dang Gui moves the blood to help relieve swelling and pain. It also moistens the intestines and frees the flow of the stools.

Comments: This medicine can either be used alone for damp or depressive heat in the intestines leading to hemorrhoidal bleeding or it may be combined with other ready-made medicines, such as *Xiao Chai Hu Tang Wan* (Minor Bupleurum Decoction Pills) when there is damp or depressive heat hemorrhoidal bleeding.

Tian Qi Wan (Pseudoginseng Pills)

Radix Pseudoginseng (*Tian Qi*)

Functions: Quickens the blood and stops bleeding

Indications: Various types of bleeding

Main signs & symptoms: Bleeding, especially but not only due to traumatic injury

Dosage: 8 pills three times per day

Formula explanation: Pseudoginseng, the sole ingredient in this medicine, quickens the blood and stops bleeding.

Comments: This medicine can be used alone for first aid purposes or combined with other Chinese ready-made medicines in order to stop any type of bleeding.

11
Wind-treating Medicines

The formulas in this category are mostly composed of either acrid, scattering medicinals which expel wind or ingredients which extinguish wind and stop tetany. The first group course and scatter external wind, while the second group level and extinguish internal wind. Thus the treatment of wind comprises these two subdivisions of formulas. External wind is due to wind evils entering into the human body from the outside.[1] These may enter the flesh, channels, sinews, joints, or bones and give rise to rashes, dizziness, numbness, difficulty moving, and joint pain. It is also possible for external wind to cause the movement of internal wind, giving rise to muscular tetany, clenched jaws, opisthotonis, facial paralysis, and other disorders characterized by spasming of the muscles.

Internal wind is due to the stirring of liver wind internally. This in turn is most often due to liver-kidney dual vacuity and ascendant hyperactivity of liver yang. Internal wind may also be generated by extreme internal heat. The signs and symptoms of stirring of internal wind include headache, dizziness, blurred vision, tinnitus, and muscle twitching. When extreme, stirring of internal wind may give rise to wind stroke with sudden loss of consciousness, paralysis, tetany, and aphasia. It should be remembered that internal wind is nothing other than counterflowing yang qi moving recklessly and moving upward and outward. Thus formulas for internal wind often include blood-nourishing and yin-enriching medicinals, since blood is the mother of qi.

Other medicines which treat wind may be found under other categories, such as exterior-resolving medicines and dispelling wind, overcoming dampness formulas in the dispelling dampness chapter.

---

[1] While this is the "textbook" explanation, I believe the formulas in this group can also be used to treat wind evils located in the exterior which may or may not be externally invading. For instance, at least one of these formulas may be used to treat wind evils associated with external genital itching and inflammation and with urticaria due to food or medication allergies.

Coursing & scattering external wind formulas

Chuan Xiong Cha Tiao Wan (Ligusticum & Tea Mixed Pills)

Radix Ligustici Wallichii (*Chuan Xiong*)
Flos Seu Herba Schizonepetae Tenuifoliae (*Jing Jie Sui*)
Radix Angelicae Dahuricae (*Bai Zhi*)
Radix Et Rhizoma Notopterygii (*Qiang Huo*)
Radix Glycyrrhizae (*Gan Cao*)
Herba Asari Cum Radice (*Xi Xin*)
Radix Ledebouriellae Divaricatae (*Fang Feng*)
Herba Menthae Haplocalycis (*Bo He*)
green Folium Camelliae Theae (*Qing Cha Ye*)

Functions: Courses wind and stops pain

Indications: External invasion of wind evils headache. Common cold and flus with headache, migraines, tension headache, neurogenic headache, acute and chronic rhinitis and sinusitis, vertigo

Main signs & symptoms: Headache in any part of the head accompanied by fever, aversion to wind and cold, fever, possible dizziness, nasal congestion, a thin, white tongue coating, and a floating, tight pulse

Contraindications:

1. Do not use to treat liver yang ascendant hyperactivity or liver-kidney dual vacuity, *i.e.*, yin vacuity, headache.
2. Do not use to treat qi and blood vacuity headache.

Dosage: 8 pills three times per day

Formula explanation: Within this formula, Ligusticum Wallichium, Angelica Dahurica, and Notopterygium course wind and stop pain. Ligusticum has an affinity for treating *shao yin* and *jue yin* channel headaches. Notopterygium has an affinity for treating *tai yang* channel headaches, and Angelica has an affinity for treating *yang ming* channel headaches. These are the sovereign medicinals in this prescription. Asarum scatters cold and stops pain. It is able to treat *shao yin* channel headaches. Mint is able to clear and disinhibit the head and eyes. It tracks down wind and scatters heat. Schizonepeta and Ledebouriella are acrid, scattering, and move upward. They course and scatter wind evils from the upper parts. Each of these medicinals assist the sovereign medicinal and strengthen the coursing of wind and stopping of pain. They are also able to relieve the exterior and are the minister medicinals. Licorice regulates and harmonizes all these other medicinals. Green Tea's nature and flavor are bitter and cold. Thus, it is able to clear the head and eyes above. Together, these last two are able to restrain the other warm, drying, upbearing, and scattering medicinals. Therefore, they are the assistant and messenger medicinals.

Xiao Huo Luo Dan (Minor Quicken the Network Vessels Elixir)

Radix Aconiti Carmichaeli (*Chuan Wu*)
Radix Aconiti Kusnezoffii (*Cao Wu*)
Lumbricus (*Di Long*)
Rhizoma Arisaematis (*Tian Nan Xing*)
Resina Olibani (*Ru Xiang*)
Resina Myrrhae (*Mo Yao*)

Functions: Dispels wind and eliminates dampness, transforms phlegm and frees the flow of the network vessels, quickens the blood and stops pain

Indications: Wind, cold, damp evils lodged and stagnating in the channels and network vessels. Hemiplegia as the sequella of a cerebrovascular accident, rheumatoid arthritis, osteoarthritis, peripheral nerve disorders

Main signs & symptoms: Body and limb sinew vessel spasm and pain, inhibition of the bending and stretching of the joints, fixed or migrating aching and pain, insensitivity of the hands and feet which has endured for many days and not healed, low back and lower leg heaviness and weakness, dampness, phlegm and dead, static blood in the channels and network vessels after wind stroke, and slimy, white tongue fur

Contraindications: Do not use in cases of yin vacuity or during pregnancy. Use only in patients with a relatively replete bodily constitution.

Dosage: 6 pills three times per day

Formula explanation: Within this formula, the two Aconites are the sovereign medicinals. They are both acrid, warm ingredients which are able to dispel wind and eliminate dampness, warm and free the flow of the channels and network vessels. They both have a relatively strong pain-stopping function. Arisaema is the minister medicinal. It dries dampness and transforms phlegm in order to eliminate phlegm dampness within the channels and network vessels. It likewise is effective for stopping pain. The assistant medicinals are Frankincense and Myrrh. These move the qi and quicken the blood in order to transform static blood within the network vessels, thus promoting the coursing and smooth flow of the qi and blood. Earthworm is the messenger medicinal. It is a good ingredient for entering specifically the network vessels. Its function is to free the flow of the channels and quicken the network vessels. When these medicinals are used together, wind, cold, and damp evils as well as phlegm turbidity and static blood are all able to be dispelled and eliminated. Hence the channels and network vessels obtain free flow, and all the symptoms can thus be cured.

Xiao Feng Wan (Disperse Wind Pills)

Radix Ledebouriellae Divaricatae (*Fang Feng*)
Radix Sophorae Flavescentis (*Ku Shen*)
Gypsum Fibrosum (*Shi Gao*)
uncooked Radix Rehmanniae (*Sheng Di*)
Herba Seu Flos Schizonepetae Tenuifoliae (*Jing Jie*)
Periostracum Cicadae (*Chan Tui*)
Fructus Arctii Lappae (*Niu Bang Zi*)
black Semen Sesami Indici (*Hei Zhi Ma*)
Rhizoma Anemarrhenae Aspheloidis (*Zhi Mu*)
Radix Angelicae Sinensis (*Dang Gui*)
Rhizoma Atractylodis (*Cang Zhu*)
Caulis Akebiae (*Mu Tong*)
Radix Glycyrrhizae (*Gan Cao*)

Functions: Dispels wind and eliminates dampness, clears heat and cools the blood

Indications: Externally invading wind heat or wind dampness mutually wrestling with internal damp heat resulting in various skin lesions. Urticaria, eczema, psoriasis, contact dermatitis, such as poison ivy and poison oak, ringworm, and diaper rash

Main signs & symptoms: Wet, red, itchy skin lesions, white or yellow tongue fur, and a floating, slippery, rapid pulse

Contraindications: This formula is contraindicated in case of qi and/or blood vacuity.

Dosage: 8 pills three times per day

Formula explanation: Schizonepeta, Ledebouriella, Arctium, and Cicada Moultings all resolve the exterior and dispel wind. Atractylodis strongly dries dampness, while Sophora clears heat and eliminates dampness. Akebia drains dampness and heat by disinhibiting urination. Gypsum and Anemarrhena clear heat and drain fire internally. Uncooked Rehmannia cools the blood, while Dang Gui both nourishes and quickens the blood. Black Sesame Seeds nourish the blood and moisten dryness. Since wind is nothing other than qi and blood is the mother of qi, it is said that, "To treat wind, first treat the blood." Uncooked Licorice clears heat and resolves toxins while harmonizing all the other medicinals in this prescription.

Hua She Jie Yang Wan (Flower & Snake Resolve Itching Pills)

Fructus Cnidii Monnieri (*She Chuang Zi*)
Rhizoma Atractylodis (*Cang Zhu*)
Radix Sophorae Flavescentis (*Ku Shen*)
Radix Ledebouriellae Divaricatae (*Fang Feng*)
Cortex Radicis Moutan (*Dan Pi*)
Radix Angelicae Sinensis (*Dang Gui*)
Zaocys Dhumnades (*Wu Shao She*)
Calculis Syntheticum Bovis (*Ren Gong Niu Huang*)

Functions: Dispels wind and eliminates dampness, clears heat and stops itching, frees the flow of the network vessels

Indications: Wind, heat, and dampness combined with blood stasis in the network vessels. Acute or chronic but especially recurrent or recalcitrant dermatoses accompanied by itching, including urticaria and external vaginal inflammation and itching

Main signs & symptoms: Skin redness, heat, swelling, and itching, possible sores or suppuration

Dosage: 4-5 pills three times per day or as needed

Formula explanation: Cnidium eliminates dampness, kills worms or parasites, and stops itching. It also dispels wind and eliminates dampness. The Chinese concept of worms includes both *Candida albicans*, scabies, and possibly other dermatomycoses. Atractylodis strongly dries dampness as well as dispels wind. Sophora clears heat and eliminates dampness and is an important medicinal for damp heat dermatoses. Ledebouriella resolves the exterior and dispels wind, treats wind dampness and stops pain. Moutan clears heat from and quickens the blood. Any one of the six depressions (qi, blood, dampness, phlegm, food, and fire or heat) tends to give rise to others of the six. Therefore, if there is enduring heat and dampness, eventually there will also be blood stasis, remembering that the qi moves the blood and blood and fluids move together. Dang Gui assists Moutan in quickening the blood but also nourishes the blood. This is based on the saying, "To treat wind, first treat the blood." Wind is nothing other than frenetically moving qi, and blood is the mother of qi. In addition, static blood tends to impair the creation of new or fresh blood, while evil dampness is often due to spleen vacuity, and the spleen is the root of qi and blood engenderment and transformation. Zaocys powerfully frees the flow of the channels and extinguishes wind, especially dispelling wind from the skin. As a *chong* or worm species of Chinese medicinal, Zaocys also opens the network vessels in the same way that snakes can wiggle into small cracks and crevices. Synthetic Cow Bezoar clears heat and resolves toxins as well as opens the orifices. It is especially effective for treating various types of hot sores and welling abscesses. Like other orifice-opening medicinals, Bezoar is able to penetrate turbidity and free the flow of the network vessels.

Comments: This is a very nice formula for treating damp heat skin problems associated with itching. It can be used for either acute or chronic dermatoses, but, because of several of its ingredients, it is especially good at treating recalcitrant and recurrent conditions, which many dermatological diseases are. It may be combined with other Chinese ready-made medicines depending on the patient's personal pattern. For instance, if dampness is due to spleen vacuity and there is also liver depression, this formula can be combined with *Xiao Chai Hu Tang Wan* (Minor Bupleurum Decoction Pills). Or it might be combined with *Jia Wei Xiao Yao Wan* (Added Flavors Rambling Pills).

Leveling & extinguishing internal wind medicines

Tian Ma Gou Teng Wan (Gastrodia & Uncaria Pills)

Rhizoma Gastrodiae Elatae (*Tian Ma*)
Ramulus Uncariae Cum Uncis (*Gou Teng*)
Sclerotium Poriae Cocos (*Fu Ling*)
Fructus Gardeniae Jasminoidis (*Shan Zhi Zi*)
Radix Scutellariae Baicalensis (*Huang Qin*)
Radix Cyathulae (*Chuan Niu Xi*)
Cortex Eucommiae Ulmoidis (*Du Zhong*)
Herba Leonuri Heterophylli (*Yi Mu Cao*)
Ramulus Loranthi Seu Visci (*Sang Ji Sheng*)
Caulis Polygoni Multiflori (*Ye Jiao Teng*)[2]

Functions: Levels the liver and extinguishes wind, clears heat and quickens the blood, and supplements and boosts the liver and kidneys

Indications: Ascendant hyperactivity of liver yang, liver wind harassing above. Cerebrovascular disease, transitory ischemic attacks, hemiplegia, essential hypertension,

---

[2] The ingredients in these pills deviate from the standard composition of this formula in that they do not include Concha Haliotidis (*Shi Jue Ming*).

renal hypertension, hypertensive encephalopathy, aphasia, apraxia, epilepsy, puerperal eclampsia, trigeminal neuralgia, and neurosis

Main signs & symptoms: Headache, dizziness, vertigo, insomnia, paralysis or convulsions, deviation of the mouth and eyes, a quivering, red tongue, and a wiry, rapid pulse

Dosage: 8 pills three times per day

Formula explanation: In this formula, Gastrodia and Uncaria level the liver and extinguish wind. They are the sovereign medicinals. Gardenia and Scutellaria clear heat and drain fire. Therefore, they assist in keeping liver channel heat from ascending upward. These are the minister medicinals. Leonurus quickens the blood and disinhibits water. Cyathula conducts the blood and moves it downward. Eucommia and Loranthus combined together are able to supplement and boost the liver and kidneys. Caulis Polygoni Multiflori and Poria quiet the spirit and tranquilize the will or mind. These are the assistant and messenger medicinals.

Comments: This medicine can be used alone or combined with other medicines to treat more complicated pattern presentations. For instance, if there is kidney yin vacuity with ascendant hyperactivity of liver yang, then it can be combined with *Liu Wei Di Huang Wan* (Six Flavors Rehmannia Pills), *Qi Ju Di Huang Wan* (Lycium & Chrysanthemum Rehmannia Pills), *Zuo Gui Wan* (Restore the Left [Kidneys] Pills), or *Da Bu Yin Wan* (Greatly Supplementing Yin Pills). If liver wind is complicated by blood vacuity, this medicine can be combined with *Si Wu Tang Wan* (Four Materials Decoction Pills).

Zhen Gan Xi Feng Wan (Settle the Liver & Extinguish Wind Pills)

Radix Achyranthis Bidentatae (*Niu Xi*)
Haematitum (*Dai Zhen Shi*)
Plastrum Testudinis (*Gui Ban*)
Radix Scrophulariae Ningpoensis (*Xuan Shen*)
Radix Albus Paeoniae Lactiflorae (*Bai Shao*)
Tuber Asparagi Cochinensis (*Tian Men Dong*)
Os Draconis (*Long Gu*)
Concha Ostreae (*Mu Li*)
Fructus Meliae Toosendan (*Chuan Lian Zi*)
Fructus Germinatus Hordei Vulgaris (*Mai Ya*)
Herba Artemisiae Capillaris (*Yin Chen Hao*)
Radix Glycyrrhizae (*Gan Cao*)

Functions: Settles the liver and extinguishes wind, nourishes yin and subdues yang

Indications: Liver-kidney yin vacuity with internal stirring of liver wind or ascendant liver yang hyperactivity dizziness, vertigo, and headache. Essential hypertension, renal hypertension, hypertensive encephalopathy, focal disorders of the higher nervous functions, such as aphasia and apraxia, epilepsy, cerebral arteriosclerosis, arteriosclerotic heart disease, and postpartum fever

Main signs & symptoms: Dizziness, vertigo, distention in the head and eyes, tinnitus, hot feelings in the head, headache, irritability, a flushed red facial complexion, and a bowstring, forceful pulse

Contraindications: Use cautiously and for only short periods of time in case of spleen qi vacuity.

Dosage: 8 pills three times per day

Formula explanation: Achyranthes is the sovereign medicinal in this formula. It leads the blood to move downward at the same time as it supplements liver and kidney yin. Hematite, Dragon Bone, and Oyster Shell all heavily subdue yang and level upward counterflow. Tortoise Plastrum, Scrophularia, Asparagus, and Peony all nourish yin and engender fluids. Hence yin becomes sufficient to control yang. Artemisia Capillaris, Melia, and Hordei all drain repletion from the liver. It is depressive liver qi which transforms into heat and stirs up liver yang. Licorice harmonizes all the other medicinals in this prescription. When combined with Hordei, it especially protects the stomach from damage by the heavy shells and minerals and the slimy, enriching yin supplements.

Comments: Although this formula's name suggests it extinguishes wind, which it does, it is actually better for subduing ascendant liver yang hyperactivity transforming from enduring depressive heat which has damaged yin fluids.

12
Dryness-treating Medicines

This category of formulas is composed of formulas which treat externally contracted dryness and those which treat internal dryness due to yin vacuity. The former subcategory of formulas uses medicinals which gently diffuse dry evils, while the latter are composed of medicinals which enrich yin and moisten dryness. External dryness is primarily due to external invasion by dry evils. These evils may combine with wind or cold and may easily transform into heat or fire. Internal dryness is due to essence deficiency and fluid consumption of the viscera and bowels. In turn, this may be due to excessive loss of body fluids through vomiting, sweating, or diarrhea, excessive urination, sexual taxation, or overindulgence in spicy foods. The lungs, spleen, kidneys, and large intestine are the viscera and bowels most commonly affected by fluid dryness.

Cautions & Contraindications:

1. Do not use moistening, enriching medicines with patients who have a damp body constitution.
2. Use with care in cases of diarrhea due to spleen vacuity.
3. Use with care in cases of qi stagnation since greasy, enriching, and supplementing ingredients can further obstruct the free flow of qi.

Medicines which gently diffuse & moisten dryness

Qing Zao Jiu Fei Tang (Clear Dryness & Rescue the Lungs Decoction)

Folium Mori Albi (*Sang Ye*)
Gypsum Fibrosum (*Shi Gao*)
Tuber Ophiopogonis Japonici (*Mai Dong*)
Gelatinum Corii Asini (*E Jiao*)
black Semen Sesami Indici (*Hei Zhi Ma*)
Semen Pruni Armeniacae (*Xing Ren*)
Folium Eriobotryae Japonicae (*Pi Pa Ye*)
Radix Panacis Ginseng (*Ren Shen*)

Radix Glycyrrhizae (*Gan Cao*)

Functions: Clears dryness and moistens the lungs

Indications: Warm, dry damage to the lungs. Upper respiratory tract infection, influenza, acute and chronic bronchitis, pulmonary tuberculosis, pneumonia, pertussis

Main signs & symptoms: Headache, body heat, a dry cough with no phlegm, counterflow qi and panting, dry, parched throat, dry nose, chest fullness, rib-side pain, heart vexation, oral thirst, a dry tongue with no fur, and a vacuous, large, rapid pulse

Contraindications: Use cautiously in patients with spleen-stomach vacuity due to the enriching, slimy nature of some of the ingredients in this formula.

Dosage: 5 tablets three times per day

Formula explanation: Within this formula, Folium Mori is the sovereign medicinal. It clears and diffuses lung dryness. The ministers are Gypsum and Ophiopogon. The first of these clears heat from the lung channel, while the second moistens lung metal dryness. When all of these are combined, there is clearing within diffusion and moistening within clearing. In terms of assistant medicinals, Armeniaca and Eriobotrya disinhibit the lung qi, thus insuring that the lungs' depurating and downbearing does its duty. Donkey Skin Glue and black Sesame Seeds moisten the lungs and nourish yin. They enable the lungs to obtain their moist nature. Ginseng and Licorice boost the qi and harmonize the center. They make earth effulgent so as to engender metal. Hence the lung qi automatically becomes effulgent as well.

Comments: This medicine is for the treatment of wind heat evils which have not been completely eliminated but which have damaged lung fluids or for contraction of wind, heat, and dry evils superimposed on a vacuity condition.

Sha Shen Mai Dong Wan (Glehnia & Ophiopogon Pills)

Radix Glehniae Littoralis (*Bei Sha Shen*)
Radix Adenophorae Strictae (*Nan Sha Shen*)
Tuber Ophiopogonis Japonici (*Mai Dong*)
Rhizoma Polygonati Odorati (*Yu Zhu*)
Folium Mori Albi (*Sang Ye*)
Radix Trichosanthis Kirlowii (*Tian Hua Fen*)

Semen Dolichoris Lablab (*Bai Bian Dou*)
Radix Glycyrrhizae (*Gan Cao*)

Functions: Clears and nourishes the lungs and stomach, engenders fluids and moistens dryness

Indications: Dryness damaging the lungs and stomach, fluid and humor depletion and detriment

Main signs & symptoms: A dry cough which will not stop, no or scanty, sticky phlegm, dry throat, oral thirst, a red tongue with scanty fur, and a fine, rapid pulse

Dosage: 8 pills three times per day

Formula explanation: Glehnia, Adenophora, Ophiopogon, Polygonatum Odoratum, and Radix Trichosanthis are all sweet in flavor and slightly cold in nature. They nourish lung and stomach yin fluids as well as clear dry heat from the lungs and stomach. Folium Mori diffuses the lungs and stops cough. When combined with the above medicinals, it assists the lung qi's opening, diffusion, and depurative downbearing. Dolichos' flavor is sweet and level. It harmonizes and nourishes the stomach qi, while it assists the transformation and upbearing of fluids by the spleen and stomach. Thus it promotes the circulation of fluids and humors up to the lungs.

Comments: This medicine is similar in function to the previous one. However, it only treats patterns in which yin and fluids have been damaged but not qi.

Enriching yin, moistening dryness medicines

Bai He Gu Jin Wan (Lily Secure the Lungs Pills)

uncooked Radix Rehmanniae (*Sheng Di*)
cooked Radix Rehmanniae (*Shu Di*)
Tuber Ophiopogonis Japonici (*Mai Dong*)
Bulbus Lilii (*Bai He*)
Radix Albus Paeoniae Lactiflorae (*Bai Shao*)
Radix Angelicae Sinensis (*Dang Gui*)
Bulbus Fritillariae Cirrhosae (*Chuan Bei Mu*)
Radix Glycyrrhizae (*Gan Cao*)
Radix Scrophulariae Ningpoensis (*Xuan Shen*)

Radix Platycodi Grandiflori (*Jie Geng*)

Functions: Nourishes yin and moistens the lungs, transforms phlegm and stops cough

Indications: Lung-kidney yin vacuity. Chronic bronchitis, bronchiectasis, hemoptysis, chronic pharyngitis, laryngitis, polyps on the vocal cords, carcinoma of the larynx, spontaneous pneumothorax, cor pulmonale, silicosis, and pulmonary tuberculosis

Main signs & symptoms: Cough with bloody phlegm, dry, painful throat, heat in the hands, feet, and heart, steaming bones, night sweats, a red tongue with scant coating, and a thready, rapid pulse

Contraindications:

1. Do not use unmodified in cases complicated by spleen vacuity.
2. Do not use unmodified in cases complicated by food stagnation.

Dosage: 8 pills three times per day

Formula explanation: In this formula, the two Rehmannias are the sovereigns. They enrich yin and supplement the kidneys. In particular, uncooked Rehmannia is also able to cool the blood and stop bleeding. Ophiopogon, Lily, and Sichuan Fritillaria are the ministers. They moisten the lungs and nourish yin but are also able to transform phlegm and stop coughing. These are assisted by Scrophularia which enriches yin, cools the blood, and clears vacuity heat. Dang Gui nourishes the blood and moistens dryness. Peony nourishes the blood and boosts yin. Platycodon diffuses and disinhibits the lung qi, stops coughing and transforms phlegm. Licorice is the messenger. It regulates and harmonizes all the other medicinals. Combined with Platycodon, these two disinhibit the throat.

Comments: This medicine should be used in combination with modern Western medicine when used to treat pulmonary tuberculosis.

13
Dampness-dispelling Medicines

The medicines in this chapter are primarily composed of dampness-dispelling medicinals which transform dampness and disinhibit water, free the flow of strangury and discharge turbidity. They treat water dampness disease. Because dampness is a yin evil whose nature is heavy and stagnant, in humans, damp diseases tend to progress slowly and also to linger. Damp evils may either enter the body from the outside or be internally engendered. Externally contracted dampness may be due to lying in damp places, rainy weather, soaking in dampness, or getting wet from having sweat. Such external dampness mostly damages the muscles of the human body, the exterior, and the channels and network vessels. This results in aversion to cold, fever, heaviness and distention of the head, vexatious aching of the joints of the limbs, and possible facial and periocular edema.

Internal dampness is usually due to unrestrained eating of uncooked, chilled foods, excessive drinking of alcohol, and over thinking, worry, and anxiety. These result in damp turbidity becoming exuberant internally. In turn, this damages the spleen qi which loses its control over transportation and transformation. In this case, the manifestations typically include glomus and oppression of the chest and stomach duct, nausea, vomiting, diarrhea, jaundice, turbid strangury, edema of the lower legs and feet, etc. Because the muscles and exterior are connected with the viscera and bowels and the exterior and interior are mutually related, exterior dampness will eventually affect the viscera and bowels, while interior dampness may overflow outside into the muscles and skin. In that case, one may see manifestations of external and internal dampness occurring simultaneously.

External dampness is primarily treated by using the sweating method. Internal dampness is treated by any of several techniques. It may be aromatically transformed. One may use bitter warm medicinals to dry dampness, or one may use sweet, bland ingredients to disinhibit urination and percolate dampness. Each of these methods has its own uses and indications. In addition, if prolonged, dampness may be associated with cold. In that case, one must warm yang and transform dampness. Or, dampness, by impeding the free flow of yang qi, may become associated with heat. In that case, the heat must be cleared and the dampness eliminated.

There are five subcategories of damp-dispelling formulas: 1) Drying dampness, harmonizing the stomach formulas. This type of formula aromatically transforms dampness affecting the spleen-stomach and disturbing digestion. 2) Heat-clearing, dampness-eliminating formulas. These are used for various types of damp heat, such as damp heat jaundice, urinary and vaginal tract diseases, and foot qi. 3) Water-disinhibiting, dampness-percolating formulas. These are mostly used for treating urinary disturbances and edema. 4) Warming and transforming water dampness formulas. These are used when dampness is associated with internal cold. 5) Wind-dispelling, dampness-overcoming formulas. These are used to treat wind damp impediment, *i.e.*, rheumatoid, arthritic conditions.

Cautions & Contraindications:

1. Use the medicines in this chapter with extreme caution in case of yin vacuity or consumption of fluids.
2. Because these medicines may be strongly attacking, they must be combined with righteous-supporting medicinals in those with bodily vacuity or during pregnancy.

Dampness-drying, stomach-harmonizing medicines

Ping Wei San (Leveling the Stomach Powder)[1]

Rhizoma Atractylodis (*Cang Zhu*)
Cortex Magnoliae Officinalis (*Hou Po*)
Pericarpium Citri Reticulatae (*Chen Pi*)
Radix Glycyrrhizae (*Gan Cao*)
dry Rhizoma Zingiberis (*Gan Jiang*)
Fructus Zizyphi Jujubae (*Da Zao*)

Functions: Dries dampness and transports the spleen, moves the qi and harmonizes the stomach

Indications: Damp stagnation of the spleen and stomach. Acute and chronic gastritis, gastrectasis, gastric ulcer, peptic ulcer, indigestion, especially pediatric indigestion, gastric neurosis, obesity, chronic pancreatitis, and parasitic diseases

---

[1] The Chinese word *ping* means level and calm or peaceful. However, when used medically, the word always implies a spatial connotation which the word calm does not capture. Leveling medicinals and formulas level and downbear upward counterflow. They do not just calm agitation.

Main signs & symptoms: Epigastric and abdominal distention and fullness, no thought for food or drink, a bland taste in the mouth or lack of taste, vomiting, nausea, acid eructation, a heavy, sagging feeling in the extremities, easy fatigue and a desire to lie down, white, slimy, or thick tongue fur, and a moderate, *i.e.*, slightly slow, or possibly bowstring pulse

Contraindications:

1. Use with caution during pregnancy.
2. Use with caution and/or modification in cases with yin and blood vacuity.

Dosage: 8 pills three times per day

Formula explanation: In this formula, a relatively large dose of Atractylodes is the sovereign. It is bitter, warm, and drying in nature. It is used to eliminate dampness and transport the spleen. Magnolia is the minister. It moves the qi and transforms dampness, disperses distention and eliminates fullness. Orange Peel is the assistant. It rectifies the qi and transforms stagnation. Licorice is the messenger. It is sweet and relaxing and harmonizes the stomach. It also regulates and harmonizes all the other medicinals. Fresh Ginger and Red Dates also regulate and harmonize the spleen and stomach. Therefore, the medicinals in this formula work together to transform damp turbidity, to regulate and smooth the qi dynamic, to augment and fortify the spleen and stomach, and to harmonize and downbear the stomach qi. Thus all the disease conditions associated with this formula are automatically eliminated.

Huo Xiang Zheng Qi Wan (Agastaches Correct the Qi Pills)

Pericarpium Arecae Catechu (*Da Fu Pi*)
Radix Angelicae Dahuricae (*Bai Zhi*)
Folium Perillae Frutescentis (*Zi Su Ye*)
Sclerotium Poriae Cocos (*Fu Ling*)
Rhizoma Pinelliae Ternatae (*Ban Xia*)
Rhizoma Atractylodis Macrocephalae (*Bai Zhu*)
Pericarpium Citri Reticulatae (*Chen Pi*)
Cortex Magnoliae Officinalis (*Hou Po*)
Radix Platycodi Grandiflori (*Jie Geng*)
Herba Agastachis Seu Pogostemi (*Huo Xiang*)
Radix Glycyrrhizae (*Gan Cao*)

Functions: Resolves the exterior and transforms dampness, rectifies the qi and harmonizes the center

Indications: External contraction of wind cold, internal damage by damp stagnation, sudden turmoil, vomiting, diarrhea. Influenza, intestinal flu, nonspecific acute colitis, acute gastroenteritis

Main signs & symptoms: Vomiting, diarrhea, effusion of heat, aversion to cold, headache, chest and diaphragmatic fullness and oppression, stomach duct and abdominal aching and pain, slimy, white tongue fur, and a moderate, *i.e.*, slightly slow, soggy or soft pulse

Contraindications: Do not use in case of wind heat or fire due to vacuity.

Dosage: 8 pills three times per day

Formula explanation: Within this formula, Agastaches is the main medicinal used in relatively large proportions. It acridly scatters cold wind at the same time that it is able to aromatically penetrate and transform turbidity. Hence it upbears the clear and downbears the turbid. It is combined with Folium Perillae and Angelica Dahurica which are acrid, aromatic, emitting, and scattering. These assist Agastaches to externally resolve wind cold at the same time as penetrating and transforming dampness and turbidity. Pinellia and Orange Peel dry dampness and harmonize the stomach, downbear counterflow and stop vomiting. Atractylodes and Poria fortify the spleen and move dampness, harmonize the center and stop diarrhea. Magnolia and Pericarpium Arecae move the qi and transform dampness, ease the flow of the center and eliminate fullness. Platycodon diffuses the lungs and disinhibits the diaphragm. Thus it benefits the resolution of the exterior as well as boosts the transformation of dampness. Ginger, Red Dates, and Licorice regulate and harmonize the spleen and stomach as well as harmonize the natures of all the medicinals in this formula. When used together, these medicinals scatter wind cold externally, transform damp turbidity internally, upbear the clear and downbear the turbid, and free and smooth the flow of the qi mechanism. Therefore, all the symptoms are automatically cured.

Comments: Typically, this medicine is used by itself. Some Chinese sources categorize it as an exterior-resolving formula, resolving wind dampness. Other Chinese sources suggest it for pediatric damp heat vomiting and diarrhea.

Heat-clearing, dampness-eliminating medicines

Ba Zheng San (Eight Correcting [Ingredients] Powder)

Semen Plantaginis (*Che Qian Zi*)
Herba Dianthi (*Qu Mai*)
Herba Polygoni Avicularis (*Bian Xu*)
Talcum (*Hua Shi*)
Fructus Gardeniae Jasminoidis (*Shan Zhi Zi*)
Radix Glycyrrhizae (*Gan Cao*)
Caulis Akebiae (*Mu Tong*)
Radix Et Rhizoma Rhei (*Da Huang*)
Medulla Junci Effusi (*Deng Xin Cao*)

Functions: Clears heat and drains fire, disinhibits water and frees the flow of strangury

Indications: Damp heat pouring downward. Acute urinary tract infection, urinary calculi, cystitis, urethritis, acute prostatitis, acute nephritis, acute pyelonephritis, glomerulonephritis, and acute gonorrhea

Main signs & symptoms: Hot strangury, bloody strangury, urination cloudy and red, astringent and painful, dribbling and dripping, uneasy flow, if severe, complete urinary blockage, lower abdominal tension and fullness, a dry mouth and tongue, a slimy, yellow tongue coating, and a slippery, rapid pulse

Contraindications:

1. Do not use long-term since it may cause light-headedness, palpitations, and diminished appetite.
2. Use only with care during pregnancy.
3. Do not use for vacuity cold.
4. Do not use in persons with bodily vacuity.

Dosage: 8 pills three times per day

Formula explanation: In this formula, Akebia, Talcum, Plantaginis, Dianthus, and Polygonum Avicularis all disinhibit water and open strangury. They also clear heat and disinhibit dampness. Gardenia clears and drains damp heat from the three burners. Rhubarb discharges heat and downbears fire. Juncus conducts heat and moves it downward. Licorice harmonizes these medicinals and relaxes urgency or cramping.

Bi Xie Sheng Shi Wan (Dioscorea Hypoglauca Overcome Dampness Pills)[2]

Rhizoma Dioscoreae Hypoglaucae (*Bi Xie*)
Semen Coicis Lachryma-jobi (*Yi Yi Ren*)
Cortex Radicis Moutan (*Dan Pi*)
Sclerotium Poriae Cocos (*Fu Ling*)
Cortex Radicis Dictamni Dasycarpi (*Bai Xian Pi*)
Medulla Tetrapanacis Papyriferi (*Tong Cao*)
Fructus Gardeniae Jasminoidis (*Shan Zhi Zi*)
Cortex Phellodendri (*Huang Bai*)
Rhizoma Atractylodis (*Cang Zhu*)
Rhizoma Alismatis (*Ze Xie*)

Functions: Clears heat and eliminates dampness, disinhibits dampness and stops abnormal vaginal discharge

Indications: Damp heat in the lower burner. Genital sores of various kinds, vaginal candidiasis and trichomoniasis, chlamydia, anal fissures and fistulas, eczema, and other damp heat skin lesions, chronic prostatitis

Main signs & symptoms: A yellow or thick, white vaginal discharge with possible foul odor, vaginal itching, redness, and heat, inflamed, wet, oozing skin lesions, scanty, frequent, burning, painful, and/or rough urination, possible white, turbid urination, a fat, possibly red or red-tipped tongue with slimy or dry,[3] white or yellow fur, and a slippery, bowstring, possibly rapid pulse

Dosage: 8 pills three times per day

Formula explanation: Within this formula, Dioscorea Hypoglauca is the main medicinal which percolates dampness and divides the clear from the turbid, upbearing the clear and downbearing the turbid. It is assisted in the elimination of dampness by Coix, Tetrapanax, and Alisma which all also percolate dampness and disinhibit water as well

---

[2] This is a modified version of *Bi Xie Shen Shi Tang* (Dioscorea Hypoglauca Percolate Dampness Decoction).

[3] Although textbooks typically say to expect a slimy tongue coating in cases of damp heat, because the tongue is in the upper body, heat due to its yang nature tends to rise, and heat consumes and exhausts body fluids, the tongue fur may not be slimy but may be dry instead, especially if there is concomitant spleen vacuity.

as by Atractylodes which aromatically dries dampness. Gardenia and Phellodendron both clear heat and eliminate dampness, while Moutan clears heat from the blood division and also quickens the blood and dispels stasis. It is common for damp heat evils to enter the blood division where they lie deeply (or hide) or force the blood to move frenetically, resulting in bleeding of various sorts. Damp heat in the lower burner also has a tendency to bind with static blood. In addition, heat in the lower burner still does tend to ascend to harass the heart spirit. The combination of Gardenia and Moutan clears heat and eliminates vexation.

Comments: This formula is a very useful one for treating Western patients. It addresses damp heat in the lower burner either due to or associated with spleen vacuity. It is far more useful than *Long Dan Xie Gan Wan* (Gentiana Drain the Liver Pills), and I am very happy that this formula is now available in pill form. For more pronounced spleen vacuity, it can be combined with *Bu Zhong Yi Qi Wan* (Supplement the Center & Boost the Qi Pills).

Yu Dai Wan (Cure Vaginal Discharge Pills)

Cortex Ailanthi Altissimi (*Chun Gen Pi*)
Radix Albus Paeoniae Lactiflorae (*Bai Shao*)
Radix Rehmanniae (*Di Huang*)
Radix Angelicae Sinensis (*Dang Gui*)
Cortex Phellodendri (*Huang Bai*)
Rhizoma Alpiniae Officinari (*Gao Liang Jiang*)
Radix Ligustici Wallichii (*Chuan Xiong*)

Functions: Clears heat and transforms dampness, stops vaginal discharge

Indications: Lower burner damp heat with red and white vaginal discharge

Dosage: 8 pills three times per day

Formula explanation: Ailanthus is the main ingredient in this formula. It clears heat and eliminates dampness and is especially effective for stopping abnormal vaginal discharge due to damp heat. This is combined with Phellodendron in order to increase the strength of clearing heat and eliminating dampness from the lower burner. Alpinia Officinarum warms the center and dispels cold. Thus it fortifies the spleen which is the source of the downward pouring dampness resulting in the white part of the vaginal discharge. The remaining medicinals nourish, quicken, and cool the blood in order to stop bleeding. In addition, Peony acts to astringe and secure yin.

Comments: This medicine is for red and white vaginal discharge due to a combination of spleen vacuity and damp heat. While this combination of patterns is not uncommon in Western female patients, red and white vaginal discharge is not a commonly met complaint in Western clinical practice.

Si Miao Wan (Four Wonders Pills)

Cortex Phellodendri (*Huang Bai*)
Semen Coicis Lachryma-jobi (*Yi Yi Ren*)
Rhizoma Atractylodis (*Cang Zhu*)
Radix Achyranthis Bidentatae (*Niu Xi*)

Functions: Clears heat and eliminates dampness

Indications: Damp heat wilting and impediment conditions, especially in the lower half of the body

Main signs & symptoms: Muscular atrophy or weakness or joint soreness and pain accompanied by redness, swelling, and heat

Dosage: 8 pills three times per day

Formula explanation: Phellodendron clears heat and eliminates dampness, while Atractylodis warmly and aromatically dries dampness. These are the two sovereign medicinals in this prescription. Coix assists the elimination of dampness through percolating and disinhibiting. Achyranthes nourishes the liver and enriches the kidneys, thus strengthening the sinews and bones and treating low back and leg soreness and weakness. However, it also has some ability to clear heat and eliminate dampness.

Comments: This formula can be used either alone or in combination with other Chinese ready-made medicines. It is for the treatment of damp heat wilting and/or impediment conditions. According to Li Dong-yuan's theory of yin fire, damp heat pouring downward damages the liver and kidneys. With the inclusion of Achyranthes, this formula takes this disease mechanism into account. However, since most conditions of damp heat impediment in Westerners tend to be associated with spleen qi and even possible kidney yang vacuity, this pill will most often be used in combination with others. Patients with such conditions need to be advised to stick to a clear bland, hypoallergenic, yeast-free diet as much as possible.

Water-disinhibiting, dampness-percolating medicines

Wu Ling San (Five [Ingredients] Poria Powder)

Sclerotium Polypori Umbellati (*Zhu Ling*)
Rhizoma Alismatis (*Ze Xie*)
Rhizoma Atractylodis Macrocephalae (*Bai Zhu*)
Sclerotium Poriae Cocos (*Fu Ling*)
Ramulus Cinnamomi Cassiae (*Gui Zhi*)

Functions: Disinhibits water and percolates dampness, warms yang and transforms qi

Indications: 1) Exterior pattern with interior collection of water dampness, 2) water dampness collected internally, and 3) phlegm rheum. Chronic nephritic edema, acute and chronic nephritis, chronic renal failure, acute gastritis, cardiac edema from congestive heart failure, gastroptosis, gastrectasis, ascites due to liver cirrhosis, infectious hepatitis, urinary retention, scrotal hydrocele, acute gastroenteritis with diarrhea, Meniere's disease, genitourinary tract infections, and neurogenic bladder syndrome

Main signs & symptoms: 1) Headache, fever, vexatious thirst, a desire to drink but vomiting upon entering of water into the stomach, inhibited urination, white tongue fur with a floating pulse; 2) puffy swelling, diarrhea, inhibited urination, cholera-like vomiting and diarrhea patterns; and 3) throbbing palpitations below the umbilicus, vomiting frothy saliva, and vertigo or shortness of breath and coughing

Contraindications:

1. Do not use or overuse in patients with spleen and kidney vacuity or combine with medicines which supplement and nourish the spleen and stomach and supplement and enrich the kidneys.
2. Do not use for the treatment of yin vacuity dysuria.
3. Do not use for prolonged periods of time.

Dosage: 5 pills three times per day

Formula explanation: Within this formula, relatively heavy doses of Alisma are used as the sovereign medicinal. Alisma is sweet, bland, and percolating, while its nature is cold. It out-thrusts the bladder, disinhibits water, and percolates dampness. The minister medicinals are Poria and Polyporus which also blandly percolate. They help strengthen the disinhibition of water. Added to these is Atractylodes which fortifies spleen qi and transports and transforms water dampness. The assistant medicinal is Cinnamon Twigs which is a single medicinal with two uses. First, it resolves the *tai yang* on the exterior. Secondly, it aids the bladder qi internally. When these five medicinals are combined together, water is moved and qi is transformed, the exterior is resolved and the spleen is fortified.

Wu Pi Yin Wan (Five Skins Drink Pills)[4]

Cortex Radicis Mori Albi (*Sang Bai Pi*)
Cortex Rhizomatis Zingiberis (*Sheng Jiang Pi*)
Cortex Sclerotii Poriae Cocos (*Fu Ling Pi*)
Pericarpium Citri Reticulatae (*Chen Pi*)
Pericarpium Arecae Catechu (*Da Fu Pi*)

Functions: Disinhibits dampness and disperses swelling, rectifies the qi and fortifies the spleen

Indications: Spleen vacuity damp exuberance, skin edema. Edema during pregnancy, protein-deficiency edema, ascites from cirrhosis, congestive heart failure, urticaria, menopausal edema

Main signs & symptoms: Generalized edema, heavy, encumbered limbs, heart and abdominal distention and fullness, ascending qi panting and hasty breathing, inhibited urination, edema during pregnancy, slimy, white tongue fur, and a deep, moderate, *i.e.*, slightly slow, pulse

Dosage: 8 pills three times per day

Formula explanation: Within this formula, Poria Skin disinhibits water and percolates dampness while simultaneously supplementing the spleen and assisting movement and transformation. Ginger Peel acridly scatters water rheum. Morus Bark depurates and downbears the lung qi in order to free the flow of and regulate the water passageways. Pericarpium Arecae moves water qi and disperses distention and fullness. Orange Peel harmonizes the stomach qi and transforms damp turbidity. When these five ingredients are used together, their effect of regulating the qi and fortifying the spleen, disinhibiting dampness and dispersing swelling is very good.

---

[4] Although the Mayway catalog calls this medicine *Wu Pi Yin Wan*, its ingredients are that of *Wu Pi San* (Five Skins Powder).

Comments: Because edema is so often due to spleen vacuity failing to control movement and transformation, this medicine is most often combined with spleen-supplementing formulas, such as *Bu Zhong Yi Qi Wan* (Supplement the Center & Boost the Qi Pills) and *Si Jun Zi Wan* (Four Gentlemen Pills).

Fang Ji Huang Qi Wan (Stephania & Astragalus Pills)

Radix Stephaniae Tetrandrae (*Fang Ji*)
Radix Astragali Membranacei (*Huang Qi*)
Radix Glycyrrhizae (*Gan Cao*)
Rhizoma Atractylodis Macrocephalae (*Bai Zhu*)
Fructus Ziziphi Jujubae (*Da Zao*)

Functions: Boosts the qi and dispels wind, fortifies the spleen and disinhibits water

Indications: Defensive exterior insecurity, wind water or wind dampness. Rheumatic heart disease, ascites, acute glomerulonephritis, chronic nephritis

Main signs & symptoms: Sweating, aversion to wind, bodily heaviness, inhibited urination, a pale tongue with white fur, and a floating pulse

Contraindications: This medicine is contraindicated for acute, repletion pattern edema.

Dosage: 8 pills three times per day

Formula explanation: Within this formula, Stephania dispels wind and moves water. Astragalus boosts the qi and secures the exterior. It is also able to move water and disperse swelling. When these two medicinals are combined, they support the righteous and dispel evils simultaneously. Thus they are the sovereign medicinals in this formula. The minister is Atractylodes. It supplements the qi and fortifies the spleen, thus assisting the spleen's movement and transformation. When combined with Astragalus, it has the function of making the defensive replete. Licorice banks earth and harmonizes the center as well as regulates and harmonizes all the other medicinals. Ginger and Red Dates regulate and harmonize the constructive and defensive. When these five ingredients are used together, the exterior qi is secured, wind evils are eliminated, the water passageways are freed and disinhibited, and the spleen qi is fortified and moved. Therefore, the symptoms of wind water and wind dampness are all automatically resolved.

Warming & transforming water dampness medicines

Zhen Wu Tang Wan (True Warrior Decoction Pills)

Sclerotium Poriae Cocos (*Fu Ling*)
Rhizoma Atractylodis Macrocephalae (*Bai Zhu*)
Radix Lateralis Praeparatus Aconiti Carmichaeli (*Fu Zi*)
Radix Albus Paeoniae Lactiflorae (*Bai Shao*)
dry Rhizoma Zingiberis (*Gan Jiang*)

Functions: Warms yang and disinhibits water

Indications: 1) Spleen-kidney yang vacuity, water qi collecting internally; 2) *tai yang* disease. Chronic nephritis, rheumatic valvular heart disease, congestive heart failure, cirrhosis of the liver, chronic hepatic disease, other causes of edema and ascites, chronic enteritis, intestinal tuberculosis, other causes of chronic diarrhea, Meniere's disease, primary hypertension, primary hyperaldosteronism, hypothyroidism, rheumatoid arthritis, chronic bronchitis

Main signs & symptoms: 1) Inhibited urination, heaviness, sagging, aching and pain of the four limbs, abdominal pain, downward precipitation (*i.e.*, diarrhea), puffy swelling of the limbs and body, white tongue fur, no thirst, and a deep pulse. 2) Sweating, no resolution after sweating, continuing effusion of heat, palpitations below the heart, dizziness, shivering, slimy, white tongue fur, and a deep, fine, forceless pulse

Dosage: 8 pills three times per day

Formula explanation: Within this formula, prepared Aconite is the sovereign. It is greatly acrid and greatly hot. It warms the kidneys and warms earth, thus invigorating yang qi. The minister medicinal is Poria. It is sweet and bland and percolates and disinhibits. It fortifies the spleen and percolates dampness, thus disinhibiting water evils. Ginger is also a minister medicinal in this formula. It is acrid and warm and it assists Aconite's warming of yang and dispelling of cold. When combined with Poria, it also warms and scatters water qi. Atractylodes is the assistant which fortifies the spleen and dries dampness, thus supporting the spleen's movement and transformation. And Peony relaxes urgency and stops abdominal pain. When all these medicinals are used together, there is scattering within warming and transforming within disinhibiting. Both the spleen and kidneys are supplemented, while yin water is controlled.

Comments: This medicine treats some very serious conditions and diseases. Therefore, one should exercise great care when treating patients with the corresponding pattern.

Bi Xie Fen Qing Wan (Dioscoreae Hypoglauca Divide the Clear Pills)

Fructus Alpiniae Oxyphyllae (*Yi Zhi Ren*)
Rhizoma Dioscoreae Hypoglaucae (*Bi Xie*)
Rhizoma Acori Graminei (*Shi Chang Pu*)
Radix Linderae Strychnifoliae (*Wu Yao*)
Sclerotium Poriae Cocos (*Fu Ling*)
Radix Glycyrrhizae (*Gan Cao*)[5]

Functions: Warms the lower source, disinhibits dampness and transforms turbidity

Indications: Lower burner vacuity cold, turbid urine. Chronic prostatitis, nephrotic syndrome, acute exacerbations of chronic pyelonephritis, chronic pelvic inflammatory disease, vaginal candidiasis, trichomoniasis, and senile vaginitis

Main signs & symptoms: White, turbid urine like rice-washing water, extremely frequent, repeated urination, a chilly, enduring white, watery vaginal discharge

Contraindications: This formula is contraindicated for the treatment of damp heat pattern chyluria.

Dosage: 8 pills three times per day

Formula explanation: Within this formula, Dioscorea Hypoglauca disinhibits dampness and transforms turbidity. It is the main medicinal for treating white, turbid urine. Alpinia Oxyphylla warms kidney yang and controls urination. Its stops slippage of turbidity and frequent urination. Lindera warms kidney cold and warms the urinary bladder. It also treats frequent, repeated urination. Acorus transforms turbidity and eliminates dampness, dispels vacuity cold from the urinary bladder. This is based on the saying that, "Warming the stomach and intestines stops uninhibited urination." The combination of Acorus and Dioscorea Hypoglauca can especially eliminate dampness, divide the clear, and transform turbidity. While the combination of Acorus, Alpinia, and Lindera is able to warm the interior and stop frequent, repeated urination. Thus when all these medicinals are used together, they are especially effective for warming the lower source, dividing the clear, and transforming turbidity.

Comments: Although this medicine is very effective for treating the patterns of chyluria and leukorrhea for which it is indicated, this is not the most common pattern of these conditions encountered in Westerners where damp heat complicated by spleen and

---

[5] The Plum Flower brand of this medicine contains Poria and Licorice which the standard, textbook formula of this name does not.

even kidney vacuity is frequently seen. Therefore, either this medicine is not correct or it must be combined with other medicines for other contributory disease mechanisms and patterns.

Wind-dispelling, dampness-overcoming medicines

Du Huo Ji Sheng Wan (Angelica Pubescens & Loranthus Pills)

Radix Angelicae Pubescentis (*Du Huo*)
Ramulus Loranthi Seu Visci (*Ji Sheng*)
Cortex Eucommiae Ulmoidis (*Du Zhong*)
Radix Achyranthis Bidentatae (*Niu Xi*)
Herba Asari Cum Radice (*Xi Xin*)
Radix Gentianae Macrophyllae (*Qin Jiao*)
Sclerotium Poriae Cocos (*Fu Ling*)
Cortex Cinnamomi Cassiae (*Rou Gui*)
Radix Ledebouriellae Sesloidis (*Fang Feng*)
Radix Ligustici Wallichii (*Chuan Xiong*)
Radix Codonopsitis Pilosulae (*Dang Shen*)
Radix Glycyrrhizae (*Gan Cao*)
Radix Angelicae Sinensis (*Dang Gui*)
Radix Albus Paeoniae Lactiflorae (*Bai Shao*)
dry Radix Rehmanniae (*Gan Di Huang*)

Functions: Dispels wind dampness, stops impediment pain, boosts the liver and kidneys, supplements the qi and blood

Indications: Chronic impediment patterns, liver-kidney dual vacuity, qi and blood insufficiency. Chronic rheumatoid arthritis, osteoarthritis, rheumatic sciatica, lumbar strain, lumbar intervertebral disc herniation, pain in the midline and back during pregnancy, hemiplegia due to stroke, and the sequellae of poliomyelitis

Main signs & symptoms: Low back and knee aching and pain, inhibition of the joints of the limbs, possible numbness and loss of feeling, intolerance to cold and liking warmth, palpitations, shortness of breath, a pale tongue with white coating, and a fine, weak pulse

Contraindications: Do not use for acute arthritis.

Dosage: 8 pills three times per day

Formula explanation: In this formula, Angelica Pubescens is the sovereign. It rectifies hidden wind and dispels wind, cold, damp evils from the lower burner and sinews and bones. Asarum emits and scatters wind cold from the yin channels and sweeps away wind dampness from out of the sinews and bones, thus stopping pain. Ledebouriella dispels wind evils and overcomes dampness. Gentiana Macrophylla eliminates wind dampness and relaxes the sinews. Loranthus, Eucommia, and Achyranthes dispel wind dampness while simultaneously supplementing the liver and kidneys. Dang Gui, Ligusticum Wallichium, Rehmannia, and Peony nourish the blood while simultaneously quickening the blood. Ginseng and Poria supplement the qi and fortify the spleen. Cinnamon Bark warms and frees the flow of the blood vessels, and Licorice regulates and harmonizes all these other medicinals. Thus this prescription as a whole dispels evils and supports the righteous.

San Bi Wan (Three Impediments Pills)

Radix Dipsaci (*Xu Duan*)
Cortex Eucommiae Ulmoidis (*Du Zhong*)
Radix Ledebouriellae Divaricatae (*Fang Feng*)
Cortex Cinnamomi Cassiae (*Rou Gui*)
Herba Asari Cum Radice (*Xi Xin*)
Radix Panacis Ginseng (*Ren Shen*)
Sclerotium Poriae Cocos (*Fu Ling*)
Radix Angelicae Sinensis (*Dang Gui*)
stir-fried Radix Albus Paeoniae Lactiflorae (*Bai Shao*)
stir-fried Radix Astragali Membranacei (*Huang Qi*)
wine stir-fried Radix Achyranthis Bidentatae (*Niu Xi*)
mix-fried Radix Glycyrrhizae (*Gan Cao*)
Radix Gentianae Macrophyllae (*Qin Jiao*)
uncooked Radix Rehmanniae (*Sheng Di*)
Radix Ligustici Wallichii (*Chuan Xiong*)
Radix Angelicae Pubescentis (*Du Huo*)

Functions: Supplements the liver and kidneys and boosts the qi, dispels wind and overcomes dampness

Indications: Liver-kidney yin and blood vacuity complicated by wind damp impediment, qi vacuity, and blood stasis

Main signs & symptoms: Joint soreness and pain, low back and knee soreness and weakness, possible tremors or numbness of the hands and feet, a pale, fat tongue with possible teeth marks on its edges and white fur, and a soggy pulse in the right bar, and a fine, bowstring pulse in the left bar and both cubits

Dosage: 8 pills three times per day

Formula explanation: This medicine is for the treatment of wind damp impediment pain with simultaneous liver blood-kidney yin vacuity, spleen qi vacuity, and blood stasis. In this case, Dipsacus, Eucommia, Dang Gui, Peony, Rehmannia, and Achyranthis all nourish the liver and supplement the kidneys, strengthening the sinews and bones. Ginseng, Astragalus, mix-fried Licorice, and Poria all fortify the spleen and supplement the qi. Ledebouriella, Angelica Pubescens, and Gentiana Macrophylla dispel wind and eliminate dampness, free the flow of impediment and assuage pain. Cortex Cinnamomi and Asarum warm the channels and network vessels, thus promoting the flow of qi and blood. Likewise, Ligusticum Wallichium moves the qi within the blood, thus quickening the blood and transforming stasis. In addition, Astragalus and Poria help eliminate dampness through percolating and disinhibiting.

Comments: This is a good, complex formula for the treatment of a mixed vacuity-repletion impediment pattern. Most systemic disease characterized by joint pain do manifest, in fact, such complicated pattern discriminations. In particular, this formula is a good one for wind damp cold impediment rheumatoid arthritis and poly/dermato-myositis, and fibromyalgia.

Juan Bi Wan (Alleviate Impediment Pills)

Ramulus Mori Albi (*Sang Zhi*)
Caulis Piperis Futokadsurae (*Hai Feng Teng*)
Radix Angelicae Sinensis (*Dang Gui*)
Radix Et Rhizoma Notopterygii (*Qiang Huo*)
Radix Angelicae Pubescentis (*Du Huo*)
Radix Gentianae Macrophyllae (*Qin Jiao*)
Radix Ligustici Wallichii (*Chuan Xiong*)
Radix Auklandiae Lappae (*Mu Xiang*)
Ramulus Cinnamomi Cassiae (*Gui Zhi*)
Resina Olibani (*Ru Xiang*)
mix-fried Radix Glycyrrhizae (*Gan Cao*)

Functions: Supplements and harmonizes the constructive and defensive, dispels wind and overcomes dampness

Indications: Wind cold damp impediment with simultaneous qi vacuity and an element of blood stasis having entered the network vessels

Main signs & symptoms: Generalized bodily heaviness, neck, shoulder, and upper back stiffness, numbness in the extremities, difficulty walking, white tongue fur, and a moderate, *i.e.*, slightly slow, pulse

Dosage: 8 pills three times per day

Formula explanation: Morus Twigs, Cinnamon Twigs, Piper Futokadsura, Notopterygium, Angelica Pubescens, and Gentiana Macrophylla all dispel wind, scatter cold, and overcome dampness, free the flow of impediment and stop pain. Dang Gui and Ligusticum Wallichium quicken the blood and transform stasis. Frankincense frees the flow of the network vessels and stops pain. Auklandia moves the qi and stops pain while also fortifying the spleen and regulating the intestines. Mix-fried Licorice fortifies the spleen and supplements the qi, supplements the heart and quiets the spirit.

Comments: This formula is not as supplementing as the previous prescription. It only supplements the spleen, not the blood or yin. Therefore, compared to the previous medicine, this ready-made pill is more appropriate for enduring impediment conditions due to wind cold dampness where there is some spleen qi vacuity but not very much. Although it attacks and supports at the same time, it is mostly an attacking rather than a supporting formula.

Xuan Bi Wan (Diffuse Impediment Pills)

Semen Coicis Lachryma-jobi (*Yi Yi Ren*)
Radix Stephaniae Tetrandrae (*Fang Ji*)
Semen Pruni Armeniacae (*Ku Xing Ren*)
Fructus Forsythiae Suspensae (*Lian Qiao*)
Radix Achyranthis Bidentatae (*Niu Xi*)
Cortex Phellodendri (*Huang Bai*)
Rhizoma Atractylodis (*Cang Zhu*)
Fructus Gardeniae Jasminoidis (*Zhi Zi*)
ginger-processed Rhizoma Pinelliae Ternatae (*Ban Xia*)
Caulis Akebiae (*Mu Tong*)

Functions: Clears heat and eliminates dampness, frees the flow of the channels and diffuses impediment

Indications: Damp hot impediment conditions. Rheumatic fever, rheumatoid arthritis, gouty arthritis, poly/dermatomyositis, and fibromyalgia

Main signs & symptoms: Redness, swelling, heat, and pain in the joints, reduced mobility, possible fever and chills with shivering, a lusterless, yellow facial complexion, dark, scanty urination, slimy, grey or yellow tongue fur, and a slippery, bowstring, rapid pulse

Dosage: 8 pills three times per day

Formula explanation: Phellodendron, Coix, Atractylodes, and Achyranthes clear heat and eliminate dampness in cases of damp heat impediment. Stephania increases Atractylodes's ability to dispel wind and overcome dampness, while Gardenia increases Phellodendron's ability to clear heat and eliminate dampness. Armeniaca diffuses and downbears the lung qi. The lungs are the "upper source of water." If the lung qi diffuses and downbears properly, this helps insure the free flow of the water passageways and the movement of water dampness down to the bladder for excretion with urination. Akebia percolates dampness and disinhibits the urination, thus helping eliminate dampness. In addition, Akebia has some ability to quicken the blood. Forsythia clears heat and resolves toxins. Toxic heat is usually akin to damp heat, and Forsythia clears heat without damaging the spleen. Pinellia dries dampness and transforms turbidity. It is the gathering and accumulation of dampness which impedes the free flow of yang qi, causing depressive heat which then unites with dampness and transforms into damp heat. Therefore, the addition of Pinellia seeks to undercut the root of damp heat engenderment and transformation.

Comments: The Plum Flow Brand version of this formula differs from the standard composition of this formula in that it does not contain Talcum (*Hua Shi*), Semen Phaseoli Calcarati (*Chi Xiao Dou*), or Excrementum Bombycis Mori (*Can Sha*) but does include Phellodendron and Atractylodis. This change is at least in part due to Talcum and Aduki Beans not lending themselves to inclusion in pill-form ready-made medicines.

This formula does not address spleen qi vacuity, and most Western patients suffering from chronic damp heat impediment conditions do exhibit signs and symptoms of spleen qi vacuity. Therefore, this medicine may have to be combined with other Chinese ready-made medicines in order to address the full pattern discrimination. For instance, one might combine this medicine with *Bu Zhong Yi Qi Wan* (Supplement the Center & Boost the Qi Pills) or with *Xiao Chai Hu Tang Wan* (Minor Bupleurum Decoction Pills). If blood stasis has entered the network vessels, one might want to combine it with *Huo Luo Xiao Ling Wan* (Quicken the Network Vessels Cleverly Effective Pills).

14
Phlegm-dispelling Medicines

Phlegm is a yin evil. It is congealed from body fluids and water dampness. Body fluids are transported and transformed by qi. If qi becomes insufficient or depressed, fluids and humors may not be transported and transformed properly. In that case, they may gather and accumulate, eventually congealing into phlegm. It is also possible for heat and fire to steam the juices and congeal body fluids into phlegm. Once generated, phlegm itself may hinder and obstruct the free flow of qi, blood, and body fluids. Depending upon its cause and the patient's bodily constitution, phlegm may be either hot or cold, damp or dry, and may exist either under the skin, in the channels and network vessels, or in the viscera.

There are five subcategories of phlegm-dispelling formulas. These are: 1) Formulas which dry dampness and transform phlegm. These fortify the spleen and transform phlegm and are used to treat cough with phlegm dampness. 2) Formulas which clear heat and transform phlegm. These are used to treat hot phlegm patterns. 3) Formulas which moisten dryness and transform phlegm. These are used to treat dry phlegm patterns. 4) Formulas which warm and transform cold phlegm. These warm the lungs and transform phlegm and are typically used to treat phlegm due to spleen yang vacuity or phlegm rheum obstructing the lungs patterns. 5) Formulas which treat wind and transform phlegm. These are used to treat either external wind invading the lungs resulting in phlegm accumulation or retention of turbid phlegm with internal stirring of liver wind. However, there are only Chinese ready-made medicines available from the suppliers included in this book from three of these categories of phlegm-dispelling medicines.

Dampness-drying, phlegm-transforming medicines

Er Chen Wan (Two Aged [Ingredients] Pills)

Rhizoma Pinelliae Ternatae (*Ban Xia*)
Pericarpium Citri Reticulatae (*Chen Pi*)
Sclerotium Poriae Cocos (*Fu Ling*)
Radix Glycyrrhizae (*Gan Cao*)

Functions: Dries dampness and transforms phlegm, rectifies the qi and harmonizes the center

Indications: Damp phlegm cough. Chronic tracheitis, chronic bronchitis, pulmonary emphysema, goiter, chronic gastritis, peptic ulcer, eclampsia, hangover, gastroptosis, Meniere's disease, and neurosis

Main signs & symptoms: Profuse phlegm which is white in color and easily spit out, chest and diaphragm glomus and oppression, nausea and vomiting, fatigue of the body and limbs, possible vertigo and heart palpitations, moist, white tongue fur, and a slippery pulse

Contraindications: Do not use unmodified for lung yin vacuity cough.

Dosage: 8 pills three times per day

Formula explanation: In this formula, Pinellia is the sovereign. It is acrid and warm and its nature is drying. It is able to dry dampness and transform phlegm as well as to downbear counterflow and harmonize the stomach and thus stop vomiting. Orange Peel is the minister. It rectifies the qi and dries dampness. It aids in normalizing the qi and dispersing phlegm. The assistant is Poria. Poria fortifies the spleen and percolates dampness. Once dampness is removed, the spleen may become effulgent and phlegm can no longer be engendered. Licorice is the messenger. It regulates and harmonizes all these other medicinals. Simultaneously it moistens the lungs and harmonizes the center.

Comments: This medicine can be used alone. However, it is most commonly used in combination with other Chinese ready-made medicines. Whenever phlegm dampness complicates other patterns, one can consider adding this medicine. For instance, asthma always includes deep-lying phlegm even during the remission stage or phase. During that phase, one can administer *Er Chen Wan* with *Bu Zhong Yi Qi Wan* (Supplement the Center & Boost the Qi Pills) and/or *Yu Ping Feng San Wan* (Jade Windscreen Powder Pills) in order to supplement spleen and lung qi, secure the exterior, and transform and eliminate deep-lying phlegm.

Heat-clearing, phlegm-transforming medicines

Qing Qi Hua Tan Wan (Clear the Qi & Transform Phlegm Pills)

Semen Trichosanthis Kirlowii (*Gua Lou Ren*)
Pericarpium Citri Reticulatae (*Chen Pi*)
Radix Scutellariae Baicalensis (*Huang Qin*)

Semen Pruni Armeniacae (*Xing Ren*)
Fructus Immaturus Citri Aurantii (*Zhi Shi*)
Sclerotium Poriae Cocos (*Fu Ling*)
bile-treated Rhizoma Arisaematis (*Dan Nan Xing*)
Rhizoma Pinelliae Ternatae (*Ban Xia*)

Functions: Clears heat and transforms phlegm, rectifies the qi and stops coughing

Indications: Phlegm heat internally binding. Chronic tracheitis, acute and chronic bronchitis, bronchiectasis, pneumonia, chronic rhinitis, and nasosinusitis

Main signs & symptoms: Cough with yellow phlegm which is thick and difficult to expectorate, chest and diaphragm glomus and fullness, short, red urination, a red tongue with slimy, yellow fur, and a slippery, rapid pulse

Dosage: 6 pills three times per day

Formula explanation: Bile-treated Arisaema is the sovereign medicinal in this formula. Its flavor is bitter and its nature is cold. It clears heat and transforms phlegm and it treats replete phlegm and replete fire obstruction and blockage. Scutellaria and Semen Trichosanthis are the minister medicinals. They downbear lung fire and transform hot phlegm. They assist the power of Arisaema. Because the treatment of phlegm also requires the rectification of the qi, Immature Aurantium and Orange Peel descend the qi and open glomus, disperse phlegm and scatter nodulation. Poria is one of the assistants. It fortifies the spleen and percolates dampness. Armeniaca is another assistant. It diffuses and disinhibits the lung qi. Pinellia is the third assistant. It dries dampness and transforms phlegm. When all these medicinals are combined together, they clear heat and transform phlegm, rectify the qi and stop coughing. Once heat is cleared and fire downborne, qi normalized and phlegm dispersed, all pathological conditions associated with this pattern are automatically resolved.

Comments: This medicine is usually used alone. However, the recommended dose of this medicine commonly needs to be increased in order to effectively treat the conditions for which it is indicated.

Wen Dan Tang Wan (Warm the Gallbladder Decoction Pills)

Caulis Bambusae In Taeniis (*Zhu Ru*)
Fructus Immaturus Citri Aurantii (*Zhi Shi*)
Rhizoma Pinelliae Ternatae (*Ban Xia*)

Pericarpium Citri Reticulatae (*Chen Pi*)
Sclerotium Poriae Cocos (*Fu Ling*)
Radix Glycyrrhizae (*Gan Cao*)
uncooked Rhizoma Zingiberis (*Sheng Jiang*)
Fructus Zizyphi Jujubae (*Da Zao*)

Functions: Rectifies the qi and transforms phlegm, clears heat and eliminates vexation

Indications: Liver depression-depressive heat complicated by phlegm and an element of heart-spleen vacuity. Chronic gastritis, peptic ulcers, chronic hepatitis, neuroses, nightmares, insomnia, palpitations, emotional depression, early stage schizophrenia, Meniere's disease, and chronic bronchitis

Main signs & symptoms: Dizziness, vertigo, nausea and/or vomiting, insomnia and especially waking from sleep in a terror, heart palpitations, timidity or susceptibility to fright, profuse phlegm, chest oppression and venter glomus, a bitter taste in the mouth, slimy, yellow tongue fur, and a slippery, bowstring, rapid pulse

Dosage: 8 pills three times per day

Formula explanation: This formula is built on a basis of *Er Chen Wan* (Two Aged [Ingredients] Pills) discussed above, the basic phlegm-transforming prescription in Chinese medicine. Immature Aurantium rectifies the qi and disperses accumulations, while Bamboo Shavings clear heat and transform phlegm, eliminate vexation and quiet the spirit. Licorice and Red Dates not only act as harmonizing medicinals in this formula, they also supplement both the heart and spleen qi and blood. This helps to quiet the spirit. Only if the spirit obtains sufficient qi and blood can it rest quietly in the mansion of the heart.

Comments: The pattern this medicine treats is actually a complex one. It is sometimes called gallbladder qi timidity for short. However, it has mostly to do with the spleen, stomach, liver, and heart, phlegm and heat. Depressive heat mixes with dampness due to spleen vacuity and leads to congelation of phlegm heat. Spleen vacuity leads to qi and blood vacuity and thus malnourishment of the heart spirit at the same time that depressive heat ascends to harass the heart spirit above.

Patients with this pattern are usually obese. However, this is typically a *tai yang* obesity as opposed to a *tai yin* obesity. *Tai yang* obesity describes a person who is overweight but with a strong musculature underneath. *Tai yin* obesity describes a person who is even more grossly overweight with very poor, underdeveloped muscle tone. If one suspects this pattern, one should ask if the patient startles easily and/or if they wake in panic from sleep. If they then have a slippery, bowstring pulse and other symptoms of liver depression and profuse phlegm, then one may use this medicine. In clinical practice, this medicine may be combined with a number of other famous formulas, such as *Xiao Chai Hu Tang Wan* (Minor Bupleurum Decoction Pills), *Xiao Yao Wan* (Rambling Pills), *Jia Wei Xiao Yao Wan* (Added Flavors Rambling Pills), and *Ban Xia Xie Xin Tang Wan* (Pinellia Drain the Heart Decoction Pills). In some menopausal women, it might even be combined with *Er Xian Wan* (Two Immortals Pills).

Medicines which warm and transform phlegm cold

Jie Geng Wan (Platycodon Pills)

Radix Platycodi Grandiflori (*Jie Geng*)

Functions: Depurates and downbears the lung qi, promotes the expulsion of pus, disinhibits the throat, and guides other medicinals upward to the chest and throat regions

Indications: Cold phlegm conditions, chest and throat conditions

Dosage: 8 pills three times per day

Formula explanation: This single ingredient medicine warms and transforms phlegm cold, depurates and downbears the lungs, promotes the expulsion of pus, and guides other medicines upward to the chest and throat regions.

Comments: This medicine is mainly used in combination with other Chinese ready-made medicines. It can be combined with a wide variety of other medicines any time one wants to add Platycodon to a formula. Platycodon is a useful medicinal for warming and transforming phlegm cold. However, it is an important messenger medicinal which guides the effects of other medicinals upward to the chest and throat. Platycodon specifically disinhibits the throat. Although Platycodon comes from the warming and transforming category of phlegm-dispelling medicinals, it can be used to treat phlegm heat when combined with other medicinals which clear heat. For instance, this medicine may be combined with *Xiao Chai Hu Tang Wan* (Minor Bupleurum Decoction Pills) in order to treat bronchitis with profuse, white, wet phlegm and/or a sore, swollen throat with phlegm nodulations under the jaw.

15
Food-dispersing, Stagnation-abducting Medicines

Formulas within this category disperse food stagnation. Food stagnation may be due to either lack of discipline and regularity in eating, liver qi stagnation, or spleen/stomach vacuity with loss of promotion of transportation and transformation. Because stagnant food is a yin accumulation which obstructs the free flow of yang qi, this obstruction to the flow of qi may give rise to transformative heat. However, if there is spleen vacuity or overeating chilled, uncooked foods, food stagnation may also be complicated by cold.

Bao He Wan (Protecting Harmony Pills)

Fructus Crataegi (*Shan Zha*)
Massa Medica Fermentata (*Shen Qu*)
Rhizoma Pinelliae Ternatae (*Ban Xia*)
Sclerotium Poriae Cocos (*Fu Ling*)
Pericarpium Citri Reticulatae (*Chen Pi*)
Fructus Forsythiae Suspensae (*Lian Qiao*)
Semen Raphani Sativi (*Lai Fu Zi*)

Functions: Disperses food and harmonizes the stomach

Indications: Food accumulation. Indigestion, diarrhea, abdominal pain, gastrointestinal flu, belching, acute exacerbation of chronic gastritis, hepatitis, acute pancreatitis, and acute or chronic cholecystitis.

Main signs & symptoms: Stomach duct glomus, fullness, distention, and pain, acid eructation, nausea on eating, vomiting of undigested food, possible diarrhea, a foul mouth odor, thick, slimy, possibly yellow tongue fur, and a slippery pulse

Contraindications: Do not use alone in case of spleen vacuity.

Dosage: 8 pills three times per day

Formula explanation: Within this formula, Crataegus is the sovereign. It disperses food and drink accumulations and stagnation. In particular, it disperses accumulations of meat and greasy, slimy substances. Massa Medica Fermentata disperses food and fortifies the spleen. It also transforms alcohol and eliminates accumulations of rotten food. Radish Seeds precipitate the qi and disperse food and particularly disperse accumulation of grains. These are the minister medicinals in this prescription. When used together, these three medicinals disperse all types of accumulated and stagnant food stuffs. The assistants, Pinellia and Orange Peel, move the qi and transform stagnation, harmonize the stomach and stop vomiting. Poria fortifies the spleen and disinhibits dampness, harmonizes the center and stops diarrhea. Since food accumulations easily transform into heat, another assistant is added. Forsythia clears heat and scatters nodulation. When all these medicinals are combined together, food accumulation is transformed and the stomach qi is harmonized.

Comments: This medicine can be either used alone or combined with other formulas when food stagnation complicates other patterns. For instance, for spleen vacuity and food stagnation, this medicine may be combined with *Si Jun Zi Wan* (Four Gentlemen Pills), *Xiang Sha Liu Jun Zi Wan* (Auklandia & Amomum Six Gentlemen Pills), or *Shen Ling Bai Zhu Wan* (Ginseng, Poria & Atractylodes Pills).

Mu Xiang Bing Lang Wan (Auklandia & Areca Pills)

Radix Auklandiae Lappae (*Mu Xiang*)
Semen Arecae Catechu (*Bing Lang*)
Pericarpium Citri Reticulatae Viride (*Qing Pi*)
Pericarpium Citri Reticulatae (*Chen Pi*)
Semen Pharbiditis (*Qian Niu Zi*)
Fructus Citri Aurantii (*Zhi Ke*)
Rhizoma Coptidis Chinensis (*Huang Lian*)
Cortex Phellodendri (*Huang Bai*)
Radix Et Rhizoma Rhei (*Da Huang*)
Rhizoma Cyperi Rotundi (*Xiang Fu*)
Rhizoma Curcumae Zedoariae (*E Zhu*)

Functions: Moves the qi and abducts stagnation, attacks accumulations and discharges heat

Indications: Accumulation and stagnation collecting internally, dampness brewing and engendering heat. Diarrhea and dysentery

Main signs & symptoms: Stomach duct and abdominal glomus, fullness, distention, and pain, red and white dysentery, tenesmus, possible constipation, slimy, yellow tongue fur, and a deep, replete pulse

Contraindications: This medicine is contraindicated in vacuity patterns. Otherwise it may damage the righteous qi since it is strongly attacking.

Dosage: 4 tablets three times per day

Formula explanation: Within this formula, Auklandia and Semen Arecae move the qi and transform stagnation, disperse stomach duct and abdominal distention and fullness. They are also able to eliminate tenesmus. Morning Glory Seeds and Rhubarb attack accumulation and abduct stagnation, drain heat and free the flow of the stools. Green Orange Peel and Orange Peel move the qi and transform accumulation. They increase Auklandia and Semen Arecae's power. Cyperus and Zedoaria course the liver and resolve depression, break the qi within the blood. Aurantium descends the qi and loosens the intestines, while it moves stagnant qi in the chest and abdomen. Coptis and Phellodendron clear heat and dry dampness. They also stop dysentery. Taken as a whole, this medicine, therefore, combines qi-moving and attacking and precipitating medicinals. Therefore, it is quite good at moving the qi and abducting stagnation, attacking accumulation and discharging heat.

Comments: Even though diarrhea and dysentery are already conditions of uninhibited flow, when they are due to food stagnation and brewing damp heat, these evils need to be precipitated and discharged. Therefore, medicinals are used which free the flow even though there seems already to be free flow. Because this medicine is strongly attacking and precipitating, it should be used with care and not unwarrantedly. It can, however, be a good medicine to take on trips to places where dysentery is common.

16
Worm-killing Medicines

In Chinese, the word *chong* means insect, worm, or bug. However, it also covers frogs, lizards, and snakes. Medically, it refers to parasites within the body. Most of these are species of worms. According to Chinese medical theory, worms arise in a damp, hot terrain. Typically, such damp heat is associated with spleen vacuity. If spleen vacuity is more severe, there may be accompanying coldness rather than heat, or both cold and heat.

General symptoms of worms include intermittent, periumbilical pain, gnawing hunger and the ability to eat even when there is abdominal pain, white spots on the cheeks, bruxism, vomiting of clear fluids, a peeled tongue coating, and a pulse which abruptly changes from large to small. Long-term parasitosis results in emaciation, fatigue, loss of appetite, poor vision and hearing, dry hair, and a large, distended abdomen.

Cautions & contraindications:

1. For best effect, take worm-killing medicines on an empty stomach.
2. Do not use in the elderly or constitutionally weak.
3. Do not use during pregnancy.
4. After the parasites have been expelled, supplement the spleen and stomach to secure and consolidate the treatment.

Wu Mei Wan (Mume Pills)

Fructus Pruni Mume (*Wu Mei*)
Herba Asari Cum Radice (*Xi Xin*)
dry Rhizoma Zingiberis (*Gan Jiang*)
Rhizoma Coptidis Chinensis (*Huang Lian*)
Radix Angelicae Sinensis (*Dang Gui*)
Radix Lateralis Praeparatus Aconiti Carmichaeli (*Fu Zi*)
Fructus Zanthoxyli Bungeani (*Shu Jiao*)
Ramulus Cinnamomi Cassiae (*Gui Zhi*)
Radix Panacis Ginseng (*Ren Shen*)
Cortex Phellodendri (*Huang Bai*)

Functions: Warms the viscera and quiets roundworms

Indications: Roundworm inversion patterns. Ascariasis, biliary ascariasis, chronic dysentery, chronic gastritis, gastric ulcer, post-gastrectomy syndrome, neurosis, insomnia, and menstrual, premenstrual, and menopausal complaints associated with candidiasis and a combination of hot and cold, vacuity and repletion signs and symptoms, including endometriosis

Main signs & symptoms: Heart vexation, vomiting, sometimes have, sometimes stops, vomiting of food containing roundworms, inversion chill of the hands and feet, abdominal pain, possible prolonged dysentery or diarrhea, a peeled tongue coating, and a deep-lying or bowstring, tight pulse

Contraindications:

1. Do not use this medicine in case of explosive diarrhea.
2. Do not use with damp heat dysentery.

Dosage: 10 tablets 2-3 times per day

Formula explanation: In this formula, heavy doses of Mume are used based on the ability of the sour flavor to control roundworms. Before being calmed, these were stirring and harassing. Zanthoxylum and Asarum are acrid flavored and are able to expel worms. Their nature is also warm, so they can warm the viscera and dispel cold. Coptis and Phellodendron are bitter and this bitterness is able to precipitate the roundworms. In addition, their coldness is able to clear heat above. The use of the above ingredients is based on the saying:

> When roundworms obtain (*i.e.*, encounter) sourness, they are calmed. When they obtain acridity, they subside. When they obtain bitter, they are able to be precipitated.

Additionally, Ginger, Cinnamon Twigs, and Aconite warm the viscera and dispel and precipitate cold. Ginseng and Dang Gui supplement and nourish the qi and blood. When combined with medicinals which warm the center, they boost the qi and warm the center at the same time as warming and supplementing lower burner vacuity cold, nourishing the blood and freeing the vessels, and regulating and harmonizing yin and yang. This then treats the inversion chilling of the four extremities.

Comments: Although this is the prototypical worm-dispelling formula in Chinese medicine and is especially effective for treating ascariasis or roundworm infestation, it can also be used for a number of other, complex complaints as well. In general, there should be a combination of hot and cold and vacuity and repletion. The heat may be damp heat and the cold may involve the spleen or spleen and kidneys. The vacuity is spleen qi vacuity and possible blood vacuity, while the repletion is not only the heat or damp heat but blood stasis and qi stagnation. Patients with this presentation will be fatigued and will have chronic digestive complaints. Frequently, they have been previously diagnosed as suffering from candidiasis, parasitosis, intestinal dysbiosis, leaky gut syndrome, or multiple food allergies. They may also have been told that they have hypoglycemia to boot.

When using this formula, for such complex conditions, it is extremely important that patients also eat a clear, bland diet and avoid all foods made with yeast or through fermentation, all sweet and sour fruits, such as tomatoes and oranges, and sugars and sweets in general. Without such dietary changes, use of this medicine alone will not achieve either satisfactory or lasting results.

17
Spirit-quieting Medicines

Spirit-quieting medicines seek to treat emotional disturbances causing vexation and agitation, insomnia, profuse dreams, and heart palpitations. There are two basic types of spirit-quieting formulas. One subcategory is used for emotional disturbances due to vacuity and the other is used for emotional disturbances due to repletion. In the case of repletion, replete fire arising from the liver or stomach ascends to the heart where it disquiets the spirit. In the case of vacuity, blood and yin fail to nourish the spirit and thus it is not calm. Therefore, the subcategory of spirit-quieting formulas which mostly deals with repletion is called heavy, settling spirit-quieting formulas. These formulas are mostly made from bitter, cold medicinals to drain fire and heavy, settling ingredients to press down ascendant yang. The subcategory of formulas which mostly deals with vacuity agitation and restlessness is called enriching and nourishing spirit-quieting formulas. These formulas mostly consist of blood-nourishing and yin-enriching medicinals assisted by vacuity heat clearing ingredients. However, because vacuity and repletion often go hand in hand in the kinds of counterflow inversion conditions associated with mental and emotional agitation, most formulas that quiet the spirit include a combination of heavy, settling ingredients, heat-clearing ingredients, and nourishing and supplementing ingredients.

Heavy, settling spirit-quieting medicines

Chai Hu Long Gu Mu Li Wan (Bupleurum, Dragon Bone & Oyster Shell Pills)

Radix Bupleuri (*Chai Hu*)
Rhizoma Pinelliae Ternatae (*Ban Xia*)
Sclerotium Poriae Cocos (*Fu Ling*)
Ramulus Cinnamomi Cassiae (*Gui Zhi*)
Radix Scutellariae Baicalensis (*Huang Qin*)
Fructus Zizyphi Jujubae (*Da Zao*)
Radix Panacis Ginseng (*Ren Shen*)
Os Draconis (*Long Gu*)
Concha Ostreae (*Mu Li*)
dry Rhizoma Zingiberis (*Gan Jiang*)

Radix Et Rhizoma Rhei (*Da Huang*)

Functions: Harmonizes and resolves the *shao yang*, transforms phlegm and settles fright, supports the righteous and dispels evils

Indications: Evil heat sinking into the *shao yang* (*i.e.*, the liver and gallbladder). Neurosis, schizophrenia, hysteria, epilepsy, hypertension, first or second degree A-V block, hyperthyroidism, Meniere's disease, spasm of the sternocleidomastoid muscle, gastritis, menopausal syndrome, post-concussion syndrome

Main signs & symptoms: Chest and rib-side fullness and distention, vexatious thirst, delirious speech, susceptibility to fright, disquietude or restlessness, insomnia, easy anger, whole body encumbrance and heaviness, a red tongue with yellow fur, and a bowstring, rapid pulse, disease categorized as mixed vacuity and repletion, alternating cold and heat, exterior and interior disease

Dosage: 8 pills three times per day

Formula explanation: This formula is made from *Xiao Chai Hu Tang* (Minor Bupleurum Decoction) minus Licorice and plus Cinnamon Twigs, Rhubarb, Poria, Dragon Bone, and Oyster Shell. When used for evil heat sinking into the *shao yang*, Cinnamon Twigs and Bupleurum acridly scatter so as to out-thrust evil qi which has sunken internally. Bupleurum and Scutellaria are then combined to clear and discharge evil heat. Rhubarb, bitter and cold, clears heat which has already sunken deeply internally. Pinellia and Ginger transform phlegm and scatter nodulation. Dragon Bone and Oyster Shell heavily settle and quiet the spirit. While Ginseng, Red Dates, and Poria fortify the spleen and boost the qi. Thus this medicine supports the righteous at the same time as it dispels evils.

However, when used as a spirit-quieting medicine in the absence of a *shao yang* condition, this formula's explanation is somewhat different. In that case, Bupleurum courses the liver and rectifies the qi. Scutellaria clears transformative heat from the liver, gallbladder, stomach, and lungs. Heat in any of these may ascend to harass the heart spirit. Dragon Bone and Oyster Shell heavily settle and quiet the spirit. Ginseng, Poria, and Red Dates fortify the spleen and boost the qi, but Ginseng and Poria also quiet the spirit. Cinnamon Twigs leads upwardly counterflowing ministerial fire downward to its lower source, while Pinellia and Ginger transform phlegm and regulate upbearing and downbearing. Rhubarb discharges heat downward, draining the stomach and, therefore, the heart.

Comments: The usual textbook formula representative of this category is *Zhu Sha An Shen Wan* (Cinnabar Quiet the Spirit Pills) which have been taken off the market due to the toxicity of Cinnabar. In actual fact, the formula above is much more clinically useful, since it addresses liver depression-depressive heat and spleen vacuity as the source of heat harassing the heart spirit. This is a common pattern in Western clinical practice.

Enriching & nourishing spirit-quieting medicines

Suan Zao Ren Tang Wan (Zizyphus Seed Decoction Pills)

Semen Zizyphi Spinosae (*Suan Zao Ren*)
Radix Glycyrrhizae (*Gan Cao*)
Rhizoma Anemarrhenae Aspheloidis (*Zhi Mu*)
Sclerotium Poriae Cocos (*Fu Ling*)
Radix Ligustici Wallichii (*Chuan Xiong*)

Functions: Nourishes the blood and quiets the spirit, clears heat and eliminates vexation

Indications: Vacuity taxation, vacuity vexation, inability to sleep. Insomnia, nervous exhaustion, night sweats, poor memory, nightmares, rapid heart palpitations, crying and irritability in teething infants, neurasthenia, and schizophrenia

Main signs & symptoms: Heart palpitations, night sweats, dizziness and vertigo, dry throat and mouth, a red tongue, and a fine, rapid pulse

Dosage: 2 pills three times per day

Formula explanation: Zizyphus Spinosa nourishes liver blood and is the ruling medicinal for quieting the heart spirit. Its assistant is Ligusticum Wallichium which regulates and nourishes liver blood. Poria tranquilizes the heart and quiets the spirit. Anemarrhena supplements insufficiency of yin at the same time as clearing internal flaring of fire. Thus it has the functions of enriching and clearing simultaneously, and Licorice clears heat and harmonizes the other medicinals.

Comments: When this formula is used for fever and fretfulness accompanying teething in infants, it can be crushed and mixed with a little sugar and water to be given in a baby oral syringe. The dose should be reduced for children and infants according to their body weight.

An Shen Bu Xin Wan (Quiet the Spirit & Supplement the Heart Pills)[1]

Concha Margaritiferae (*Zhen Zhu Mu*)
Caulis Polygoni Multiflori (*Ye Jiao Teng*)
Cortex Albizziae Julibrissin (*He Huan Pi*)
Fructus Ligustri Lucidi (*Nu Zhen Zi*)
Herba Ecliptae Prostratae (*Han Lian Cao*)
Radix Salviae Miltiorrhizae (*Dan Shen*)
Semen Cuscutae Chinensis (*Tu Si Zi*)
Fructus Schisandrae Chinensis (*Wu Wei Zi*)
Rhizoma Acori Graminei (*Shi Chang Pu*)

Functions: Nourishes the heart and quiets the spirit

Indications: Heart blood and yin vacuity. Heart palpitations, insomnia, dizziness, tinnitus

Main signs & symptoms: Heart palpitations, insomnia, profuse dreams, dizziness, tinnitus, a pale tongue with a red tip or a red tongue with scant fur, and a fine, rapid or vacuous pulse

Dosage: 8 pills three times per day

Formula explanation: Ligustrum and Eclipta, called the Two Ultimates (*Er Zhi*), nourish the blood and enrich yin. Salvia nourishes and quickens the blood and supplements the heart. Schisandra is an astringent, while Cuscuta is a yang supplement. However, both also fill the essence. As Li Dong-yuan has said, "When essence accumulates, it renders the spirit wholesome." Caulis Polygoni nourishes the heart and quiets the spirit. Cortex Albizziae quiets the spirit and resolves depression. Both medicinals quicken the blood and free the flow of the network vessels, and the vessels are the place where the spirit resides. Mother of Pearl heavily settles, quiets the liver and subdues yang , while Acorus opens the orifices, transforms phlegm, and quiets the spirit.

Comments: This medicine can be combined with other Chinese ready-made medicines when there are more complex patterns needing yin and blood supplementation and spirit-quieting. For instance, it may be combined with *Jia Wei Xiao Yao Wan* (Added Flavors Rambling Powder) when there is liver depression transforming heat accompanied by heart blood and yin vacuity with pronounced disquietude of the spirit.

---

[1] The Nuherbs version of this formula does not contain Albizzia, Caulis Polygoni Multiflori, or Ligustrum Lucidum.

The effect of most of the medicines in this category is cumulative. This means that they cannot be used like Western tranquilizers for immediate symptomatic relief. Rather, they tend to work over a period of several days.

Tian Wang Bu Xin Dan (Heavenly Emperor Supplement the Heart Elixir)

uncooked Radix Rehmanniae (*Sheng Di*)
Radix Scrophulariae Ningpoensis (*Xuan Shen*)
Fructus Schisandrae Chinensis (*Wu Wei Zi*)
Tuber Asparagi Cochinensis (*Tian Dong*)
Tuber Ophiopogonis Japonici (*Mai Dong*)
Radix Angelicae Sinensis (*Dang Gui*)
Semen Biotae Orientalis (*Bai Zi Ren*)
Semen Zizyphi Spinosae (*Suan Zao Ren*)
Radix Polygalae Tenuifoliae (*Yuan Zhi*)
Sclerotium Poriae Cocos (*Fu Ling*)
Radix Salviae Miltiorrhizae (*Dan Shen*)
Radix Codonopsitis Pilosulae (*Dang Shen*)
Radix Platycodi Grandiflori (*Jie Geng*)

Functions: Enriches yin and nourishes the blood, supplements the heart and quiets the spirit

Indications: Yin debility and scanty blood. Heart disease, menopausal syndrome, chronic urticaria, apthous ulcers, neurasthenia

Main signs & symptoms: Vacuity vexation, scanty sleep, heart palpitations, lassitude of the spirit, profuse dreams, impaired memory, dry, bound stools, sores arising in the mouth and on the tongue, a red tongue with scanty fur, and a fine, rapid pulse

Dosage: 8 pills three times per day

Formula explanation: This formula uses a heavy dose of uncooked Rehmannia. One reason is to enrich kidney water in order to supplement yin. Another reason is that it enters the blood division and nourishes the blood. If the blood is not dry, then fluids are automatically moistened. It is the main or ruling medicinal in this formula. Scrophularia, Asparagus, and Ophiopogon are all sweet, cold, enriching, and moistening. They are in order to clear vacuity fire. Salvia and Dang Gui supplement the blood. By nourishing the blood, they assist the above medicinals in enriching yin. The foregoing medicinals as a group all supplement the blood. Codonopsis and Poria boost the qi and calm the heart, while Zizyphus Seeds and Schisandra, both sour, restrain and constrain the heart qi. Thus, they also quiet the heart spirit. Semen Biotae and Polygala nourish the heart and quiet the spirit. These are the medicinals which as a group supplement the heart qi, calm the heart, and quiet the spirit. One group of medicinals supplements the root which is yin-blood insufficiency, while another group treats the branch of vacuity vexation and scanty sleep. Hence root and branch are treated at the same time. If yin and blood are not vacuous, from where can such conditions be engendered?

Bai Zi Yang Xin Wan (Biota Seed Nourish the Heart Pills)

Semen Biotae Orientalis (*Bai Zi Ren*)
Fructus Lycii Chinensis (*Gou Qi Zi*)
Radix Scrophulariae Ningpoensis (*Xuan Shen*)
cooked Radix Rehmanniae (*Shu Di*)
Tuber Ophiopogonis Japonici (*Mai Dong*)
Radix Angelicae Sinensis (*Dang Gui*)
Sclerotium Pararadicis Poriae Cocos (*Fu Shen*)
Rhizoma Acori Graminei (*Shi Chang Pu*)
Radix Glycyrrhizae (*Gan Cao*)

Functions: Nourishes the heart and quiets the spirit, supplements the kidneys and enriches yin

Indications: Constructive and blood insufficiency. Loss of regulation of the kidneys and heart. Heart palpitations, insomnia, poor memory

Main signs & symptoms: Essence spirit abstraction (*i.e.*, disorientation), racing heart, fright palpitations, insomnia, profuse dreams, impaired memory, night sweats

Dosage: 8 pills three times per day

Formula explanation: Semen Biotae nourishes the heart and quiets the spirit. Dang Gui, cooked Rehmannia, and Lycium Berries nourish the blood and enrich yin. Poria fortifies the spleen and supplements the qi. It also percolates water, thus leading fire to move downwards. Therefore, Poria also quiets the spirit. Ophiopogon engenders fluids, transforms phlegm, and clears heat, while Scrophularia clears vacuity heat and transforms phlegm. Together, they nourish the heart, while draining fire which might be harassing the heart spirit and phlegm which might be obstructing the orifices of the heart. Likewise, Acorus opens the orifices, transforms phlegm, and quiets the spirit. Licorice supplements the qi and nourishes the heart. It also harmonizes and regulates all the other medicinals in this formula.

Comments: Compared to *Tian Wang Bu Xin Dan* (Heavenly Emperor Supplement the Heart Elixir) above, this formula emphasizes treating the root. That root is liver blood-kidney yin. Therefore, the previous formula is better when the symptoms of spirit disquietude are more pronounced, and this formula is better for securing or consolidating the therapeutic effect after the patient has calmed down a bit.

Gan Mai Da Zao Wan (Licorice, Wheat & Red Dates Pills)

Radix Glycyrrhizae (*Gan Cao*)
Fructus Levis Tritici Aestivi (*Fu Xiao Mai*)
Fructus Zizyphi Jujubae (*Da Zao*)
Bulbus Lilii (*Bai He*)
Cortex Albizziae Julibrissin (*He Huan Pi*)
Caulis Polygoni Multiflori (*Ye Jiao Teng*)[2]

Functions: Nourishes the heart and quiets the spirit, harmonizes the center and relaxes urgency (*i.e.*, tension), also supplements the spleen qi

Indications: Visceral agitation. Hysteria, neurosis, depression, menopausal syndrome, autonomic dystonia, enuresis, and fever of unknown origin

Main signs & symptoms: Essence spirit abstraction, constant sorrow and a desire to cry which one is not able to control, restless sleep, if severe, erratic speech and behavior, crying and laughing without constancy, a red tongue with scanty fur, and a fine rapid pulse

Dosage: 8 pills three times per day

Formula explanation: Within this formula, Licorice's sweetness moderates or relaxes and harmonizes the center as well as nourishes the heart. Therefore, it is the main ingredient for relaxing urgency and compulsion. It is assisted by Blighted Wheat which is slightly cold. It nourishes the heart and calms the spirit. Red Dates supplement and boost the spleen qi, relax liver urgency, and treat heart vacuity all at the same time. When these three sweet medicinals are combined, they are sweetly relaxing, enriching, and supplementing. Their effect is to emolliate the liver and relax urgency, calm the heart and quiet the spirit. Lily moistens the lungs and nourishes the heart, Albizzia nourishes the heart and quiets the spirit, Caulis Polygoni nourishes the liver and calms the spirit, and Poria supplements the spleen and quiets the spirit. Therefore, each of these additional ingredients supplements one of the viscera involved in this scenario.

---

[2] This version of this famous formula contains several additional ingredients that the standard formula does not. The standard ingredients are the first three listed above.

Comments: This very simple medicine can either be used alone or combined with other Chinese ready-made medicines. However, its simplicity should not deceive one. It is based on very sophisticated Chinese medical theory. In describing the disease mechanisms of visceral agitation, Profs. Song and Yu state:

> The cause of this disease is mainly heart constructive insufficiency and heart fire upward dazzling lung metal. The heart rules joy and the lungs rule sorrow. The heart produces laughter and the lungs produce crying. Therefore, there is distress due to sorrow and deep grief, crying and laughing with no constancy. The kidneys rule yawning. If heart yin is already vacuous, heart fire is hyperactive above and is not able to descend and join with the kidneys. Thus there is much yawning and stretching.[3]

That being said, this formula does not use any bitter, cold medicinals to clear heart fire. Rather, it uses Li Dong-yuan's approach of treating yin fire with sweet, warm medicinals which fortify the spleen and upbear the clear. Once the clear is upborne, the turbid is downborne and the qi mechanism is disinhibited. Depression is resolved and the root of yin fire is cut. This is like taking the wood out from under a cauldron. This method also does not use a lot of slimy, enriching ingredients which might gum up the qi mechanism even more. This is why I say this seemingly simple medicine is quite sophisticated.

An Shui Wan (Quiet Sleep Pills)

Radix Polygalae Tenuifoliae (*Yuan Zhi*)
Semen Biotae Orientalis (*Bai Zi Ren*)
Radix Platycodi Grandiflori (*Jie Geng*)
cooked Radix Rehmanniae (*Shu Di*)
Pericarpium Citri Reticulatae (*Chen Pi*)
Semen Zizyphi Spinosae (*Suan Zao Ren*)
Radix Glycyrrhizae (*Gan Cao*)
Radix Scrophulariae Ningpoensis (*Xuan Shen*)
Sclerotium Poriae Cocos (*Fu Ling*)
Radix Dioscoreae Oppositae (*Shan Yao*)
Radix Codonopsitis Pilosulae (*Dang Shen*)
Radix Angelicae Sinensis (*Dang Gui*)
Tuber Ophiopogonis Japonici (*Mai Dong*)
Rhizoma Atractylodis Macrocephalae (*Bai Zhu*)
Rhizoma Acori Graminei (*Shi Chang Pu*)
Fructus Schisandrae Chinensis (*Wu Wei Zi*)

---

[3] Song Guang-ji & Yu Xiao-zhen, *A Handbook of Traditional Chinese Gynecology*, trans. by Zhang Ting-liang & Bob Flaws, Blue Poppy Press, Boulder, CO, 1995, p. 227

Herba Stephaniae Sinicae (*Jin Bu Huan*)

Functions: Enriches yin and nourishes the blood, supplements the heart and quiets the spirit

Indications: Yin debility and scanty blood. Heart disease, menopausal syndrome, chronic urticaria, apthous ulcers, neurasthenia

Main signs & symptoms: Vacuity vexation, scanty sleep, heart palpitations, lassitude of the spirit, profuse dreams, impaired memory, dry, bound stools, sores arising in the mouth and on the tongue, a red tongue with scanty fur, and a fine, rapid pulse

Dosage: Two as needed[4]

Formula explanation: This formula uses a heavy dose of cooked Rehmannia. One reason is to enrich kidney water in order to supplement yin. Another reason is that it enters the blood division and nourishes the blood. If the blood is not dry, then fluids are automatically moistened. It is the main or ruling medicinal in this formula. Scrophularia and Ophiopogon are sweet, cold, enriching, and moistening. They clear vacuity fire. Dang Gui supplements the blood. By nourishing the blood, it assists the above medicinals to enrich yin. The foregoing medicinals as a group all supplement yin and blood. Codonopsis, Dioscorea, and Poria boost the qi and calm the heart, while Zizyphus Seeds and Schisandra, both sour, restrain and constrain the heart qi. Thus, they also quiet the heart spirit. Semen Biotae and Polygala nourish the heart and quiet the spirit. Acorus opens the orifices, transforms phlegm, and quiets the spirit. These are the medicinals which as a group supplement the heart qi, calm the heart, and quiet the spirit. One group of medicinals supplements the root which is yin-blood insufficiency, while another group treats the branch of vacuity vexation and scanty sleep. Finally, Licorice harmonizes all the other medicinals in this prescription.

The one unusual ingredient in this formula which is otherwise a modification of *Tian Wang Bu Xin Dan* (Heavenly Emperor Supplement the Heart Elixir) is Stephania Sinica. This medicinal is bitter and cold. When used in decoction in doses from 6-15g, it clears heat and resolves toxins, fortifies the stomach and stops pain, scatters stasis and disperses swelling. It is normally used for the treatment of throat pain due to external contraction, mouth and tongue sores, vomiting and diarrhea, stomach pain, welling and flat abscesses, swellings and toxins, and injury due to fall and strike. In this formula, it clears heat from the lungs, stomach, and, therefore, also the heart and moves the blood,

---

[4] According to Alisa Wrinkle at Mayway USA, the reason the dosage of this Chinese ready-made medicine is so low and why it can be used on a symptomatic or as needed basis is because the Stephania Sinica is used in concentrated extract form.

remembering that either a qi or yin-blood vacuity is easily complicated by an element of stasis. When used in concentrated form, this medicinal functions as a sedative.

Comments: This formula is very similar in composition and rationale to *Tian Wang Bu Xin Dan* (Heavenly Emperor Supplement the Heart Elixir). However, its distributors suggest that it can be used on an as needed basis. Because it includes a concentrated extract of Stephania Sinica, care should be taken in its use, especially long-term for chronic, recalcitrant insomnia. I also think that, unlike other Chinese ready-made medicines whose doses should routinely be increased above the recommended doses on their packaging, one should be careful when increasing the dosage of this medicine.

18
Securing & Astringing Medicines

One of the five functions of the qi is to restrain or hold the blood, essence, and fluids within the body. Medicines within the securing and astringing category are meant to control the unwanted loss or discharge of blood, essence, or body fluids to the outside of the body. Typically, such medicines are made up of a combination of qi-supplementing medicinals with astringent ingredients, since loss of securing is ascribed to vacuity and insufficiency of the lungs, spleen, and/or kidneys. There are four main subcategories of securing and astringing formulas within Chinese medicine: 1) formulas which secure the exterior and stop sweating, 2) formulas which astringe the intestines and stem desertion (*i.e.*, prolonged diarrhea or dysentery), 3) formulas which astringe the essence and stop loss of semen, and 4) formulas which secure flooding (*i.e.*, uterine bleeding) and stop abnormal vaginal discharge. There are only ready-made medicines available from the suppliers contained in this book representative of two of these categories—formulas which secure the exterior and formulas which secure the essence. Although the lungs, spleen, and kidneys all share in the control of qi, the kidneys especially control opening and closing in general and closing of the treasuries in particular. Thus most of the formulas in this category contain kidney-supplementing medicinals.

Cautions & contraindications:

1. Do not use securing and astringing medicines in cases of loss, discharge, and emission due to repletion.
2. Do not use if there are retained or hidden evils.
3. In the treatment of diseases characterized by unwanted loss of blood, essence, and body fluids due to vacuity of righteous qi, it is necessary to treat both the root and branch simultaneously.

Exterior-securing, perspiration-stopping medicines

Yu Ping Feng San Wan (Jade Windscreen Powder Pills)

Radix Astragali Membranacei (*Huang Qi*)
Radix Atractylodis Macrocephalae (*Bai Zhu*)
Radix Ledebouriellae Divaricatae (*Fang Feng*)

Functions: Boosts the qi, secures the exterior, and stops sweating

Indications: Exterior vacuity spontaneous perspiration, easy contraction of wind evils. Upper respiratory tract infection, exacerbation of chronic bronchitis, mild bronchitis, especially in children, allergic rhinitis, hyperthyroid condition, autonomic dystonia

Main signs & symptoms: Spontaneous sweating on slight or no movement, aversion to wind, recurrent or easy contraction of external wind evils, a pale white complexion, a pale tongue with white fur, and a floating, vacuous or soggy, soft pulse

Dosage: 8 pills three times per day

Formula explanation: Within this formula, Astragalus is the sovereign medicinal which boosts the qi and secures the exterior. Atractylodes is then the minister medicinal which fortifies the spleen and boosts the qi. It assists Astragalus by increasing its power of boosting the qi and securing the exterior. The combination of these two ingredients makes the qi effulgent and the exterior replete. Thus sweat is not able to be discharged externally and evils also cannot easily invade internally. The assistant medicinal is Ledebouriella. It mildly dispels any wind evils lodged in the exterior. Thus the combination of Astragalus with Ledebouriella insures that the exterior is secured but evils are not retained, the combination of Ledebouriella with Astragalus insures that evils are dispelled without damaging the righteous. Hence there is scattering within supplementation and supplementation within scattering.

Comments: In modern clinical practice, this medicine is most commonly used during the remission stages between acute allergic or infectious episodes. In that case, it is usually used in combination with other supplementing medicines and formulas with the intention of preventing further acute attacks. These other medicines are typically either lung and spleen supplements, spleen and kidney supplements, or lung, spleen, and kidney supplements. For instance, this medicine is commonly combined with *Bu Zhong Yi Qi Wan* (Supplement the Center & Boost the Qi Pills) which supplement the lungs and spleen. This is based on the principle of treating the root during remission. During acute attacks or episodes, other more scattering and diffusing medicines are then used in order to emphasize treatment of the branch.

Essence-astringing, loss-stopping medicines

Jin Suo Gu Jing Wan (Golden Lock Secure the Essence Pills)

Semen Astragali Complanati (*Sha Yuan Ji Li*)
Semen Euryalis Ferocis (*Qian Shi*)
Stamen Nelumbinis Nuciferae (*Lian Zi Xin*)

Os Draconis (*Long Gu*)
Concha Ostreae (*Mu Li*)
Semen Nelumbinis Nuciferae (*Lian Zi*)

Functions: Supplements the kidneys and secures the essence

Indications: Kidney vacuity and essence debility, seminal emission. Neurasthenia, premature ejaculation, myasthenia gravis

Main signs & symptoms: Seminal emission, seminal discharge, lassitude of the spirit, loss of strength, aching and weakness of the four limbs, low backache, tinnitus, a pale tongue with white fur, and a fine, weak pulse

Contraindications:

1. Do not use for seminal emission or urinary enuresis or incontinence due to damp heat in the lower burner.
2. Do not use alone for seminal emission due to heart and kidneys not interacting.

Dosage: 8 pills three times per day

Formula explanation: Within this formula, Semen Astragali is the sovereign medicinal. It supplements the kidneys and astringes the essence. Semen Nelumbinis and Euryales are the minister medicinals which assist the sovereign to supplement the kidneys and astringe the essence. This combination of sovereign and minister medicinals is mainly in order to supplement insufficiency. Stamen Nelumbinis, Dragon Bone, and Oyster Shell are all astringent, restraining, and constraining in nature. Their purpose is thus to astringe the essence, and they are the assistant medicinals in this formula. When all these ingredients are used together, they can astringe the external discharge of essence and fluids as well as supplement kidney essence insufficiency. Although it mainly secures and astringes, once seminal emission and seminal discharge are stopped, it goes on to treat the root by supplementing vacuity and securing the kidneys.

Comments: This medicine can be used alone for the treatment of pediatric enuresis due to kidney qi immaturity and weakness manifesting as bed-wetting and frequent urination. In that case, there will be no particular signs of spleen qi vacuity nor of damp heat in the lower burner. Children suffering from enuresis are usually old enough to swallow pills. In that case, this is a cheap and easy cure.

For the treatment of seminal emission, this medicine is usually combined with other Chinese ready-made medicines. This is because, in adults, kidney qi vacuity will usually also involve either yin vacuity, yang vacuity, or both. In that case, this medicine should be used in combination with yang-supplementing medicines, such as *Jin Gui Shen Qi*

Wan (*Golden Cabinet* Kidney Qi Pills), or with yin-supplementing, heat-clearing medicines, such as *Zhi Bai Di Huang Wan* (Anemarrhena & Phellodendron Rehmannia Pills). That being said, although the Chinese clinical literature universally includes the disease category of seminal emission, this is a rarely seen complaint in the West.

Sang Piao Xiao Wan (Mantis Eggcase Pills)

Os Draconis (*Long Gu*)
mix-fried Plastrum Testudinis (*Gui Ban*)
Ootheca Mantidis (*Sang Piao Xiao*)
Radix Panacis Ginseng (*Ren Shen*)
Sclerotium Pararadicis Poriae Cocos (*Fu Shen*)
Rhizoma Acori Graminei (*Shi Chang Pu*)
Radix Angelicae Sinensis (*Dang Gui*)
Radix Polygalae Tenuifoliae (*Yuan Zhi*)

Functions: Regulates and supplements the heart and kidneys, secures the essence and stops leakage

Indications: Heart-kidney qi vacuity urinary and seminal incontinence. Diabetes mellitus, stress incontinence, uterine prolapse, autonomic dystonia

Main signs & symptoms: Frequent urination, if severe, urinary incontinence, turbid urine, possible spermatorrhea, impaired memory, spirit abstraction, a pale tongue with white fur, and a slow, fine or faint pulse

Contraindications: This medicine is contraindicated in cases of incontinence due to fire effulgence in the lower burner or damp heat.

Dosage: 8 pills three times per day

Formula explanation: Mantis Eggcases supplement the kidneys, secure the essence, and stop leakage. Dragon Bones help secure the essence as well as stabilize the will, *i.e.*, the emotions, and quiet the spirit. Ginseng greatly supplements the qi which is then upborne to accumulate to become the heart spirit. Spirit of Poria assists in this process while also leading any upwardly stirring ministerial to move downward due to its disinhibiting urination. Acorus transforms phlegm, opens the orifices, and quiets the spirit. Thus the heart spirit above is made quiet via four different mechanisms. Tortoise Plastrum and Dang Gui nourish the liver and enrich the kidneys, thus supplementing the kidneys below. Polygala then promotes the interconnection between the heart and kidneys.

Comments: In Western clinical practice, one of this medicine's most important day to day uses is in the treatment of stress incontinence. This condition occurs primarily in women and is usually associated with spleen-kidney dual vacuity. In such cases, this medicine might be combined with *Bu Zhong Yi Qi Wan* (Supplement the Center & Boost the Qi Pills) for a better, more long-lasting effect.

19
Supplementing & Boosting Medicines

Medicines which enrich and nourish and supplement and boost insufficiency of the body's qi and blood, yin and yang are called supplementing medicines. This category of formulas is further divided into five subcategories: 1) formulas which supplement the qi, 2) formulas which supplement the blood, 3) formulas which supplement both the qi and blood simultaneously, 4) formulas which supplement yin, and 5) formulas which supplement yang. Because of the interrelationship between the qi and blood and between yin and yang, frequently formulas which supplement the qi will contain medicinals which nourish blood and *vice versa*. Likewise, formulas which supplement yin will often contain ingredients to strengthen yang and *vice versa*. Nevertheless, when using supplementing formulas, the practitioner must accurately identify whether qi, blood, yin, or yang is predominantly vacuous and should choose a formula from the appropriate category. Because Chinese medicine works by restoring balance to the system, supplementing formulas should not be used unless there is diagnosable vacuity and insufficiency. To do so only supplements repletion.

Because simple vacuity patterns typically present as chronic, enduring diseases, they commonly require enduring, protracted treatment where regularity of small doses is what's called for. Therefore, vacuity patterns lend themselves to treatment by ready-made medicines, mostly in the form of pills, and that is why there are so many Chinese ready-made medicines included in this chapter.

Qi-supplementing medicines

Si Jun Zi Wan (Four Gentlemen Pills)

Radix Panacis Ginseng (*Ren Shen*)
Rhizoma Atractylodis Macrocephalae (*Bai Zhu*)
Sclerotium Poriae Cocos (*Fu Ling*)
Radix Glycyrrhizae (*Gan Cao*)

Functions: Boosts the qi and fortifies the spleen

Indications: Spleen and stomach qi vacuity. Chronic gastritis, gastric and duodenal ulcer, gastrointestinal weakness and dysfunction, gastroptosis, irritable bowel syndrome, diabetes mellitus, periodic paralysis, uterine fibroids, anemia, vomiting, and diarrhea

Main signs & symptoms: A withered, white facial complexion, a faint, lethargic voice, diminished appetite, lack of strength of the four extremities, loose stools, a pale tongue, and a fine, moderate, *i.e.*, slightly slow, pulse

Contraindications:

1. Do not use this medicine alone in high fever, yin vacuity with exuberant fire, accumulation and stagnation with qi distention, or fluid insufficiency.
2. Prolonged use of this medicine may result in a dry mouth, vexatious thirst, agitation, easy anger, and constipation.

Dosage: 8 pills three times per day

Formula explanation: Ginseng is the sovereign medicinal in this formula. It is sweet and warm and greatly supplements the source qi. It also fortifies the spleen and nourishes the stomach. Atractylodes is the minister. It is bitter and warm and fortifies the spleen and dries dampness. The assistant is Poria which is sweet and bland and percolates dampness and fortifies the spleen. Used together, Poria and Atractylodes' ability to fortify the spleen and eliminate dampness are strengthened, thus promoting transportation and transformation. The messenger is Licorice. It is sweet and warm and regulates the center. Taken as a whole, this formula has the functions of boosting the qi and fortifying the spleen.

Comments: This medicine is rarely prescribed by itself to Western patients. Usually, because of diet, stress, overwork, and under-exercise, Western patients do suffer from spleen vacuity. However, this is usually only part of a larger, more complex picture. When there is spleen vacuity causing lack of appetite, fatigue, cold hands and feet, and a tendency to loose stools or diarrhea with an absence of any heat signs and symptoms, this is a good medicine to use in combination with a wide variety of other Chinese ready-made medicines. For instance, if one wants to increase the spleen-fortifying, qi-supplementing of *Xiao Chai Hu Tang Wan* (Minor Bupleurum Decoction Pills) or *Xiao Yao Wan* (Rambling Pills), one can combine either of these with *Si Jun Zi Wan*. If one wants to supplement the spleen qi as well as kidney yin, then one can combine these pills with *Liu Wei Di Huang Wan* (Six Flavors Rehmannia Pills). Or, if one wants to supplement the spleen qi as well as kidney yang, one can combine these pills with *Jin Gui Shen Qi Wan* (*Golden Cabinet* Kidney Qi Pills), etc.

Xiang Sha Liu Jun Zi Wan (Auklandia & Amomum Six Gentlemen Pills)

Radix Codonopsitis Pilosulae (*Dang Shen*)
Rhizoma Pinelliae Ternatae (*Ban Xia*)
Rhizoma Atractylodis Macrocephalae (*Bai Zhu*)
Sclerotium Poriae Cocos (*Fu Ling*)
Pericarpium Citri Reticulatae (*Chen Pi*)
Radix Glycyrrhizae (*Gan Cao*)
Fructus Amomi (*Sha Ren*)
Radix Auklandiae Lappae (*Mu Xiang*)

Functions: Fortifies the spleen and harmonizes the stomach, rectifies the qi and stops pain

Indications: Spleen-stomach qi vacuity, cold dampness stagnating in the middle burner

Main signs & symptoms: Torpid intake, burping and belching, stomach duct and abdominal distention and fullness or aching and pain, vomiting, diarrhea

Dosage: 8 pills three times per day

Formula explanation: This formula is based on *Si Jun Zi Wan* above. To that basic prescription, Pinellia and Orange Peel are added in order to harmonize the stomach and downbear counterflow as well as transform and eliminate dampness. This then makes *Liu Jun Zi Tang* (Six Gentlemen Decoction). Auklandia moves the qi and stops pain, regulates and rectifies the intestinal qi, while Amomum acridly and aromatically transforms dampness and stops vomiting, moves the qi and fortifies the stomach.

Comments: This medicine treats a combination of spleen qi vacuity, dampness, and qi stagnation. However, this qi stagnation is primarily stomach and intestinal qi, not liver qi. Although this medicine has its definite uses in clinical practice, it is probably one of the more often erroneously prescribed formulas in the West.

Xiang Sha Yang Wei Wan (Auklandia & Amomum Nourish the Stomach Pills)

Rhizoma Pinelliae Ternatae (*Ban Xia*)
Sclerotium Poriae Cocos (*Fu Ling*)
Pericarpium Citri Reticulatae (*Chen Pi*)
Rhizoma Atractylodis Macrocephalae (*Bai Zhu*)
Herba Agastachis Seu Pogostemi (*Huo Xiang*)
Cortex Magnoliae Officinalis (*Hou Po*)

Fructus Cardamomi (*Dou Kou*)
Fructus Immaturus Citri Aurantii (*Zhi Shi*)
Radix Auklandiae Lappae (*Mu Xiang*)
Fructus Amomi (*Sha Ren*)
Rhizoma Cyperi Rotundi (*Xiang Fu*)
Fructus Zizyphi Jujubae (*Da Zao*)
uncooked Rhizoma Zingiberis (*Sheng Jiang*)
Radix Glycyrrhizae (*Gan Cao*)

Functions: Fortifies the spleen, harmonizes the stomach, and transforms dampness

Indications: Spleen qi vacuity and stomach disharmony with dampness

Main signs & symptoms: Torpid intake, scanty eating, a bland or slimy taste in the mouth, lack of taste, stomach duct glomus, fullness, and distention after eating, fatigue, lack of strength in the four extremities

Dosage: 8 pills three times per day

Formula explanation: On a base of *Si Jun Zi Wan*, other medicinals are added to A) rectify the qi and B) transform dampness. Amomum, Cardamon, Cyperus, Aurantium Immaturus, and Auklandia all rectify the qi. Magnolia and Agastaches aromatically transform dampness. While Licorice, uncooked Ginger, and Red Dates fortify the spleen, harmonize the stomach, and harmonize all the other ingredients in this medicine.

Comments: Compared to the previous medicine, in this case there is even more pronounced dampness and qi stagnation of the stomach. Many Western patients with a combination of chronic digestive complaints and chronic fatigue exhibit patterns of spleen vacuity with considerable dampness and qi stagnation. In such cases, this medicine can be combined with others to treat these aspects of the patient's total pattern. Most such Western patients also suffer from an element of heat, frequently heat in the lungs and stomach. In that case, this medicine can be combined with *Xiao Chai Hu Tang Wan* (Minor Bupleurum Decoction Pills) to good effect.

Shen Ling Bai Zhu Wan (Ginseng, Poria & Atractylodes Pills)

Radix Panacis Ginseng (*Ren Shen*)
Rhizoma Atractylodis Macrocephalae (*Bai Zhu*)
Sclerotium Poriae Cocos (*Fu Ling*)
Radix Glycyrrhizae (*Gan Cao*)
Radix Dioscoreae Oppositae (*Shan Yao*)
Semen Dolichoris Lablab (*Bai Bian Dou*)

Semen Nelumbinis Nuciferae (*Lian Zi*)
Semen Coicis Lachryma-jobi (*Yi Yi Ren*)
Fructus Amomi (*Sha Ren*)
Radix Platycodi Grandiflori (*Jie Geng*)

Functions: Boosts the qi and fortifies the spleen, percolates dampness and stops diarrhea

Indications: Spleen-stomach vacuity weakness. Chronic gastritis, chronic hepatitis, chronic bronchitis, chronic nephritis, diabetes mellitus, malabsorption syndromes, and malnutrition, especially in children

Main signs & symptoms: Scanty eating, loose stools or diarrhea, possible vomiting, lack of strength in the four limbs, bodily emaciation, chest and stomach duct oppression and distention, a sallow yellow facial complexion, a pale red tongue with white fur, and a fine, moderate (*i.e.*, slightly slow) or vacuous, moderate pulse

Contraindications: Do not use alone if there is yin vacuity/vacuity heat.

Dosage: 10 tablets two times per day

Formula explanation: This formula is also created on a basis of *Si Jun Zi Wan*. Those four ingredients are mainly to supplement the qi of the spleen and stomach. These are combined with Dolichos, Coix, and Dioscorea, all sweet and bland, and with Semen Nelumbinis, sweet and astringent, in order to assist Atractylodes in fortifying the spleen and also to percolate dampness and stop diarrhea. In addition, Amomum, acrid, warm, aromatic, and penetrating, arouses the spleen. It assists the Four Gentlemen to promote the central islet's movement and transformation, thus freeing the flow of the qi mechanism's ascension and descension and stopping vomiting and diarrhea. Platycodon is a guiding medicinal for the hand *tai yin* lung channel. Combined with the root formula, it helps lead the other medicinals upward, spreading their effect to the upper burner in order to boost the lungs. This is why this formula can also be used to treat lung qi vacuity with enduring cough and profuse phlegm. This is based on the principle of banking earth in order to engender metal.

Comments: This formula warms and supplements the spleen and transforms and eliminates phlegm without being drying. However, because it does not include any heat-clearing medicinals, I do not find it all that useful in my clinical practice where most of my patients exhibit some kind of evil heat.

Bu Zhong Yi Qi Wan (Supplement the Center & Boost the Qi Pills)

Radix Astragali Membranacei (*Huang Qi*)
Radix Glycyrrhizae (*Gan Cao*)

Radix Codonopsitis Pilosulae (*Dang Shen*)
Radix Angelicae Sinensis (*Dang Gui*)
Pericarpium Citri Reticulatae (*Chen Pi*)
Rhizoma Cimicifugae (*Sheng Ma*)
Radix Bupleuri (*Chai Hu*)
Rhizoma Atractylodis Macrocephalae (*Bai Zhu*)

Functions: Supplements the center and boosts the qi, upbears yang and lifts the fallen

Indications: 1) Spleen/stomach qi vacuity, 2) qi vacuity downward falling. Debility after prolonged disease, common cold in a person with bodily vacuity, chronic bronchitis, prolapsed uterus, prolapsed rectum, chronic hemorrhoids, gastroptosis, hernia, chronic gonorrhea, diarrhea, persistent malaria, habitual miscarriage, functional uterine bleeding and other hemorrhagic disorders, abnormal vaginal discharge, various postpartum problems, such as urinary incontinence, lochioschesis, and agalactia, chronic hepatitis, peritonitis, tuberculosis, neurasthenia, impotence, corneal ulcers, cerebral arteriosclerosis, pernicious anemia, leukopenia, chronic nephritis, and myasthenia gravis

Main signs & symptoms: 1) Fever, spontaneous sweating, thirst with a desire for warm drinks, shortness of breath, disinclination to speak, dyspnea on minor movement, bodily fatigue and chilled extremities, an ashen white or faded yellow facial color, loose stools, a pale tongue with thin white coating, and a flooding, vacuous or large, vacuous pulse; 2) anal prolapse, first and second degree uterine prolapse, prolonged diarrhea, prolonged dysentery, prolonged malaria, and other such complaints due to downward falling of clear yang

Contraindications:

1. Do not use this medicine for fever due to yin vacuity. However, it can be used for fever due to qi vacuity.
2. Only use for prolapse due to central qi vacuity, not for prolapse due to kidney qi vacuity or damp heat.

Dosage: 8 pills three times per day

Formula explanation: Within this formula, Astragalus is the sovereign. It boosts the qi. Codonopsis, Atractylodes, and Licorice fortify the spleen and boost the qi. They are the ministers. Together, they are able to supplement the center and boost the qi. Orange Peel is added to rectify the qi. Dang Gui is added to supplement the blood. These two are the assistant medicinals. Bupleurum and Cimicifugae upbear and lift downfallen clear yang. Thus they are the messengers within this qi-supplementing formula.

Comments: This medicine is one of the most important formulas in Chinese medicine. It has a very wide scope of application, and is, in my opinion, more useful than *Si Jun Zi Wan* (Four Gentlemen Pills). Although this medicine is first and foremost thought of as treating central qi fall with various kinds of visceral prolapse, it is an excellent formula for spleen qi vacuity conditions characterized mainly by fatigue. Because of the inclusion of Bupleurum, Orange Peel, and Cimicifuga, this medicine does rectify the qi. When the clear is upborne, the turbid is then downborne. This means that the qi mechanism must be disinhibited. Therefore, this formula treats a combination of spleen qi vacuity with liver depression where the qi vacuity is more prominent than the qi stagnation. In addition, it should be remembered that Li Dong-yuan originally designed this formula to treat fever due to yin fire or spleen qi vacuity. Upbearing of clear yang goes hand in hand with out-thrusting, and out-thrusting is a valid way of dealing with internal and depressive heat.

Although this medicine may be used alone, it is commonly combined with a wide range of other formulas. For instance, if there is emotional depression and fatigue, this medicine might be combined with *Gan Mai Da Zao Wan* (Licorice, Wheat & Red Dates Pills). For liver depression and more spleen qi vacuity, it might be combined with *Xiao Yao Wan* (Rambling Pills). For liver depression, stomach and/or lung heat, and more prominent spleen vacuity, it might be combined with *Xiao Chai Hu Tang Wan* (Minor Bupleurum Decoction Pills). For spleen qi vacuity with phlegm dampness, it might be combined with *Er Chen Wan* (Two Aged [Ingredients] Pills). For kidney yin and yang vacuity with spleen vacuity, it might be combined with *Ba Ji Yin Yang Wan* (Morinda & Epimedium Pills), and on and on.

Sheng Mai San (Engender the Pulse Powder)

Radix Panacis Ginseng (*Ren Shen*)
Tuber Ophiopogonis Japonici (*Mai Dong*)
Fructus Schisandrae Chinensis (*Wu Wei Zi*)

Functions: Boosts the qi and engenders fluids, constrains yin and stops sweating

Indications: 1) Summerheat heat excessive sweating with consumption of qi and damaged fluids; 2) enduring cough lung vacuity, qi and yin both damaged. Chronic bronchitis, pulmonary tuberculosis, supraventricular arythmias, rheumatic heart disease, coronary artery disease, post-bypass debility

Main signs & symptoms: 1) Bodily fatigue, shortness of breath, dry throat, oral thirst, a vacuous, fine pulse. 2) Dry cough with scant phlegm, shortness of breath, spontaneous perspiration, a dry mouth and parched tongue with thin fur and scanty fluids, and a vacuous, rapid or vacuous, fine pulse[1]

Contraindications: Use this medicine with extreme caution in cases with high fever or in which evils have not been completely eliminated or have yet to damage fluids. If this medicine is used in cases where external evils still remain, due to Schisandra's astringing action, it is like locking a thief inside the house. Due to Ginseng's supplementing function, it will supplement what is already replete (*i.e.*, will only make the evil qi stronger). This will only prolong the disease.

Dosage: 8 pills three times per day

Formula explanation: Ginseng is sweet, level, and supplements the lungs. It greatly supports the source qi. It is the sovereign medicinal in this medicine. Ophiopogon is sweet and cold. It nourishes yin and engenders fluids, clears vacuity heat and eliminates vexation. It is the minister medicinal. Schisandra is sour. It restrains and constrains the lungs and stops sweating. It is the assistant medicinal. This formula's rationale is based on the saying that, "When the lungs desire restraint, quickly eat sour to restrain them." Taken as a whole, this formula supplements the lungs, nourishes the heart, and enriches yin. It is very effective for boosting the qi and engendering fluids.

Comments: This medicine may be administered alone or may be combined with other ready-made medicines. For instance, in cases where depressive heat has damaged lung and/or stomach fluids and there is the complication of qi vacuity, one might combine this medicine with either *Xiao Yao Wan* (Rambling Pills) or *Xiao Chai Hu Tang Wan* (Minor Bupleurum Decoction Pills).

Shen Qi Da Bu Wan (Codonopsis & Astragalus Greatly Supplementing Pills)

Radix Codonopsitis Pilosulae (*Dang Shen*)
Radix Astragali Membranacei (*Huang Qi*)

Functions: Supplements the qi

Indications: Qi vacuity

---

[1] Vacuous pulse used here only means a weak, fine, forceless pulse. Actually, I prefer to use the vacuous pulse (*xu mai*) much more specifically as the proper name of a separate pulse image. In that case, it is defined as floating, large, and forceless. Since large means wide in Chinese pulse examination, using this definition, a pulse cannot be both wide and fine. These are mutually opposites.

Main signs & symptoms: Fatigue, lack of strength in the four limbs, possible spontaneous perspiration and shortness of breath on slight exertion, a forceless pulse

Dosage: 8 pills three times per day

Formula explanation: Codonopsis and Astragalus both greatly supplement the lung and spleen qi.

Comments: This medicine can be combined with many other Chinese ready-made medicines whenever one wants to supplement the qi more, and particularly the lung and spleen qi. Since qi vacuity complicates so many chronic, enduring conditions, these pills are potentially very useful.

Shen Qi Wu Wei Zi Wan (Codonopsis, Astragalus & Schisandra Pills)

Fructus Schisandrae Chinensis (*Wu Wei Zi*)
Radix Astragali Membranacei (*Huang Qi*)
Radix Codonopsitis Pilosulae (*Dang Shen*)
Semen Zizyphi Spinosae (*Suan Zao Ren*)

Functions: Supplements the qi, secures the exterior, and stops sweating

Indications: Qi vacuity spontaneous perspiration, yin vacuity night sweats

Main signs & symptoms: Enduring disease or bodily vacuity due to age, fatigue, lack of strength in the four limbs, spontaneous perspiration and/or shortness of breath on slight exertion, night sweats, a fat, red tongue with teeth marks on its edges and scanty fur, and a fine, rapid or vacuous, rapid pulse

Dosage: 8 pills three times per day

Formula explanation: Within this formula, Schisandra restrains, constrains, and astringes the lung qi, thus securing the exterior and stopping sweating due to vacuity. Astragalus and Codonopsis supplement the lung and spleen qi, thus stopping sweating due to exterior qi vacuity. Zizyphus Spinosa nourishes the heart and supplements the liver. However, it also stops sweating, whether spontaneous perspiration or night sweats.

Comments: This formula can be prescribed by itself when either spontaneous perspiration due to qi vacuity or night sweats due to yin vacuity are the main complaints. However, in clinical practice, both of those conditions are usually symptoms within a larger disease context, such as menopausal syndrome. In that case, this medicine can be combined with other Chinese ready-made medicines to treat such complicated conditions.

For instance, for night sweats due to yin vacuity/vacuity heat, this medicine can be combined with *Da Bu Yin Wan* (Greatly Supplementing Yin Pills), *Zuo Gui Wan* (Restore the Left [Kidney] Pills), *Liu Wei Di Huang Wan* (Six Flavors Rehmannia Pills), or *Zhi Bai Di Huang Wan* (Anemarrhena & Phellodendron Rehmannia Pills). For menopausal night sweats due to yin and yang vacuity, they might be combined with *Cong Rong Bu Shen Wan* (Cistanches Supplement the Kidneys Pills) and/or *Ba Ji Yin Yang Wan* (Morinda & Epimedium Pills).

Ren Shen Jian Pi Wan (Ginseng Fortify the Spleen Pills)

Fructus Immaturus Citri Aurantii (*Zhi Shi*)
Radix Panacis Ginseng (*Ren Shen*)
Rhizoma Atractylodis Macrocephalae (*Bai Zhu*)
Fructus Germinatus Hordei Vulgaris (*Mai Ya*)
Pericarpium Citri Reticulatae (*Chen Pi*)
Fructus Crataegi (*Shan Zha*)

Functions: Fortifies the spleen and supplements the qi, transforms food and disperses accumulation

Indications: Spleen qi vacuity complicated by food stagnation

Main signs & symptoms: Fatigue, lack of strength in the four limbs, no thought for eating or drinking, abdominal distention, bad breath, slimy tongue fur, and a soggy, slippery, or fine, slippery, bowstring pulse

Dosage: 6 pills three times per day

Formula explanation: Ginseng and Atractylodes are the sovereign medicinals within this formula which fortify the spleen and supplement the qi. Orange Peel, Immature Aurantium, and Malted Barley all rectify the qi and eliminate distention. These are the minister medicinals within this formula. Crataegus transforms food and disperses accumulations. It is the assistant medicinal. In addition, Malted Barley especially disperses and eliminates cereal foods, while Crataegus particularly disperses and transforms meaty foods, including milk and milk products.

Comments: Although this medicine can be prescribed alone for a combination of spleen vacuity and food stagnation, it is more usually combined with other formulas when a combination of spleen supplements and food dispersers are wanted. For instance, it might be combined with *Xiao Yao Wan* (Rambling Pills) or *Xiao Chai Hu Tang Wan* (Minor Bupleurum Decoction Pills) for patient's whose cases are compli-cated by food stagnation. These pills can also be given to children on a semi-regular basis in order to fortify their spleen, disperse stagnation, and transform turbidity.

Zi Sheng Wan (Enrich Life Pills)[2]

Radix Codonopsitis Pilosulae (*Dang Shen*)
Rhizoma Atractylodis Macrocephalae (*Bai Zhu*)
Semen Coicis Lachryma-jobi (*Yi Yi Ren*)
Massa Medica Fermentata (*Shen Qu*)
Pericarpium Citri Reticulatae (*Chen Pi*)
Fructus Crataegi (*Shan Zha*)
Semen Euryalis Ferocis (*Qian Shi*)
Radix Dioscoreae Oppositae (*Shan Yao*)
Semen Dolichoris Lablab (*Bai Bian Dou*)
Fructus Germinatus Hordei Vulgaris (*Mai Ya*)
Sclerotium Poriae Cocos (*Fu Ling*)
Semen Nelumbinis Nuciferae (*Lian Zi*)
Radix Platycodi Grandiflori (*Jie Geng*)
Herba Agastachis Seu Pogostemi (*Huo Xiang*)
Radix Glycyrrhizae (*Gan Cao*)
Fructus Cardamomi (*Dou Kou*)
Rhizoma Coptidis Chinensis (*Huang Lian*)

Functions: Boosts the qi and fortifies the spleen, harmonizes the stomach and quiets the fetus

Indications: Spleen qi vacuity with qi and food stagnation complicated by heat vomiting during pregnancy and threatened miscarriage

Main signs & symptoms: Scanty eating, nausea and vomiting, diarrhea, lack of strength, and bodily emaciation

Dosage: 8 pills three times per day

Formula explanation: This formula is an expanded modification of *Shen Ling Bai Zhu Wan* (Ginseng, Poria & Atractylodes Pills) discussed above. Agastaches and Cardamon have been added to increase the strength of this formula to transform dampness and turbidity. Crataegus and Malted Barley have been added to transform food and disperse accumulation. Alisma has been added to percolate dampness, while

---

[2] The usual standard name of this formula is *Bao Tai Zi Sheng Wan* (Protect the Fetus & Enrich Life Pills).

Euryales has been added to stop diarrhea and prevent enduring spleen vacuity from reaching the kidneys. Coptis has been added to clear and eliminate dampness and heat.

Comments: Two things often happen during pregnancy. First, the spleen often gets vacuous and weak. This is because it is the spleen which primarily transforms and engenders the blood which nourishes the fetus and it is the spleen qi which holds up the fetus as it grows ever larger and heavier. Secondly, dampness and heat often accumu-late during pregnancy. Blood and body fluids share a common source and blood and fluids move together. This helps explain why dampness tends to gather and accumulate during pregnancy. If this dampness inhibits the free flow of qi, depressed qi may trans-form into depressive heat. This may then give rise to damp heat brewing and binding.

Therefore, this is a good formula for a combination of spleen qi vacuity, food stagnation, and damp heat during pregnancy, a complicated but commonly seen combination. For this condition, this medicine can be prescribed alone or it may be combined with *Ban Xia Xie Xin Tang* (Pinellia Drain the Heart Decoction). If one tries to treat enduring diarrhea or loose stools during pregnancy but does not also clear heat and eliminate dampness even in the presence of many spleen vacuity signs and symptoms, successful treatment may be hard to come by in Western patients. Therefore, this is a very useful medicine.

Bu Fei Wan (Supplement the Lungs Pills)

Radix Astragali Membranacei (*Huang Qi*)
cooked Radix Rehmanniae (*Shu Di*)
Cortex Radicis Mori Albi (*Sang Bai Pi*)
Radix Asteris Tatarici (*Zi Wan*)
Radix Codonopsitis Pilosulae (*Dang Shen*)
Fructus Schisandrae Chinensis (*Wu Wei Zi*)
Radix Panacis Ginseng (*Ren Shen*)

Functions: Boosts the qi and secures the exterior

Indications: Lung qi vacuity enduring cough

Main signs & symptoms: Shortness of breath, spontaneous perspiration, coughing and panting, a pale tongue, and a faint or vacuous pulse

Formula explanation: Ginseng, Astragalus, and Codonopsis all strongly supplement the spleen and boost the qi, thereby supplementing the lung qi. Schisandra is an astringent whose function in this formula is mainly to secure the lungs. It also enriches lung fluids. Aster and Cortex Mori both downbear counterflow, thus leveling panting and stopping cough. In addition, because Morus is cold in nature, it clears any deep-lying or hidden heat in the lungs which may be consuming and damaging both lung qi and yin. Cooked Rehmannia supplements yin fluids in the body in general and also supplements the kidneys in particular. Since the lungs and kidneys function together to control respiration, supplementation of the kidneys aids in the absorption of the qi in the lower burner. Because qi is rooted in its lower source, this helps counteract upward counterflow.

Comments: This medicine is a derivative of *Sheng Mai Wan* (Engender the Pulse Pills). Its functions are similar to *Yu Ping Feng San Wan* (Jade Windscreen Powder Pills). However, this medicine is better for enduring cough, while *Yu Ping Feng San Wan* is better for recurrent contraction of wind cold evils and spontaneous perspiration.

Blood-supplementing medicines

Si Wu Tang Wan (Four Materials Decoction Pills)

Radix Angelicae Sinensis (*Dang Gui*)
Radix Ligustici Wallichii (*Chuan Xiong*)
Radix Albus Paeoniae Lactiflorae (*Bai Shao*)
cooked Radix Rehmanniae (*Shu Di Huang*)

Functions: Supplements and regulates the blood

Indications: *Chong* and *ren* vacuity detriment, menstruation not regulated, lower abdominal pain, flooding and leaking. Dysmenorrhea, irregular menstruation, uterine bleeding, anemia due to various causes, threatened miscarriage, abdominal pain during pregnancy, postpartum weakness, scanty lactation, hemafecia, dry skin, constipation, and neurogenic headache

Main signs & symptoms: Dizziness, tinnitus, heart palpitations, loss of sleep, blurred vision, a lusterless facial complexion and nails, generalized muscular tension, irregular menstruation with scant flow or blood lumps and clots, possible amenorrhea, occasional aching and pain, restless fetus during pregnancy, downward precipitation of blood which will not stop, postpartum lochia which will not stop, abdominal masses, lower abdominal dragging pain, occasional fever and chills, a pale tongue, and a bowstring, fine or fine, choppy pulse

Contraindications:

1. Do not use this medicine for severe anemia or blood loss. In that case, boost the qi in order to supplement the blood.
2. Do not use if there is spleen and stomach vacuity and dampness with poor appetite and loose stools.

Formula explanation: In this formula, Dang Gui both supplements the blood and quickens the blood. Cooked Rehmannia supplements the blood. These two are the rulers. Ligusticum Wallichium enters the blood division where it rectifies the qi within the blood. Peony restrains yin and nourishes the blood. Thus all the ingredients in this formula are categorized as blood division medicinals.

Comments: Although this medicine is based on one of the most famous formulas in Chinese medicine, it is rarely used by itself. However, it can be combined with almost any other Chinese ready-made medicine when blood vacuity complicates the picture as long as there is not significant spleen or intestinal dampness and loose stools. This is because two of the ingredients, Dang Gui and cooked Rehmannia, are slimy and enriching and can cause or aggravate loose stools in those with dampness and turbidity. For instance, if there is more blood vacuity than addressed by *Xiao Yao Wan* (Rambling Pills) alone and an element of blood stasis, this medicine can be combined with *Xiao Yao Wan*. Or if a patient's pattern calls for *Xiao Chai Hu Tang Wan* (Minor Bupleurum Decoction Pills) but their case is complicated by blood vacuity, then this medicine can be combined with *Xiao Chai Hu Wan*.

In particular, the last combination is especially important and effective for women who "catch cold" right at the beginning of each menstruation. In that case, this combination is a very cheap, easy, and effective cure.

Bu Xue Tiao Jing Wan (Supplement the Blood & Regulate Menstruation Pills)

Herba Leonuri Heterophylli (*Yi Mu Cao*)
Radix Angelicae Sinensis (*Dang Gui*)
cooked Radix Rehmanniae (*Shu Di*)
Radix Ligustici Wallichii (*Chuan Xiong*)
Radix Albus Paeoniae Lactiflorae (*Bai Shao*)

Functions: Supplements and quickens the blood

Indications: Blood vacuity with concomitant blood stasis. Menstrual irregularities and various postpartum conditions

Main signs & symptoms: A pale facial complexion, pale lips, pale nails, dry skin, falling hair, delayed and/or scanty menstruation, painful menstruation, postpartum lower abdominal pain, postpartum dizziness and spirit clouding, postpartum retention of lochia, a pale, possibly purplish tongue or static spots or macules, and a fine, bowstring, possibly choppy pulse

Dosage: 10 tablets two times per day

Formula explanation: This formula is simply *Si Wu Tang* (Four Materials Decoction) plus Leonurus. Leonurus quickens the blood and transforms stasis. However, because it does not damage the blood by strongly attacking it, it is especially good for blood stasis complicating blood vacuity conditions as is often the case after delivery. It is also empirically especially good for gynecological blood stasis conditions. Therefore, its other name is *Kun Cao*, Women's Herb.

Comments: This medicine can either be used alone (not so common in my experience) or combined with other Chinese ready-made medicines for situations complicated by blood vacuity with an element of blood stasis. For instance, it can be combined with *Xiao Yao Wan* (Rambling Pills), *Jia Wei Xiao Yao Wan* (Added Flavors Rambling Pills), *Xiao Chai Hu Tang Wan* (Minor Bupleurum Decoction Pills), *Bu Zhong Yi Qi Wan* (Supplement the Center & Boost the Qi Pills), or *Er Xian Wan* (Two Immortals Pills) just to name several commonly used ready-made medicines.

Fu Ke Zhong Zi Wan (Gynecological Double Progeny Pills)

cooked Radix Rehmanniae (*Shu Di*)
Cortex Eucommiae Ulmoidis (*Du Zhong*)
Rhizoma Cyperi Rotundi (*Xiang Fu*)
Radix Ligustici Wallichii (*Chuan Xiong*)
Radix Angelicae Sinensis (*Dang Gui*)
Radix Dipsaci (*Xu Duan*)
Folium Artemisiae Argyii (*Ai Ye*)
Gelatinum Corii Asini (*E Jiao*)
Radix Scutellariae Baicalensis (*Huang Qin*)
Radix Albus Paeoniae Lactiflorae (*Bai Shao*)

Functions: Nourishes the blood and stops bleeding, supplements the kidneys and invigorates yang, rectifies the qi, clears heat, and quiets the fetus

Indications: Blood vacuity, kidney vacuity, and depressive heat causing fetal stirring restlessness. Threatened miscarriage, menorrhagia, and infertility

Main signs & symptoms: Vaginal bleeding during pregnancy, low back soreness, dark red, thick blood, irritability, a red tongue with possibly yellow fur or slimy, yellow fur, and a slippery, bowstring, rapid pulse

Dosage: 8 pills three times per day

Formula explanation: The main ingredients in this formula are *Si Wu Tang* (Four Materials Decoction): Dang Gui, cooked Rehmannia, Peony, and Ligusticum Wallichium. These medicinals supplement the blood and also quicken the blood. Cyperus rectifies the qi. When the Four Materials are combined with Cyperus, the liver is harmonized and emolliated, thus resolving depression. The liver's main function is to control coursing and discharge, but the liver can only function when it receives sufficient blood to nourish it. Scutellaria clears heat, while Dipsacus and Eucommia supplement the kidneys. Scutellaria, Dispacus, and Eucommia all have pronounced fetus-quieting abilities. Donkey Skin Glue aids the Four Materials to nourish and enrich the blood at the same time as it stops bleeding, while Mugwort warms the uterus and stops bleeding. Hence the Four Materials, Dipsacus, Eucommia, and Scutellaria treat the root, while Donkey Skin Glue and Mugwort treat the branch.

Comments: This medicine can be prescribed by itself for either threatened miscarriage or menorrhagia exhibiting a pattern of liver depression-depressive heat complicated by liver-kidney yang vacuity. However, in Western patients, this pattern is almost always also associated with spleen vacuity. In that case, this medicine can be combined with *Dang Gui Wan* (Dang Gui Pills), *Shen Qi Da Bu Wan* (Ginseng & Astragalus Greatly Supplementing Pills), or *Bu Zhong Yi Qi Wan* (Supplement the Center & Boost the Qi Pills) for even greater qi supplementation.

Dang Gui Su Wan (Solely Dang Gui Pills)

Radix Angelicae Sinensis (*Dang Gui*)

Functions: Supplements the blood and quickens the blood

Indications: Blood vacuity

Main signs & symptoms: A pale facial complexion, pale lips and nails, dry skin, brittle nails, night blindness, malnourished sinews, a pale tongue, and a fine pulse

Dosage: 8 pills three times per day

Formula explanation: This medicine consists of only a single ingredient, Dang Gui. Dang Gui nourishes and supplements the blood and also quickens the blood and transforms stasis. In addition, Dang Gui also moistens the intestines and frees the flow of the stools.

Comments: This medicine is rarely used alone. However, it can be combined with any other Chinese ready-made medicine when one wants to either add to or increase the dosage of Dang Gui. Therefore, it is a very useful medicine.

Shou Wu Pian (Polygonum Multiflorum Tablets)

Radix Polygoni Multiflori (*He Shou Wu*)

Functions: Supplements the liver and kidneys, secures the essence and stops leakage, clears and resolves fire toxins, moistens the intestines and frees the flow of the stools, dispels wind from the skin by nourishing the blood, treats malaria-like disorders

Indications: Liver blood-kidney qi and yin vacuity, fluid dryness constipation

Main signs & symptoms: Low back soreness and weakness, dizziness, blurred vision, seminal emission, abnormal vaginal discharge, premature greying of the hair, numbness of the extremities, itching due to wind rash in turn due to blood vacuity, chronic malaria-like disorders associated with bodily debility, as in *lao nue* or taxation "malaria", and insomnia

Dosage: 4 pills three times per day

Formula explanation: Polygonum Multiflorum supplements the blood and nourishes the liver. It also moistens the intestines and frees the flow of the stools.

Comments: This single ingredient ready-made medicine is sometimes very useful for supplementing the blood and moistening the intestines. It can be combined with a wide range of other Chinese ready-made medicines when one wants to supplement the blood or nourish the liver even more. Although it is Caulis Polygoni Multiflori (*Ye Jiao Teng*, a.k.a., *Shou Wu Teng*) which is categorized as a spirit-quieting medicinal, I believe Polygonum Root shares at least some of the same ability. Therefore, this medicine may be added to others for the treatment of blood vacuity insomnia.

Shao Yao Gan Cao Wan (Peony & Licorice Pills)

Radix Albus Paeoniae Lactiflorae (*Bai Shao*)
mix-fried Radix Glycyrrhizae (*Gan Cao*)

Functions: Emolliates the liver, relaxes cramps, and stops pain

Indications: Blood vacuity malnourishment of the sinews resulting in cramps and pain. Intercostal neuralgia, sciatica, trigeminal neuralgia, chronic pelvic inflammatory disease, primary dysmenorrhea

Main signs & symptoms: Irritability, spasms of the calf muscles, cramps in the hands and feet, abdominal cramps or pain, a pale tongue, and a fine, bowstring pulse

Dosage: 8 pills three times per day

Formula explanation: Peony nourishes the blood and emolliates the liver. The liver governs the sinews. If there is a liver blood vacuity, the sinews may be malnourished. If they do not obtain sufficient blood and yin fluids, they may become dry and contract. Hence nourishing liver blood nourishes and moistens the sinews. In addition, the liver's function of coursing and discharge is dependent on obtaining sufficient blood. If the liver obtains sufficient blood, its coursing and discharging function properly and the qi mechanism is disinhibited. Mix-fried Licorice fortifies the spleen and supplements the qi. The spleen is the postnatal or latter heaven root of the engenderment and transformation of blood. In addition, a strong, healthy spleen checks or keeps liver (qi) repletion in control.

Comments: This medicine can be combined with any other Chinese ready-made medicine when there are spasms and pain due to either blood vacuity not nourishing the sinews or liver invading the spleen. For instance, it might be combined with *Ban Xia Xie Xin Tang* (Pinellia Drain the Heart Decoction [Pills]) for the treatment of tenesmus or abdominal cramping associated with damp heat and spleen vacuity colitis, or it might be combined with *Tao Hong Si Wu Wan* (Persica & Carthamus Four Materials Pills) for blood vacuity and blood stasis restless leg syndrome or peripheral neuropathy.

Medicines which supplement both the qi & the blood

Gui Pi Wan (Restore the Spleen Pills)

Radix Codonopsitis Pilosulae (*Dang Shen*)
Radix Astragali Membranacei (*Huang Qi*)
Rhizoma Atractylodis Macrocephalae (*Bai Zhu*)
Sclerotium Pararadicis Poriae Cocos (*Fu Shen*)
Arillus Euphoriae Longanae (*Long Yan Rou*)
Semen Zizyphi Spinosae (*Suan Zao Ren*)
Radix Auklandiae Lappae (*Mu Xiang*)
Radix Glycyrrhizae (*Gan Cao*)
Radix Angelicae Sinensis (*Dang Gui*)
Radix Polygalae Tenuifoliae (*Yuan Zhi*)
Fructus Zizyphi Jujubae (*Da Zao*)

Functions: Boosts the qi and supplements the blood, fortifies the spleen and nourishes the heart

Indications: 1) Heart-spleen dual vacuity, taxation damage of the heart and spleen, qi and blood insufficiency, 2) spleen not gathering the blood. Neurasthenia, gastric and duodenal ulcers, functional uterine bleeding, thrombocytopenic purpura, aplastic anemia, common anemia, chronic hemorrhagic disorders, menorrhagia, post-concussion syndrome, myasthenia gravis, congestive heart disease, supraventricular tachycardia, palpitations, cervicitis, uterine cancer, leukemia, insomnia, poor memory, genital itching, nocturnal emission, impotence, and chronic gonorrhea

Main signs & symptoms: 1) Heart palpitations, impaired memory, insomnia, night sweats, vacuity heat (*i.e.*, feverishness), diminished appetite, bodily fatigue, a withered yellow facial complexion, a pale, fat tongue with thin, white fur, and a fine, moderate (*i.e.*, slightly slow) or fine, weak pulse; 2) hemafecia, uterine bleeding, early menstruation, excessively profuse menstruation but pale-colored blood or dribbling and dripping which will not stop, or abnormal vaginal discharge

Dosage: 8 pills three times per day

Formula explanation: In this formula, Ginseng, Astragalus, Licorice, and Red Dates are all sweet and warm and supplement the spleen and boost the qi. Dang Gui is sweet and acrid. It warms and nourishes the liver and engenders heart blood. Spirit of Poria, Zizyphus Spinosa, and Longans are sweet and neutral. They nourish the heart and quiet the spirit. Polygala joins and frees the flow between the heart and kidneys. It also stabilizes the will (or mind and emotions) and tranquilizes the heart. Auklandia recti-fies the qi and arouses the spleen. This ingredient is added because qi-boosting, blood-supplementing formulas use enriching, greasy ingredients which may stagnate the qi and hinder the spleen and stomach's function of transportation and transformation.

Comments: This medicine is especially useful for treating women's uterine bleeding or any person's bleeding due to spleen qi vacuity.

Ba Zhen Wan (Eight Pearls Pills)

cooked Radix Rehmanniae (*Shu Di*)
Radix Angelicae Sinensis (*Dang Gui*)
Radix Codonopsitis Pilosulae (*Dang Shen*)
Sclerotium Poriae Cocos (*Fu Ling*)
Radix Albus Paeoniae Lactiflorae (*Bai Shao*)
Rhizoma Atractylodis Macrocephalae (*Bai Zhu*)

Radix Ligustici Wallichii (*Chuan Xiong*)
Radix Glycyrrhizae (*Gan Cao*)

Functions: Supplements and boosts the qi and blood

Indications: Qi and blood dual vacuity

Main signs & symptoms: A somber white or sallow yellow facial complexion, dizziness, blurred vision, fatigued body and limbs, shortness of breath, faint or weak voice or disinclination to speak due to fatigue, heart palpitations, racing heart, reduced desire to eat, a pale tongue with thin, white fur, and a fine, vacuous pulse

Dosage: 8 pills three times per day

Formula explanation: Within this formula, Ginseng, Atractylodes, Poria, and Licorice supplement the spleen and boost the qi. Dang Gui, Peony, and cooked Rehmannia enrich and nourish the heart and liver. Ligusticum Wallichium is added to enter the blood division and rectify the qi. Thus Dang Gui and Rehmannia are supplemented without causing stagnation.

Comments: This medicine can be used alone when there is the simple pattern of qi and blood dual vacuity. However, such a simple pattern is not so commonly met in Western clinical practice. Therefore, in the West, this medicine is more often combined with other ready-made medicines based on the presence of other complicating patterns. For example, this formula might be combined with either *Xiao Yao Wan* (Rambling Pills) or *Xiao Chai Hu Tang Wan* (Minor Bupleurum Decoction Pills) if there is even more qi and blood vacuity than either of these two medicines address.

Shi Quan Da Bu Wan (Ten [Ingredients] Greatly & Completely Supplementing Pills)

Radix Angelicae Sinensis (*Dang Gui*)
cooked Radix Rehmanniae (*Shu Di*)
Radix Codonopsitis Pilosulae (*Dang Shen*)
Radix Astragali Membranacei (*Huang Qi*)
Rhizoma Atractylodis Macrocephalae (*Bai Zhu*)
Radix Albus Paeoniae Lactiflorae (*Bai Shao*)
Sclerotium Poriae Cocos (*Fu Ling*)
Radix Glycyrrhizae (*Gan Cao*)
Cortex Cinnamomi Cassiae (*Rou Gui*)
Radix Ligustici Wallichii (*Chuan Xiong*)

Functions: Warms and supplements the qi and blood

Indications: Qi and blood insufficiency

Main signs & symptoms: Vacuity taxation cough, scanty eating, seminal emission, lower leg and knee lack of strength, sores which do not constrain (*i.e.*, pull together and heal), women's flooding and leaking

Dosage: 8 pills three times per day

Formula explanation: This medicine contains all the same ingredients as *Ba Zhen Wan* (Eight Pearls Pills) above. However, Astragalus and Cortex Cinnamomi have been added to this base. Some Chinese sources say this formula addresses qi and blood vacuity complicated by vacuity cold, while others simply say the inclusion of these two ingredients simply results in faster, greater supplementation of the qi and blood. In other words, vacuity cold symptoms do not need to be present to use this formula.

Comments: Like *Ba Zhen Wan* above, this medicine can be used either alone or in combination with other Chinese ready-made medicines.

Yang Rong Wan (Nourish the Constructive Pills)

Radix Angelicae Sinensis (*Dang Gui*)
cooked Radix Rehmanniae (*Shu Di*)
Radix Albus Paeoniae Lactiflorae (*Bai Shao*)
Radix Ligustici Wallichii (*Chuan Xiong*)
Rhizoma Cyperi Rotundi (*Xiang Fu*)
Herba Leonuri Heterophylli (*Yi Mu Cao*)
Cortex Eucommiae Ulmoidis (*Du Zhong*)
Radix Astragali Membranacei (*Huang Qi*)
Folium Artemisiae Argyii (*Ai Ye*)
Sclerotium Poriae Cocos (*Fu Ling*)
Tuber Ophiopogonis Japonici (*Mai Dong*)
Radix Glycyrrhizae (*Gan Cao*)
Pericarpium Citri Reticulatae (*Chen Pi*)
Gelatinum Corii Asini (*E Jiao*)
Fructus Amomi (*Sha Ren*)

Functions: Supplements the qi and blood, supplements the kidneys and strengthens the low back, stops bleeding and secures the fetus

Indications: Qi and blood vacuity and kidney vacuity excessively profuse menstruation or fetus stirring restlessness. Menorrhagia, threatened miscarriage, infertility

Main signs & symptoms: Generalized qi and blood vacuity signs and symptoms as described above plus scanty eating, lack of strength in the four limbs, fatigue, low back soreness, abdominal distention, leakage of blood during pregnancy

Dosage: 8 pills three times per day

Formula explanation: Within this formula, Astragalus, Atractylodes, Poria, and Licorice all supplement the spleen and boost the qi. Dang Gui, cooked Rehmannia, and Peony supplement and nourish the heart and liver. Ligusticum Wallichium and Leonurus quicken the blood, while Cyperus, Orange Peel, and Amomum rectify the qi. Eucommia supplements the kidneys and strengthens the low back, while Ophiopogon helps supplement the heart and engenders fluid to assist the engenderment of blood. This is because the blood and fluids share a common source. Mugwort warms the uterus and stops bleeding. Mugwort and Leonurus both are especially effective at stopping bleeding, while Eucommia, Amomum, and Atractylodes are especially effective at quieting the fetus and stopping threatened miscarriage.

Comments: This medicine is mainly for the treatment of spleen-kidney dual vacuity threatened miscarriage or luteal phase defect infertility or menorrhagia also due to spleen-kidney dual vacuity. In this case, there are signs and symptoms of spleen qi vacuity with signs and symptoms of kidney yang vacuity. However, these latter may be confined to low back soreness and pain, decreased libido, cold feet, and a tendency to nocturia. Frequently, such conditions are complicated by qi stagnation and blood stasis, which this formula does address. However, if there is more pronounced liver depression qi stagnation or if there is depressive heat, then this medicine should be combined with another Chinese ready-made medicine which addresses those disease mechanisms and patterns.

Because threatened miscarriage is an emergency condition, the dose of these pills will probably have to be increased by three or even four times. Usually, bulk-dispensed, water-decocted formulas are prescribed for threatened miscarriage. However, pills can be used, at least initially, to begin medication while individually written prescriptions are being made and decocted.

Fu Ke Yang Ying Wan (Gynecological Nourishing the Constructive Pills)[3]

Radix Codonopsitis Pilosulae (*Dang Shen*)
Rhizoma Atractylodis Macrocephalae (*Bai Zhu*)
Radix Astragali Membranacei (*Huang Qi*)

---

[3] The Mayway catalog gives the Pinyin of this formula's name simply as *Yang Ying Wan*. However, the fuller name given above is what appears in Chinese characters. This formula is more usually called *Ren Shen Yang Ying Wan* (Ginseng Nourish the Constructive Pills).

Supplementing & Boosting Medicines

Radix Glycyrrhizae (*Gan Cao*)
Cortex Cinnamomi Cassiae (*Rou Gui*)
Fructus Citri Aurantii (*Zhi Ke*)
Radix Angelicae Sinensis (*Dang Gui*)
Fructus Zizyphi Jujubae (*Da Zao*)
Radix Albus Paeoniae Lactiflorae (*Bai Shao*)
cooked Radix Rehmanniae (*Shu Di*)
Fructus Schisandrae Chinensis (*Wu Wei Zi*)
Sclerotium Poriae Cocos (*Fu Ling*)
dry Rhizoma Zingiberis (*Gan Jiang*)
Radix Polygalae Tenuifoliae (*Yuan Zhi*)

Functions: Boosts the qi and supplements the blood, nourishes the heart and quiets the spirit

Indications: Qi and blood insufficiency

Main signs & symptoms: Heart palpitations, impaired memory, scanty eating, fatigue, shortness of breath and spontaneous perspiration on slight exertion, bodily emaciation, dry skin, dry mouth and parched throat, enduring sores which will not close

Dosage: 8 pills three times per day

Formula explanation: Within this formula, Astragalus, Poria, Licorice, and Red Dates supplement the spleen and boost the qi, while Dang Gui, Peony, and cooked Rehmannia nourish the blood. Cortex Cinnamomi and dry Ginger warm the middle and scatter cold, thus supplementing the spleen. Because the spleen is the latter heaven root of qi and blood engenderment and transformation, if the spleen is exuberant, then qi and blood have a place from which to be engendered. Schisandra and Polygala both supplement the heart and quiet the spirit, while Aurantium rectifies the qi and downbears counterflow. Red Dates and Poria also assist in the supplementation of the heart and quieting of the spirit, and Licorice also acts to harmonize and regulate all the ingredients in the formula.

Comments: Compared to *Shi Quan Da Bu Wan* (Ten [Ingredients] Greatly & Completely Supplementing Pills), this medicine is better for qi and blood dual vacuity where there is more disquietude of the spirit due to heart qi and blood vacuity.

Dang Gui Wan (Dang Gui Pills)

Radix Angelicae Sinensis (*Dang Gui*)
Radix Ligustici Wallichii (*Chuan Xiong*)
Rhizoma Atractylodis Macrocephalae (*Bai Zhu*)

Fructus Zizyphi Jujubae (*Da Zao*)

Functions: Nourishes the blood and supplements the qi

Indications: Blood vacuity complicated by an element of qi vacuity

Main signs & symptoms: A pale facial complexion, pale lips and nails, dry, brittle nails, night blindness, fatigue, scanty eating, lack of strength in the four limbs, a pale tongue with thin, white fur, and a fine, forceless pulse

Dosage: 8 pills three times per day

Formula explanation: Within this formula, Dang Gui is the sovereign medicinal which nourishes the blood. The minister medicinals are Atractylodes and Ligusticum Wallichium. Atractylodes fortifies the spleen and supplements the qi, while Ligusticum quickens the blood. Dead or static blood impedes the engenderment of fresh or new blood. Thus it is sometimes said that quickening the blood is supplementation. Red Dates are then the assistant medicinal. They assist Dang Gui to nourish the blood and Atractylodes to supplement the qi.

Comments: This medicine is primarily good for combining with other Chinese ready-made medicines when one wants to add to or increase those other medicine's ability to nourish the blood and, secondarily, supplement the spleen qi. Thus there are a great many Chinese ready-made medicines which might be used with this one.

Zhi Gan Cao Wan (Mix-fried Licorice Pills)

uncooked Radix Rehmanniae (*Sheng Di*)
mix-fried Radix Glycyrrhizae (*Gan Cao*)
Tuber Ophiopogonis Japonici (*Mai Dong*)
Semen Cannabis Sativae (*Huo Ma Ren*)
Ramulus Cinnamomi Cassiae (*Gui Zhi*)
uncooked Rhizoma Zingiberis (*Sheng Jiang*)
Fructus Zizyphi Jujubae (*Da Zao*)
Radix Panacis Ginseng (*Ren Shen*)
Gelatinum Corii Asini (*E Jiao*)

Functions: Supplements the qi and nourishes the blood, enriches yin and restores the pulse

Indications: Heart qi and blood vacuity. Supraventricular arrhythmia, rheumatic heart disease, mitral valve stenosis, mitral valve prolapse, hyperthyroidism, pulmonary tuberculosis, emphysema, neurasthenia

Main signs & symptoms: Heart palpitations, irritability, vexation and agitation, insomnia, emaciation, shortness of breath, constipation with dry, bound stools, a dry mouth and throat, a pale tongue with either dry or scanty fur, and a bound, regularly intermittent, or faint pulse

Contraindications: Do not use this medicine alone for severe heart yin vacuity or in cases with severe diarrhea. Because Licorice raises blood pressure, it should either not be used or used with care in patients with hypertension.

Dosage: 8 pills three times per day

Formula explanation: Mix-fried Licorice is the sovereign medicinal in this formula. It supplements both the heart qi and blood. It is assisted by Ginseng which also supplements the qi and quiets the spirit, especially when combined with mix-fried Licorice. Red Dates supplement the spleen and nourish the heart. Hence these three are the main ingredients for supplementing the heart qi and blood. Another four medicinals nourish and enrich blood and yin. Cooked Rehmannia and Donkey Skin Glue both nourish the blood and enrich yin. Ophiopogon engenders fluids in the stomach and lungs, clears heat from the heart, and transforms phlegm, and Cannabis nourishes yin and moistens the intestines. Cinnamon Twigs free the flow of the heart qi. When combined with Ginseng, it is especially effective for treating heart palpitations. Uncooked Ginger harmonizes the center and helps prevent stagnation due to slimy, enriching ingredients, while the combination of uncooked Ginger and Red Dates harmonizes the constructive and defensive.

Comments: Although this formula supplements the three vacuities of heart qi, blood, and yin, since it does not have any heat-clearing medicinals other than Ophiopogon, it should not be used or used alone where yin vacuity has led to pronounced vacuity heat. A heart qi vacuity may also manifest a moderate or relaxed, *i.e.*, slightly slow pulse. Many athletes have such a pulse. In such cases, many Chinese doctors believe that over-exercise has damaged the heart. Therefore, this might be one Chinese ready-made medicine that is appropriate for treatment of otherwise asymptomatic athletes who are looking to increase their performance.

Yin-supplementing medicines

Liu Wei Di Huang Wan (Six Flavors Rehmannia Pills)

cooked Radix Rehmanniae (*Shu Di*)
Fructus Corni Officinalis (*Shan Zhu Yu*)
Radix Dioscoreae Oppositae (*Shan Yao*)

Rhizoma Alismatis (*Ze Xie*)
Sclerotium Poriae Cocos (*Fu Ling*)
Cortex Radicis Moutan (*Dan Pi*)

Functions: Enriches and supplements the liver and kidneys

Indications: Liver-kidney yin vacuity. Retarded growth of children, lumbago, optic neuritis, central retinitis, optic nerve atrophy, pulmonary tuberculosis, diabetes, hyperthyroidism, Addison's disease, hypertension, neurasthenia, functional uterine bleeding, chronic urinary tract infection, chronic nephritis, chronic glomerulonephritis, nephroatrophy, deafness, impotence, nocturnal emission, nocturia, menopause, senility

Main signs & symptoms: Low back and knee soreness and weakness, dizziness and vertigo, tinnitus and deafness, night sweats and spermatorrhea, bone-steaming and tidal fevers, heat in the hands, feet, and heart (or heat in the centers of the hands and feet), wasting thirst, possible vacuity fire toothache, dry mouth and throat, a red tongue with scant fur, and a fine, rapid pulse

Contraindications:

1. Use this medicine with care in patients with slimy, white tongue fur and indigestion indicating spleen vacuity and dampness or food stagnation.
2. Do not use in patients with diarrhea.

Dosage: 8 pills three times per day

Formula explanation: Within this formula, cooked Rehmannia is the sovereign ingredient. It enriches kidney yin and boosts the essence and marrow. Cornus assists in warming and enriching the kidneys and boosting the liver. Dioscorea enriches the kidneys and supplements the spleen. These are the three yin-supplementing medicinals in this formula. They are called the *san bu* or three supplementers. These are then combined with three draining or opening ingredients called the *san xie*, the three drainers. Alisma aids Rehmannia by draining any exuberance of kidney fire and downbears turbidity. Moutan aids Cornus by draining liver fire. In addition, it quickens the blood and transforms stasis. Since this formula is so often used in the elderly and the chronically ill, an element of blood stasis is often found in cases for whom this formula is appropriate. Poria assists Dioscorea by percolating spleen dampness. Further, Poria and Alisma work together to eliminate dampness and disinhibit water.

Qi Ju Di Huang Wan (Lycium & Chrysanthemum Rehmannia Pills)

cooked Radix Rehmanniae (*Shu Di*)
Radix Dioscoreae Oppositae (*Shan Yao*)

Fructus Corni Officinalis (*Shan Zhu Yu*)
Sclerotium Poriae Cocos (*Fu Ling*)
Rhizoma Alismatis (*Ze Xie*)
Cortex Radicis Moutan (*Dan Pi*)
Fructus Lycii Chinensis (*Gou Qi Zi*)
Flos Chrysanthemi Morifolii (*Ju Hua*)

Functions: Enriches the kidneys and nourishes the liver, brightens the eyes

Indications: Liver-kidney yin vacuity eye and vision problems and wilting condition

Main signs & symptoms: Blurred vision, dry, scratchy eyes, easy tearing of the eyes on exposure to wind, malnourishment of the sinews, low back and knee soreness and weakness, a pale tongue with a possibly red tip, and a fine, bowstring pulse

Dosage: 8 pills three times per day

Formula explanation: This medicine is an augmented modification of *Liu Wei Di Huang Wan* (Six Flavors Rehmannia Pills) above. To that base, Lycium Berries have been added in order to nourish the liver and supplement the kidneys, while Chrysanthemum Flowers have been added to clear heat and brighten the eyes.

Comments: This medicine is the guiding prescription to use whenever there is liver blood and kidney yin vacuity without pronounced vacuity heat. Although the word blood is not included when we say liver-kidney yin vacuity, it is supposed to be understood. Therefore, this formula is not just for eye and vision diseases. For instance, it is an important formula for chronic impediment and wilting condition associated with liver-kidney yin vacuity malnourishment of the sinews.

Mai Wei Di Huang Wan (Ophiopogon & Schisandra Rehmannia Pills)

cooked Radix Rehmanniae (*Shu Di*)
Radix Dioscoreae Oppositae (*Shan Yao*)
Fructus Corni Officinalis (*Shan Zhu Yu*)
Cortex Radicis Moutan (*Dan Pi*)
Sclerotium Poriae Cocos (*Fu Ling*)
Rhizoma Alismatis (*Ze Xie*)
Tuber Ophiopogonis Japonici (*Mai Dong*)
Fructus Schisandrae Chinensis (*Wu Wei Zi*)

Functions: Constrains the lungs and grasps the kidneys

Indications: Lung-kidney yin vacuity

Main signs & symptoms: Cough, panting counterflow, tidal heat, night sweats

Dosage: 8 pills three times per day

Formula explanation: Another expansion of *Liu Wei Di Huang Wan* (Six Flavors Rehmannia Pills), Ophiopogon has been added to engender fluids, clear heat, and transform phlegm, while Schisandra has been added to engender fluids, constrain the lungs, and stop coughing.

Comments: This medicine is the guiding prescription for all conditions due to lung-kidney yin vacuity.

Zhi Bai Di Huang Wan (Anemarrhena & Phellodendron Rehmannia Pills)

cooked Radix Rehmanniae (*Shu Di*)
Fructus Corni Officinalis (*Shan Zhu Yu*)
Radix Dioscoreae Oppositae (*Shan Yao*)
Sclerotium Poriae Cocos (*Fu Ling*)
Cortex Radicis Moutan (*Dan Pi*)
Rhizoma Alismatis (*Ze Xie*)
Rhizoma Anemarrhenae Aspheloidis (*Zhi Mu*)
Cortex Phellodendri (*Huang Bai*)

Functions: Enriches yin and downbears fire

Indications: Yin vacuity fire effulgence

Main signs & symptoms: Bone-steaming, taxation heat, vacuity vexation, night sweats, lower and upper back aching and pain, seminal emission, a red tongue with scanty fur, and a fine, rapid, or vacuous rapid, possibly surging pulse

Dosage: 8 pills three times per day

Formula explanation: Yet another expanded modification of *Liu Wei Di Huang Wan* (Six Flavors Rehmannia Pills), Anemarrhena is added to enrich yin and downbear fire, while Phellodendron is added to clear vacuity and damp heat.

Comments: This medicine is a very useful one for all cases where there is yin vacuity with fire effulgence. However, even simple yin vacuity conditions will have some heat signs and symptoms, such as a red tongue and fast pulse. That does not mean that one should necessarily clear heat. Before this medicine should be used, there should be definite signs of fire effulgence. In fact, this is one of the most commonly misused Chinese medicinal formulas in the West where it tends to be over-prescribed.

Ming Mu Di Huang Wan (Brighten the Eyes Rehmannia Pills)

cooked Radix Rehmanniae (*Shu Di*)
Fructus Corni Officinalis (*Shan Zhu Yu*)
Radix Dioscoreae Oppositae (*Shan Yao*)
Concha Haliotidis (*Shi Jue Ming*)
Radix Angelicae Sinensis (*Dang Gui*)
Flos Chrysanthemi Morifolii (*Ju Hua*)
Fructus Lycii Chinensis (*Gou Qi Zi*)
Cortex Radicis Moutan (*Dan Pi*)
Rhizoma Alismatis (*Ze Xie*)
Radix Rubrus Paeoniae Lactiflorae (*Chi Shao*)
Fructus Tribuli Terrestris (*Bai Ji Li*)
Sclerotium Poriae Cocos (*Fu Ling*)

Functions: Nourishes the liver and enriches the kidneys, clears heat, subdues yang, extinguishes wind, and brightens the eyes

Indications: Liver-kidney yin vacuity eye and vision problems

Main signs & symptoms: Blurred vision, night blindness, dry, scratchy or itchy eyes, red eyes

Dosage: 8 pills three times per day

Formula explanation: This formula is an expanded version of *Qi Ju Di Huang Wan* (Lycium & Chrysanthemum Rehmannia Pills) discussed above. However, to that base, Dang Gui has been added to supplement the blood more strongly, while Red Peony quickens the blood and clears heat. Tribulus extinguishes wind, and Abalone Shell subdues yang.

Comments: This medicine is commonly prescribed by itself. Whereas *Qi Ju Di Huang Wan* may be used for conditions other than eyes diseases, this medicine is specifically for eye diseases and pretty much only eye diseases. This is a more appropriate medicine for when enduring disease has entered the network vessels.

Er Long Zuo Ci Wan (Deafness Left [Kidney] Magnetite Pills)

cooked Radix Rehmanniae (*Shu Di*)
Radix Dioscoreae Oppositae (*Shan Yao*)

Fructus Corni Officinalis (*Shan Zhu Yu*)
Cortex Radicis Moutan (*Dan Pi*)
Sclerotium Poriae Cocos (*Fu Ling*)
Rhizoma Alismatis (*Ze Xie*)
Radix Bupleuri (*Chai Hu*)
Magnetitum (*Ci Shi*)

Functions: Enriches yin and subdues yang, opens the portal of the ears and sharpens auditory acuity

Indications: Kidney yin vacuity tinnitus and deafness

Main signs & symptoms: Continuous, cicada-like tinnitus which worsens at night or when fatigued, deafness, irritability, insomnia, dizziness and vertigo, blurred vision, and a fine, weak or fine and rapid pulse

Dosage: 8 pills three times per day

Formula explanation: This formula is another expanded modification of *Liu Wei Di Huang Wan* (Six Flavors Rehmannia Pills). Bupleurum is added to guide the other medicinals into the *shao yang* channels which encircle the ears. Magnetite subdues yang and quiets the spirit, nourishes the kidneys and supplements the liver. In particular, this medicinal is known to have an empirical effect of improving both the hearing and vision.

Comments: This medicine is for the treatment of tinnitus and deafness due to kidney yin vacuity. This means tinnitus due to aging and *not* due to damage by loud sounds. It should be taken at the very first sign of this condition. If this condition becomes chronic and enduring, it may be difficult if not impossible to cure.

Gu Ben Wan (Secure the Root Pills)

Tuber Asparagi Cochinensis (*Tian Dong*)
Tuber Ophiopogonis Japonici (*Mai Dong*)
cooked Radix Rehmanniae (*Shu Di*)
uncooked Radix Rehmanniae (*Sheng Di*)
Radix Codonopsitis Pilosulae (*Dang Shen*)

Functions: Enriches yin and supplements the qi

Indications: Lung-kidney qi and yin vacuity

Main signs & symptoms: Enduring dry cough and/or panting counterflow with no or scanty phlegm, low back and knee soreness and weakness, frequent, scanty urination, a dry mouth but no desire to drink, fatigue, loss of strength of the four limbs, scanty eating

Dosage: 6 pills three times per day

Formula explanation: This medicine combines the Two Dongs with the Two Di's. The Two Dongs are Ophiopogon and Asparagus. Ophiopogon engenders fluids and moistens the lungs, while Asparagus enriches yin and supplements the kidneys. Cooked Rehmannia supplements the kidneys and enriches yin, while uncooked Rehmannia cools the blood and clears vacuity heat. Codonopsis is added to supplement and fortify the lungs and spleen, thus boosting the qi.

Comments: This is not a medicine which I would be likely to prescribe alone. However, it is a good medicine to combine with others wherever there is more serious yin fluid debility and damage with heat consuming both the qi and fluids.

Zuo Gui Wan (Restore the Left [Kidney] Pills)

cooked Radix Rehmanniae (*Shu Di*)
Radix Dioscoreae Oppositae (*Shan Yao*)
Fructus Corni Officinalis (*Shan Zhu Yu*)
Semen Cuscutae Chinensis (*Tu Si Zi*)
Fructus Lycii Chinensis (*Gou Qi Zi*)
Radix Achyranthis Bidentatae (*Niu Xi*)
Gelatinum Cornu Cervi (*Lu Jiao Jiao*)
Gelatinum Plastri Testudinis (*Gui Ban Jiao*)

Functions: Enriches yin and supplements the kidneys

Indications: True yin insufficiency

Main signs & symptoms: Vertigo and dizziness, low backache and weak knees, seminal emission, seminal discharge, spontaneous perspiration, night sweats, a dry mouth and parched throat, thirst with a desire to drink water, a smooth bare tongue with scanty fur, and a fine, possibly rapid pulse

Contraindications: Because this medicine contains slimy, enriching medicinals, it should be used with care in cases which involve spleen vacuity.

Dosage: 8 pills three times per day

Formula explanation: Within this formula, a heavy dose of cooked Rehmannia enriches the kidneys in order to fill true yin. Lycium Berries boost the essence and brighten the eyes. Cornus astringes the essence and constrains sweat. Deer Antler and Tortoise Shell Glue are both bloody, meaty natured ingredients. Deer Antler Glue tends to supplement yang, while Tortoise Shell Glue tends to enrich yin. When both glues are used together, they flow freely into the two vessels of the *ren* and *du*, boost the essence and fill the marrow. Thus within the supplementation of yin there is the supplementation of yang, for, when yang grows, yin is engendered. Cuscuta and Achyranthes together strengthen the low back and knees, and Dioscorea enriches and boosts the spleen and kidneys. Hence this formula as a whole enriches the kidneys and fills yin, fosters yin and subdues yang.

Comments: This formula is stronger and more enriching than *Liu Wei Di Huang Wan* (Six Flavors Rehmannia Pills). However, yin vacuity does not commonly present all by itself. Therefore, this medicine is typically prescribed in combination with other Chinese ready-made medicines when strong yin supplementation is wanted without the sophisticated internal checks and balances and minor themes of *Liu Wei Di Huang Wan*. Because it contains bloody, meaty ingredients, it is better for the treatment of bone and joint problems exhibiting a yin vacuity pattern.

Da Bu Yin Wan (Greatly Supplementing Yin Pills)

cooked Radix Rehmanniae (*Shu Di*)
Plastrum Testudinis (*Gui Ban*)
Rhizoma Anemarrhenae Aspheloidis (*Zhi Mu*)
Cortex Phellodendri (*Huang Bai*)

Functions: Enriches yin and downbears fire

Indications: Liver-kidney yin vacuity, vacuity fire flaming upward. Tuberculosis of the lungs, kidneys, and/or bones, bronchiectasis, diabetes mellitus, hyperthyroid conditions, neurasthenia

Main signs & symptoms: Bone-steaming, tidal heat, night sweats, seminal emission, cough, hacking blood, heart vexation, easy anger, leg and knee aching and heat or wilting and limpness, a red tongue with scanty fur, and a rapid pulse which has force in the cubit position

Contraindications: Use this medicine cautiously in patients with torpid intake and loose stools. This medicine is contraindicated in case of fire due to repletion.

Dosage: 8 pills three times per day

Supplementing & Boosting Medicines

Formula explanation: Within this formula, cooked Rehmannia and Tortoise Shell enrich and supplement true yin, subdue yang and control fire. These are the ingredients in this medicine which bank the root. Phellodendron is bitter and cold and drains ministerial fire, therefore hardening true yin. Anemarrhena is bitter and cold. Above, it clears and moistens lung heat. Below, it enriches and moistens kidney yin. These are the ingredients in this formula which clear the origin. When both these two groups of medicinals are combined together, their effect is to bank the root and clear the origin.

Comments: This medicinal can be prescribed alone but rarely is. It can be combined with any other ready-made medicine when one wants to strongly enrich yin and downbear fire. Although its functions are basically the same as *Zhi Bai Di Huang Wan* (Anemarrhena & Phellodendron Rehmannia Pills), this medicine only accomplishes these two functions. It is not as sophisticated and complicated as *Zhi Bai Di Huang Wan*. Therefore, it is a better choice for combining with other medicines when one does not want to include all the ingredients in that more complex formula.

Yi Guan Jian Wan (One Link Decoction Pills)

uncooked Radix Rehmanniae (*Sheng Di*)
Fructus Lycii Chinensis (*Gou Qi Zi*)
Radix Glehniae Littoralis (*Bei Sha Shen*)
Tuber Ophiopogonis Japonici (*Mai Dong*)
Radix Angelicae Sinensis (*Dang Gui*)
Fructus Meliae Toosendan (*Chuan Lian Zi*)

Functions: Enriches yin and courses the liver

Indications: Liver blood-kidney yin vacuity complicated by liver depression qi stagnation. Chronic active hepatitis, cirrhosis, costochondritis, peptic ulcers, essential hypertension, hypertension during pregnancy, Addison's disease, thrombocytopenic purpura, pulmonary tuberculosis, diabetes mellitus, chronic orchiditis, neurasthenia, and various gynecological complaints

Main signs & symptoms: Chest and rib-side distention and pain, venter and abdominal distention and fullness, dry mouth and throat, acid regurgitation, possible scanty, delayed menstruation, blocked, and/or painful menstruation, a red tongue with dry fur, and a fine, bowstring pulse

Dosage: 8 pills three times per day

Formula explanation: Uncooked Rehmannia and Lycium both supplement the kidneys and enrich yin, while Ophiopogon and Glehnia enrich yin and engender fluids in the stomach and lungs. Dang Gui nourishes and quickens the blood. The combination of these five ingredients is based on the saying that, "Blood and fluids share a common source." Melia courses the liver and rectifies the qi. However, Melia is not as windy and drying a qi-rectifying medicinal as most others in this category. Therefore, it moves the qi without damaging and consuming yin fluids.

Comments: This medicine can be used alone or combined with others as the case demands. For instance, for the treatment of delayed menstruation due to late ovulation in turn due to yin vacuity and liver depression, it might be prescribed alone during the post-menstrual, pre-ovulatory phase. Or it might be combined with a qi-supplementing medicine in the case of qi and yin dual vacuity conditions complicated by liver depression qi stagnation.

Wu Zi Yan Zong Wan (Five Seeds Increase Progeny Pills)

Fructus Lycii Chinensis (*Gou Qi Zi*)
Semen Cuscutae Chinensis (*Tu Si Zi*)
Fructus Rubi Chingii (*Fu Pen Zi*)
Semen Plantaginis (*Che Qian Zi*)
Fructus Schisandrae Chinensis (*Wu Wei Zi*)

Functions: Supplements the kidneys and boosts the essence

Indications: Essence insufficiency infertility

Main signs & symptoms: Delayed and/or scanty menstruation, blocked menstruation, low back and knee soreness and weakness, tinnitus, dizziness, blurred vision, infertility, a pale tongue, and a fine pulse

Dosage: 8 pills three times per day

Formula explanation: Lycium nourishes the liver and enriches the kidneys. Cuscuta supplements the spleen and kidneys as well as the blood and yang. Rubus or Raspberry nourishes the liver and invigorates yang as well as secures the kidneys. Schisandra also supplements and secures the kidneys. However, it enriches the lungs and quiets the heart spirit as well. When these four seeds or fruits are combined together, they supplement all five of the viscera which transform and store essence. Plantago clears heat and eliminates dampness by disinhibiting urination. According to Li Dong-yuan, damp heat in the lower burner can damage the liver and kidneys below and cause upward stirring of ministerial fire. Plantago thus insures that supplementation of yin and yang does not lead to upward stirring of ministerial fire. Hence essence can be fostered all the more efficiently.

Comments: This medicine can be prescribed alone for essence insufficiency conditions, such as infertility, or it can be combined with other medicines when essence insufficiency complicates other patterns. For instance, when using phased protocols for infertility, this medicine might be prescribed in the post-menstruation, pre-ovulatory phase. Although Cuscuta and Rubus both supplement yang as well as yin, their yang supplementation is definitely secondary, and most Western practitioners tend to think of essence as being yin.

Yang-supplementing medicines

Jin Gui Shen Qi Wan (Golden Cabinet Kidney Qi Pills)

cooked Radix Rehmanniae (*Shu Di*)
Fructus Corni Officinalis (*Shan Zhu Yu*)
Radix Dioscoreae Oppositae (*Shan Yao*)
Rhizoma Alismatis (*Ze Xie*)
Sclerotium Poriae Cocos (*Fu Ling*)
Cortex Radicis Moutan (*Dan Pi*)
Ramulus Cinnamomi Cassiae (*Gui Zi*)
Radix Lateralis Praeparatus Aconiti Carmichaeli (*Fu Zi*)

Functions: Warms and supplements kidney yang

Indications: Kidney yang insufficiency. Nephritis, nephrosclerosis, kidney stones, kidney tuberculosis, pyelitis, albuminuria, edema, cystitis, chronic urethritis, prostatic hypertrophy, urinary incontinence, diabetes, cerebral hemorrhage, arteriosclerosis, hypertension, hypotension, neurasthenia, spermatorrhea, impotence, lumbago, sciatica, beriberi, cataracts, glaucoma, decrease in eyesight, keratitis, eczema, senile pruritus, vaginal itching, urticaria, chronic gonorrhea, rectal prolapse, menopausal complaints, primary hyperaldosteronism, Addison's disease, hypothyroidism, postpartum urinary retention, arthritis, and chronic bronchial asthma

Main signs & symptoms: Low back pain, weak knees, a cold feeling in the lower half of the body, lower abdominal tension, inhibited urination or excessive urination, nocturia, cockcrow diarrhea, a pale, fat tongue with thin, white, moist fur, and a deep, fine pulse in the cubit position

Contraindications:

1. Do not use this medicine in cases of yin vacuity with a dry mouth and throat and a red tongue with scant fur unless there are cold feet below signifying concomitant yang vacuity.

2. Do not use in patients with chronic gastrointestinal weakness and diarrhea.

Dosage: 8 pills three times per day

Formula explanation: This formula uses cooked Rehmannia to enrich and supplement kidney yin. Cornus and Dioscorea enrich and supplement the liver and spleen, thus assisting the enrichment and supplementation of yin within the kidneys. A small amount of Ramulus Cinnamoni and Aconite are added to warm and supplement yang within the kidneys. Alisma and Poria disinhibit water and percolate dampness, while Moutan clears and drains liver fire. Thus this combination of medicinals warms and supplements kidney yang, supplements at the same time as it drains, and supplements without being greasy. It is also based on the notion of seeking yang within yin.

You Gui Wan (Restore the Right [Kidney] Pills)

cooked Radix Rehmanniae (*Shu Di*)
Radix Dioscoreae Oppositae (*Shan Yao*)
Fructus Corni Officinalis (*Shan Zhu Yu*)
Fructus Lycii Chinensis (*Gou Qi Zi*)
Cortex Eucommiae Ulmoidis (*Du Zhong*)
Semen Cuscutae Chinensis (*Tu Si Zi*)
Radix Angelicae Sinensis (*Dang Gui*)
Cortex Cinnamomi Cassiae (*Rou Gui*)
Radix Lateralis Praeparatus Aconiti Carmichaeli (*Fu Zi*)
Gelatinum Cornu Cervi (*Lu Jiao Jiao*)

Functions: Warms and supplements kidney yang, fills the essence and supplements the blood

Indications: Kidney yang insufficiency, lifegate fire debility

Main signs & symptoms: Enduring disease qi debility, lassitude of the spirit, fear of cold, chilled limbs, possible yang wilting (*i.e.*, impotence) and seminal emission, possible yang vacuity sterility, possible non-replete (*i.e.*, incomplete) stools, if severe, complete non-transformation of grains, possible urinary incontinence, possible low back and knee limpness and weakness, lower limb puffy swelling

Dosage: 8 pills three times per day

Formula explanation: Within this formula, Cortex Cinnamomi and Aconite are combined with the bloody, meaty natured Deer Antler Glue in order to warm and supplement kidney yang, fill the essence and supplement the marrow. Cooked

Rehmannia, Cornus, Dioscorea, Cuscuta, Lycium Berries, and Eucommia together enrich yin and boost the kidneys, nourish the liver and supplement the spleen. Then Dang Gui is added in order to supplement the blood and nourish the liver. When all these medicinals are combined together, their effect is to warm yang and boost the kidneys, fill the essence and supplement the blood in order to bank and supplement the source yang within the kidneys.

Comments: This medicine can either be used alone or combined with other Chinese ready-made medicines. It does not percolate dampness or quicken the blood the way *Jin Gui Shen Qi Wan* (*Golden Cabinet* Kidney Qi Pills) do, while it more strongly nourishes the blood and fills the essence.

Er Xian Wan (Two Immortals Pills)

Rhizoma Curculiginis Orchioidis (*Xian Mao*)
Herba Epimedii (*Xian Ling Pi*)
Radix Morindae Officinalis (*Ba Ji Tian*)
Cortex Phellodendri (*Huang Bai*)
Rhizoma Anemarrhenae Aspheloidis (*Zhi Mu*)
Radix Angelicae Sinensis (*Dang Gui*)

Functions: Nourishes the liver and supplements the kidneys, enriches yin and invigorates yang, clears vacuity heat

Indications: Liver blood-kidney yin and yang vacuity with vacuity heat perimenopausal complaints

Main signs & symptoms: Hot flashes, night sweats, heart palpitations, vexation and agitation, possible tinnitus and/or dizziness, low back and knee soreness and weakness, cold feet, nocturia, decreased sexual desire, and a pale tongue with red tip or a red tongue with scanty fur[4]

Dosage: 8 pills three times per day

Formula explanation: Curculigo, Epimedium, and Morinda all nourish the blood and invigorate yang. This means that they supplement liver blood-kidney yin at the same time

---

[4] Because of the combination of yin and yang vacuities, the pulse image may be quite complex. For instance, yin vacuity-vacuity heat may give rise to a floating, rapid pulse, while yang vacuity may give rise to a deep, slow pulse. Hence it is difficult to say exactly what the pulse image will be when one has both yin and yang vacuities. It very much depends on which vacuity is more severe and also the other contributing patterns and disease mechanisms.

as they supplement kidney yang. Dang Gui nourishes liver blood. It also quickens the blood, and an element of blood stasis frequently complicates yang vacuity patterns. Yang vacuity gives rise to vacuity cold, at least below, and cold's nature is constricting and congealing. Anemarrhena enriches yin at the same time as it drains fire. Phellodendron clears vacuity heat above and damp heat below. Hence these two ingredients are mainly for clearing vacuity heat counterflowing upwards.

Comments: This is one of the most famous Chinese formulas for the treatment of perimenopausal syndrome. However, in clinical practice, it is rarely used alone. If there is pronounced fatigue due to spleen qi vacuity, then it can be combined with *Shen Qi Da Bu Wan* (Ginseng & Astragalus Greatly Supplementing Pills) or with *Bu Zhong Yi Qi Wan* (Supplement the Center & Boost the Qi Pills). If there is concomitant liver depression, it can be combined with *Xiao Yao Wan* (Rambling Pills) or *Jia Wei Xiao Yao Wan* (Added Flavors Rambling Pills). If there is liver depression and phlegm heat, it may be combined with *Wen Dan Wan* (Warm the Gallbladder Pills). If there is marked insomnia due to yin vacuity, it can be combined with *Suan Zao Ren Tang Wan* (Zizyphus Spinosa Decoction Pills). If there are marked night sweats, it can be combined with *Gan Mai Da Zao Wan* (Licorice, Wheat & Red Dates Pills). If there is a heart blood-spleen qi vacuity, it can be combined with *Gui Pi Wan* (Restore the Spleen Pills). In fact, its potential combinations are legion and the foregoing are only meant as examples.

Ba Ji Yin Yang Wan (Morinda & Epimedium Pills)

Radix Morindae Officinalis (*Ba Ji Tian*)
cooked Radix Rehmanniae (*Shu Di*)
Herba Epimedii (*Yin Yang Huo*)
Radix Albus Paeoniae Lactiflorae (*Bai Shao*)
Radix Dioscoreae Oppositae (*Shan Yao*)
Rhizoma Cibotii Barometsis (*Gou Ji*)
Radix Dipsaci (*Xu Duan*)
Semen Nelumbinis Nuciferae (*Lian Zi*)
Fructus Corni Officinalis (*Shan Zhu Yu*)
Fructus Rosae Laevigatae (*Jin Ying Zi*)
Fructus Lycii Chinensis (*Gou Qi Zi*)
Cortex Eucommiae Ulmoidis (*Du Zhong*)
Radix Angelicae Sinensis (*Dang Gui*)

Functions: Nourishes the liver and invigorates yang, strengthens the low back and the sinews and bones

Indications: Liver blood-kidney yang low back and knee soreness and pain

Main signs & symptoms: Chronic low back and knee or lower leg soreness and weakness, excessive nighttime urination, enduring, clear, chilly vaginal discharge, cold feet, decreased sexual desire

Dosage: 8 pills three times per day

Formula explanation: Morinda, Epimedium, Eucommia, Dipsacus, and Cibotium all nourish the liver and invigorate the kidneys, strengthen the low back and the sinews and bones. Cooked Rehmannia and Lycium nourish the liver and enrich the kidneys, remembering that yin and yang are mutually related and that the blood and essence share a common source. Cornus, Semen Nelumbinis, and Rosa Leavigata are all astringents which help secure the essence. Dioscorea supplements the spleen and kidneys, remembering that the former and latter heaven roots mutually support and promote each other. Dang Gui and White Peony nourish the blood, while Peony also relaxes cramping. These two ingredients help nourish the sinews.

Comments: This formula is primarily for the treatment of kidney yang vacuity low back pain. However, it is also effective for treating decreased sexual desire due to kidney yang vacuity as well as abnormal vaginal discharge due to kidney yang qi vacuity.

Huan Shao Dan (Return to Lesser [Years] Elixir)

Rhizoma Acori Graminei (*Shi Chang Pu*)
Fructus Corni Officinalis (*Shan Zhu Yu*)
Fructus Schisandrae Chinensis (*Wu Wei Zi*)
Radix Dioscoreae Oppositae (*Shan Yao*)
Radix Morindae Officinalis (*Ba Ji Tian*)
Cortex Eucommiae Ulmoidis (*Du Zhong*)
Fructus Broussounetiae (*Chu Shi Zi*)
cooked Radix Rehmanniae (*Shu Di*)
Radix Achyranthis Bidentatae (*Niu Xi*)
Fructus Lycii Chinensis (*Gou Qi Zi*)
Herba Cistanchis Deserticolae (*Rou Cong Rong*)
Sclerotium Poriae Cocos (*Fu Ling*)
Radix Polygalae Tenuifoliae (*Yuan Zhi*)
Fructus Foeniculi Vulgaris (*Xiao Hui Xiang*)
Fructus Zizyphi Jujubae (*Da Zao*)

Functions: Warms and supplements kidney yang, fills the essence and quiets the spirit

Indications: Kidney yang vacuity and debility impotence and slippery essence. Aldosteronism, diabetes mellitus, hypothyroidism, chronic nephritis, prostatitis, renal tuberculosis

Main signs & symptoms: Low back and knee pain and weakness, frequent, numerous nighttime urination, lassitude of the spirit, lack of strength, dizziness and vertigo, impaired memory, no taste for food or drink, a pale tongue with glossy, white fur, and a deep, weak pulse

Dosage: 8 pills three times per day

Formula explanation: Within this formula, Cistanches, Morinda, Broussounetia, and Eucommia supplement the kidneys and invigorate yang, strengthen the sinews and fortify the bones. Based on the saying that, "If you want to supplement yang, you must search for yang in the midst of yin," cooked Rehmannia and Lycium Berries enrich and supplement kidney yin. When yang obtains yin, it assists its transformation and engenderment. The kidneys are the former heaven root. Therefore, Dioscorea, Poria, Red Dates, and Fennel are used to fortify and move the spleen and stomach. These insure that the finest essence of water and grains is transported to the five viscera. Thus latter heaven assists and supports former heaven. Polygala, Acorus, and Schisandra connect and promote the interaction of the heart and kidneys, quiet the spirit and stabilize the will or mind. Cornus secures the kidneys and astringes the essence. It treats slippery essence and polyuria. Achyranthes strengthens the low back and the sinews. It treats low back pain and lower leg weakness or limpness.

Comments: This medicine is especially good for the treatment of pitting edema in the lower extremities, aversion to cold, fatigue, a fat, pale tongue with glossy, white fur, and a sunken, weak pulse due to kidney yang vacuity with water dampness exuberant internally. However, it can also be used to treat polyuria, nocturia, seminal emission, and decreased libido all due to kidney yang vacuity. It is a complex formula and tends to be prescribed alone, although it may be used in combination with other Chinese ready-made medicines.

20
The Five Most Important Chinese Ready-made Medicines

In the West, most patients seeking treatment from professional acupuncturists and practitioners of Chinese medicine suffer from chronic diseases for which Western medicine has no ready solutions. Typically, these diseases are what in Chinese are called "difficult to treat, knotty diseases." Such difficult to treat, knotty diseases tend more often than not to exhibit complex, multifaceted patterns, not the simple, discreet patterns described in most beginner's textbooks. However, the good news is that most chronic, enduring diseases share certain characteristics. If one understands those key characteristics, then there are complex, multifaceted formulas to treat these complex, multipattern patients.

First of all, anyone with a chronic, enduring disease will have liver depression qi stagnation. If liver depression qi stagnation was not part of the original disease mechanism of the condition, just the fact of being enduringly ill will result in liver depression. The liver governs coursing and discharging and likes to spread freely. The main cause of liver depression, according to the Chinese medical literature, is not fulfilling one's desires. If one is ill, at least some of one's desires cannot be fulfilled. One cannot eat what one wants, go where one wants, do what one wants, or look the way one wants. Therefore, even if the disease did not start off with liver depression, just the fact of being chronically diseased will result in liver depression.

If the liver becomes depressed, then two things are likely. First, enduring stagnation may transform heat. Thus liver depression may transform into or engender depressive heat. Heat is yang by nature and, therefore, tends to rise upward. If depressive heat rises upward, it will tend to collect in the stomach, heart, and/or lungs, all located "above" the liver in Chinese medicine.

Secondly, if the liver becomes depressed, then that means it is replete with qi. Replete liver wood will then assail spleen-stomach earth according to five phase control cycle theory. When this happens, the spleen will tend to become vacuous and weak but also damp. This is because a vacuous spleen will fail to control the movement and transformation of water within the body. However, when the liver assails the stomach, it tends to become disharmonious, *i.e.*, counterflow upward, and hot. If heat persists, it will consume and damage stomach fluids.

Because dampness is yin, heavy, and turbid, it will tend to pour downward in the body. Although it may have been engendered in the middle burner, it commonly percolates down to the lower burner. If there is depressive heat in the body already, this dampness will readily transform into damp heat. However, even without already existing depressive heat, dampness may result in damp heat. This is because dampness impedes the free flow of yang qi. If this yang qi becomes backed up behind this accumulated dampness, the qi becomes depressed and transforms into heat. Then this heat binds with the dampness to form damp heat. Likewise, if there was no liver depression before the accumulation of dampness, because dampness hinders and obstructs the coursing and discharge of the qi, it tends, over time, to also cause liver depression.

Although we could continue any of these lines of reasoning, *i.e.*, follow any of these disease mechanisms, on to other disease mechanisms, the above several disease mechanisms form, in my experience, the core of most of the chronic diseases common in the West. These several elements are liver depression, depressive heat, spleen vacuity, and damp heat. Happily, there are several Chinese ready-made medicines which are available to treat this combination of disease mechanisms, and these comprise my list of the five most important Chinese ready-made medicines for Westerners.

These five are:

Xiao Chai Hu Tang Wan (**Minor Bupleurum Decoction Pills**)
Xiao Yao Wan (**Rambling Pills**)
Jia Wei Xiao Yao Wan (**Added Flavors Rambling Pills**)
Bu Zhong Yi Qi Wan (**Supplement the Center & Boost the Qi Pills**)
Ban Xia Xie Xin Tang (**Pinellia Drain the Heart Decoction**)

Xiao Chai Hu Tang treats the combination of liver depression qi stagnation, spleen qi vacuity, stomach disharmony, depressive heat in the liver, gallbladder, stomach, or lungs, dampness, and phlegm. Amongst these liver depression and spleen qi vacuity are primary, while patients typically have a selection of several but not necessarily all of the others.

Xiao Yao Wan treats the combination of liver depression qi stagnation, spleen qi vacuity, blood vacuity, and dampness. Again, liver depression and spleen qi vacuity are the core disease mechanisms, while blood vacuity and/or dampness are secondary and variable.

Jia Wei Xiao Yao Wan treats the same combination of disease mechanisms as *Xiao Yao Wan*, however with the addition of depressive heat. This depressive heat may be in any of the three burners. This pill is also especially good for depressive heat which has entered the blood division. When heat has entered the blood division, its main symptom is bleeding, although it may also express itself as skin rashes and lesions.

Bu Zhong Yi Qi Tang treats more serious spleen qi vacuity. Because this medicine does include Bupleurum, Cimicifuga, and Orange Peel, this formula does also rectify the qi. Because it contains Dang Gui, it does harmonize the liver. If internal heat is due to depression and it is not too severe, one valid way of eliminating that heat is to clear heat by out-thrusting depression which this medicine does.

Ban Xia Xie Xin Tang treats spleen vacuity and damp heat. In this case, the damp heat is in the stomach and intestines. In most Westerners, when the spleen gets vacuous and weak, the stomach actually gets hot and even dry. The pattern of spleen-stomach vacuity weakness is a relatively rare occurrence in adult Western patients in my experience.

If one knows how to combine other Chinese ready-made medicines with the above five key medicines, one can treat a wide variety of even the most stubborn, chronic diseases. All one has to do is determine what other disease mechanisms are also operative in the case. If there is phlegm and dampness, combine any of the above medicines with *Er Chen Wan* (Two Aged [Ingredients] Pills). If there is blood vacuity, combine with *Dang Gui Su Wan* (Solely Dang Gui Pills), *Si Wu Tang Wan* (Four Materials Decoction Pills), or *Shou Wu Pian* (Polygonum Multiflorum Tablets). If there is blood stasis, combine with *Tao Hong Si Wu Tang Wan* (Persica & Carthamus Four Materials Decoction Pills), *Xue Fu Zhu Yu Tang Wan* (Blood Mansion Dispel Stasis Decoction Pills), *Gui Zhi Fu Ling Wan* (Cinnamon Twigs & Poria Pills), or *Bu Yang Huan Wu Wan* (Supplement Yang & Restore Five [Tenths] Pills). If there is water dampness, combine with *Wu Ling San* (Five [Ingredients] Poria Powder). If there is defensive qi insecurity, combine with *Yu Ping Feng San Wan* (Jade Windscreen Powder Pills). If there is kidney yang vacuity, combine with *You Gui Wan* (Restore the Right [Kidney] Pills), *Jin Gui Shen Qi Wan* (*Golden Cabinet* Kidney Qi Pills), or *Ba Ji Yin Yang Wan* (Morinda & Epimedium Pills). If there is kidney yin vacuity, combine with *Liu Wei Di Huang Wan* (Six Flavors Rehmannia Pills), *Zhi Bai Di Huang Wan* (Anemarrhena & Phellodendron Rehmannia Pills), *Da Bu Yin Wan* (Greatly Supplementing Yin Pills), or *Zuo Gui Wan* (Restore the Left [Kidney] Pills).

In addition, one can combine even these five key medicines together. If there is more qi vacuity than *Xiao Chai Hu Tang Wan* ordinarily treats, combine it with *Bu Zhong Yi Qi Wan*. If there is more heat than *Bu Zhong Yi Qi Wan* treats, combine it with either *Xiao Chai Hu Tang Wan* or *Jia Wei Xiao Yao Wan* depending on where the heat is in the body. If there is a *Xiao Chai Hu Tang Wan* pattern but complicated by blood vacuity, combine it and *Xiao Yao Wan* or *Jia Wei Xiao Yao Wan* if one wants even more heat-clearing with Gardenia. If there are chronic digestive complaints with spleen vacuity and damp heat, one can combine *Xiao Chai Hu Tang Wan* with *Ban Xia Xie Xin Tang Wan*. Likewise, it is also possible to combine even *Bu Zhong Yi Qi Wan* with *Ban Xia Xie Xin Tang Wan*.

In order to do this kind of combining one must know the natures, flavors, functions, and indications of the individual Chinese medicinals. Then one looks at the ingredients in a ready-made medicine or even more than one ready-made medicine and decides if these ingredients are wanted or not. In other words, when combining Chinese ready-made medicines to treat more complex, multifaceted patterns, one should not be too concerned about the main conditions the formulas were originally or most often used to treat. As I've mentioned above, although *Xiao Chai Hu Tang Wan* is most famous for harmonizing *shao yang* conditions, in clinical practice that is not what it is most often used for. And although *Bu Zhong Yi Qi Wan* is the most famous Chinese formula for raising prolapse, this formula is only rarely used for prolapse conditions. In other words, as one becomes more familiar with the descriptions of individual Chinese medicines, one should be able to look at a formula and "read" all the possible uses of that formula from assessing its combination of ingredients.

In terms of dealing with complicated, chronic diseases, first look to see whether your patient has the signs and symptoms of liver depression qi stagnation: irritability, a bowstring pulse, and, in women, PMS. Then look to see if your patient has spleen qi vacuity: fatigue, a tendency to loose stools, cold hands and feet, and a fat tongue. Next look to see if there are any signs of dampness: a wet tongue, a soggy pulse, wet skin lesions, edematous swelling. Look to see if there are any signs of phlegm: profuse phlegm, slimy tongue fur, a slippery pulse, phlegm nodulations beneath the skin. Look to see if there is any heat: red skin lesions, a red tongue with yellow fur, a rapid pulse, foul-smelling, purulent discharges or odors. If there is a combination of liver depression and spleen vacuity, than you can be pretty well assured that one or more of the five key medicines listed above can be used with your patient. By determining if there is dampness, phlegm, and heat and where and what kind of heat it is, you can further narrow down the selection between these five. Then if there are any signs and symptoms of other patterns, identify those other patterns and choose one or more other Chinese ready-made medicines to deal appropriately with these other patterns. *Violà*, you now should have a pretty good match of Chinese ready-made medicines to your patient's pattern no matter how complicated.

21
The Safety of Chinese Patent Medicines

In the last several years, Chinese patent medicines have received a certain amount of bad press in the West. This is due to the discovery of heavy metals and Western pharmaceuticals in some Chinese ready-made medicines and medicinals made from endangered species in others. Therefore, many Westerners are questioning whether or not Chinese patent medicines are safe and ethically OK to use. These are valid questions.

In compiling this book, I have chosen to include only those medicines which are manufactured by Chinese companies which are working with the U.S. Food & Drug Administration and the U.S. Customs Department. There are many other Chinese ready-made medicines available in Chinatowns in North America and Europe. However, by sticking to this repertoire available from these suppliers, I feel practitioners can rest assured that the medicines they are prescribing are safe and effective, uncontaminated and unadulterated, legally imported and labeled, and ethically produced.

In 1998, the California Department of Health Services, Food and Drug Branch, released *The Compendium of Asian Patent Medicines* compiled under the direction of Richard Ko, Pharm. D., Ph.D. and Alice Au, Ph.D. This is a report on the atomic absorption analysis and gas chromatography mass spectometry of 261 Chinese patent medicines. The researchers of the California Department of Health Services were checking these medicines for the presence of heavy metals and pharmaceutical ingredients. (In actuality, Drs. Ko and Au tested over 600 Chinese patent medicines even though their published report only discusses 261 of these.) According to Drs. Ko and Au, 15-25% of the Chinese ready-made medicines studied contained either heavy metal contamination or the undisclosed addition of Western pharmaceuticals.

Although this 15-25% represents a fairly large number of contaminated and adulterated Chinese patent medicines, the good news is that at least 75% and maybe as much as 85% of all Chinese ready-made medicines are free from such contamination and adulteration. In other words, such contamination and adulteration is the exception rather than the rule. It is unreasonable to condemn a whole industry for the mistakes and transgressions of a few manufacturers. As the work of Drs. Ko and Au show, the vast majority of Chinese patent medicines are not contaminated by heavy metals and are not adulterated by Western pharmaceuticals.

If one sticks to the Chinese ready-made medicines described in this book and purchased from either Mayway Corp. or Nuherbs Co. one can be sure that the medicines they are prescribing are safe and effective when used according to professional Chinese medical standards of care and are neither contaminated or adulterated.

Bibliography

Chinese Language Sources

Fang Ji Xue (The Study of Formulas & Prescriptions), Xu Ji-qun *et al.*, Shanghai Science & Technology Press, Shanghai, 1986

Fang Ming Shi Yi (Famous Formulas Explained), Hong Wen-xu & Su Kong, Chinese National Chinese Medicine Press, Beijing, 1990

Jian Ming Zhong Yi Ci Dian (A Simple, Clear Dictionary of Chinese Medicine), Chinese National Chinese Medicine Research Institute & Guangzhou College of Chinese Medicine, People's Health & Hygiene Press, Beijing, 1986

Lao Ren Bao Kang Zhong Cheng Yao (Old People's Protecting Health Chinese Prepared Medicines), Shen Lian-sheng & Li Guo-ya, People's Healthy & Hygiene Press, Beijing, 1984

Yin Hua Chong Yong Zhong Yi Chu Fang Shou Ce (An English-Chinese Handbook of Commonly Used Chinese Medical Formulas), Ou Ming, Joint Publishing Co., Ltd., Hong Kong, 1989

Zhong Yi Cheng Yao Xue (Chinese Medicine Prepared Medicines), Liu De-yi, Tianjin Science & Technology Press, Tianjin, 1984

Zhong Yi Fang Ji Da Ci Dian (Chinese Medicine Formula & Prescription Encyclopedia), Qian You-sheng *et al.*, People's Health & Hygiene Press, Beijing, 1995

Zhong Yi Fang Yao Shou Ce (A Handbook of Chinese Medical Formulas & Medicinals), Wang Shi-min, Shandong People's Press, Jinan, 1984

English Language Sources

A Clinical Guide to Chinese Herbs & Formulae, Chen Song-yu & Li Fei, Churchill Livingstone, Edinburgh, 1993

Chinese Herbal Medicine: Formulas & Strategies, Dan Bensky & Randall Barolet, Eastland Press, Seattle, 1990

Clinical Handbook of Chinese Prepared Medicines, Chun-han Zhu, Paradigm Publications, Brookline, MA, 1989

Commonly Used Chinese Herb Formulas with Illustrations, Hong-yen Hsu & Chau-shin Hsu, Oriental Healing Arts Institute, LA, 1980

Handbook of Chinese Herbs & Formulas, Vol. II, Him-che Yeung, Self-published, LA, 1985

Seventy Essential TCM Formulas for Beginners, Bob Flaws, Blue Poppy Press, Boulder, CO, 1994

Medicine Index

An Shen Bu Xin Wan **148**
An Shui Wan **152**

Ba Ji Yin Yang Wan 91, 167, 170, **198**, 203
Ba Zhen Wan **179**, 181
Ba Zheng San **117**
Bai He Gu Jin Wan **111**
Bai Hu Tang **47**
Bai Xing Shi Gan Wan **56**
Bai Zi Yang Xin Wan **150**
Ban Xia Xie Xin Tang Wan **44**, 45, 135, 203
Bao He Wan **137**
Bi Min Gan Wan **24**
Bi Tong Wan **23**, 95
Bi Xie Fen Qing Wan **125**
Bi Xie Shen Shi Tang **118**
Bi Xie Sheng Shi Wan **118**
Bu Fei Wan **172**
Bu Xue Tiao Jing Wan **174**
Bu Yang Huan Wu Wan **95**, 203
Bu Zhong Yi Qi Wan 56, 59, 90, 91, 119, 123, 130, 132, 156, 159, **165**, 175, 176, 198, 202-204

Cang Er Zi Wan **25**
Chai Ge Jie Ji Tang **26**
Chai Hu Long Gu Mu Li Wan **145**
Chai Hu Shu Gan Wan **71**, 72
Chen Xiang Hua Qi Wan **76**
Chuan Xin Lian **52**
Chuan Xiong Cha Tiao Wan **102**
Cong Rong Bu Shen Wan **170**

Da Bu Yin Wan 93, 107, 170, **192**, 203
Da Chai Hu Wan **65**
Da Huang Jiang Zhi Wan **34**
Da Huang Mu Dan Pi Tang **33**
Dan Shen Yin Wan **94**
Dan Zhi Xiao Yao Wan 13, **43**
Dang Gui Si Ni Wan **63**
Dang Gui Su Wan **176**, 203
Dang Gui Wan 176, **183**
Dao Chi Wan **57**
Ding Chuan Wan **77**
Du Huo Ji Sheng Wan **126**

Er Chen Wan 41, **131**, 132, 134, 167, 203
Er Long Zuo Ci Wan **189**
Er Xian Wan 135, 175, **197**

Fang Feng Tong Sheng San **66**
Fang Ji Huang Qi Wan **123**
Fu Ke Yang Ying Wan **182**
Fu Ke Zhong Zi Wan **175**
Fu Zi Li Zhong Wan **62**

Gan Cao Jie Geng Tang **22**
Gan Mai Da Zao Wan **151**, 167, 198
Ge Gen Wan **18**
Ge Xia Zhu Yu Wan **83**
Gu Ben Wan **190**
Gui Pi Wan 98, **178**, 198
Gui Zhi Fu Ling Wan **90**, 203

Hua She Jie Yang Wan **105**
Huai Jiao Wan **99**
Huan Shao Dan **199**
Huang Lian Jie Du Wan **48**
Huo Luo Xiao Ling Wan **93**, 130
Huo Xiang Zheng Qi Wan **115**

Ji Sheng Ju He Wan **74**
Jia Wei Xiao Yao Wan 24, 34, **43**, 44, 56, 98, 106, 135, 148, 175, 198, 202, 203
Jiao Ai Tang **98**
Jie Geng Wan **135**
Jin Gu Die Shang Wan **87**
Jin Gui Shen Qi Wan 158, 162, **195**, 197, 203
Jin Suo Gu Jing Wan **156**
Jing Fang Bai Du Wan **28**
Juan Bi Wan **128**

Li Dan Wan **54**
Liang Ge Wan **32**
Liu Jun Zi Tang **163**
Liu Wei Di Huang Wan 107, 162, 170, **185**, 187, 188, 190, 192, 203
Long Dan Xie Gan Wan **53**, 119

Ma Xing Shi Gan Tang **57**
Ma Zi Ren Wan 13, **35**
Mai Wei Di Huang Wan **187**
Ming Mu Di Huang Wan **189**
Mu Xiang Bing Lang Wan **138**
Mu Xiang Shun Qi Wan **73**

Nei Xiao Luo Li Wan **90**
Ning Sou Wan **78**

Ping Wei San **114**

Pu Ji Xiao Du San 50

Qi Ju Di Huang Wan 107, **186**, 189
Qing Gu Wan 58
Qing Qi Hua Tan Wan 132
Qing Wei San Wan 55
Qing Zao Jiu Fei Tang 109

Ren Shen Bai Du Wan 27
Ren Shen Jian Pi Wan 170

San Bi Wan 127
Sang Ju Yin Wan 21
Sang Piao Xiao Wan 158
Sha Shen Mai Dong Wan 110
Shao Fu Zhu Yu Wan 84
Shao Yao Gan Cao Wan 177
Shen Ling Bai Zhu Wan 138, **164**, 171
Shen Qi Da Bu Wan **168**, 176, 198
Shen Qi Wu Wei Zi Wan 169
Shen Tong Zhu Yu Wan 84
Sheng Mai San 40, **167**
Shi Hui San 96
Shi Quan Da Bu Wan 180, 183   *Shu Gan Wan p 72*
Shou Wu Pian 13, **177**, 203
Si Jun Zi Wan 72, 123, 138, **161-165**, 167
Si Miao Wan 120
Si Ni San Wan 41
Si Wu Tang Wan 40, 86, 107, **173**, 203
Suan Zao Ren Tang Wan 147, 198

Tao Hong Si Wu Tang 40, 82, **86**, 203
Tao Ren Wan 35
Tian Ma Gou Teng Wan 106
Tian Qi Wan 100
Tian Tai Wu Yao San Wan 75
Tian Wang Bu Xin Dan 149, 151, 153, 154
Tong Jing Wan 89
Tong Qiao Huo Xue Wan 86
Tong Shun Wan 36
Tong Xie Yao Fang Wan 44

Wen Dan Tang Wan 133
Wen Dan Wan 198
Wen Jing Tang Wan 92
Wu Ling San 121, 203
Wu Mei Wan 141
Wu Pi San 122
Wu Pi Yin Wan 122
Wu Ren Wan 37
Wu Wei Xiao Du Yin Wan 51

Wu Zi Yan Zong Wan 194

Xi Gua Shuang 51
Xiang Lian Wan 56
Xiang Sha Liu Jun Zi Wan 138, **163**
Xiang Sha Yang Wei Wan 163
Xiao Chai Hu Tang Wan 24, 27, **39**, 40, 42, 44, 55, 56, 72, 99, 106, 130, 135, 162, 164, 167, 168, 170, 174, 175, 180, 202-204
Xiao Cheng Qi Tang 66
Xiao Feng Wan 104
Xiao Huo Luo Dan 103
Xiao Jian Zhong Wan 61
Xiao Qing Long Wan 19, 21
Xiao Yao Wan 13, 24, 27, 34, **42-44**, 56, 72, 90, 95, 98, 106, 135, 148, 162, 167, 168, 170, 174, 175, 180, 198, 202, 203
Xin Yi Wan 20
Xuan Bi Wan 129
Xue Fu Zhu Yu Tang Wan 55, **81**, 203

Yan Hu Suo Wan 95
Yang Rong Wan 181
Yi Guan Jian Wan 193
Yin Qiao Jie Du Wan 22
You Gui Wan **196**, 203
Yu Dai Wan 119
Yu Ping Feng San Wan 132, **155**, 173, 203

Zhen Gan Xi Feng Wan 107
Zhen Wu Tang Wan 124
Zhi Bai Di Huang Wan 98, 158, 170, **188**, 193, 203
Zhi Gan Cao Wan 184
Zhu Sha An Shen Wan 146
Zi Sheng Wan 171
Zuo Gui Wan 107, 170, **191**, 203
Zuo Jin Wan 56

General Index

A

abdomen, palpable lumps within the 91
abdominal and rib-side distention and pain 71
abdominal cramps 62, 177
abdominal fullness 31, 76, 92
abdominal masses 83, 84, 91, 92, 173
abdominal pain 31, 34, 44, 55, 62, 63, 66, 75, 84, 85, 89, 124, 137, 141, 142, 173, 174
abdominal pain, severe venter and 85
abscesses, welling 32, 33, 51, 52, 106
acid eructations 40
acid regurgitation 72, 76, 193
acne 43, 67, 87
acne rosacea 87
Addison's disease 186, 193
afternoon effusion of heat 92
agalactia 166
age spots 87
AIDS vii, 122, 132, 173, 176, 186
albuminuria 195
aldosteronism 199
allergic rhinitis 20, 21, 25, 156
alopecia 39
alternating cold and heat 66, 146
anal bleeding, bright red 99
anal fissures and fistulas 118
anemia 42, 62, 63, 162, 166, 173, 179
anemia, aplastic 179
anemia, common 179
anemia, pernicious 62, 166
anger, easy 82, 146, 162, 192
angina pectoris 63, 82, 94
anxiety 49, 113
aphasia 101, 107, 108
aplastic anemia 179
appendicitis 34, 51
appetite, reduced 40, 42, 117, 162, 179
apraxia 107, 108
apthous ulcers 149, 153
arteriosclerotic heart disease 108
arthritis vii, 64, 103, 124, 126, 128, 129, 195
arthritis, gouty 129
arthritis, rheumatoid vii, 64, 103, 124, 126, 128, 129
ascariasis 142
asthma, acute 77, 78
asthma, bronchial 57, 77, 78, 195
asthma, chronic 78
ascites 14, 121-124
Au, Alice 205
auditory acuity, loss of 87

autonomic dystonia 151, 156, 158
aversion to cold 17-19, 26, 27, 50, 113, 116, 200
aversion to heat 48
aversion to wind 23, 29, 102, 123, 156
A-V block 146

B

back, pain in the midline and, during pregnancy 126
balding 87
belching 69, 76, 77, 137, 163
beriberi 195
biliary ascariasis 142
bladder syndrome, neurogenic 121
bleeding gums 40, 48
bleeding, intermenstrual 92
blood, dark red, thick 175
bloody stools 63
bloody stranguary 117
blood-quickening, stasis-dispelling medicines 81
blood-rectifying medicines 81
bodily fatigue 166, 167, 179
bodily heaviness 123, 128
body and limbs, fatigue of the 132
body heat 110
body pain, generalized 29
boils 49, 53
bone-steaming 58, 59, 186, 188, 192
borborygmus 44, 45
bowel disease, inflammatory 62
breast distention 42, 71
breast distention and pain 71
breast condition, fibrocystic 41, 75
breast lumps, benign 75
breath, bad 55, 73, 76, 170
breath, shortness of 121, 126, 166, 167, 169, 172, 180, 183, 184
breath, shortness of, on slight exertion 169
breathing, hasty 77, 122
bronchial asthma 57, 77, 78, 195
bronchial pneumonia 57
bronchiolitis 57, 77
bronchitis 22, 39, 63, 70, 77, 78, 110, 112, 124, 132-135, 156, 165-167
bronchitis, acute 22
bronchitis, chronic 39, 63, 77, 78, 110, 112, 124, 132-134, 156, 165-167
burping and eructation 73

C

California Department of Health Services 205
cancer vii, 179
Candida albicans 105
carbuncles 49, 51, 53, 67
carcinoma of the larynx 112
cardiac edema 121
cataracts 195
cellulitis 49
cerebral arteriosclerosis 108, 166
cerebral hemorrhage 49, 82, 96, 195
cerebrovascular disease 106
cervical erosion 91
chest and diaphragm glomus and oppression 56, 67, 132
chest and diaphragmatic fullness and oppression 116
chest and rib-side fullness and oppression 70
chest and rib-side region bitterness 40
chest and venter fullness and glomus 28
chest and venter oppression and fullness 41
chest, external injury to the 82
chest fullness 110
chest pain 57, 73, 82, 94
chest, vexatious heat in the 32, 58
chills, severe 27, 39
chlamydia 118
cholecystitis 32, 39, 41, 49, 53-55, 65, 66, 72, 76, 137
cholelithiasis 32, 41, 54, 55, 72
chronic fatigue immune deficiency syndrome vii
cinnabar macules 67
cirrhosis of the liver 73, 84, 124
climacteric disorders 42
cold, aversion to 17-19, 26, 27, 50, 113, 116, 200
cold, fear of 196
cold, intolerance to 126
cold precipitating formulas 31
cold sores 53
colitis, chronic 35, 63
colitis, nonspecific acute 116
colitis, ulcerative 56
common cold 12, 20, 22, 23, 26, 39, 102, 166
common cold, easy contraction of wind evils 156
congestive heart failure 121, 122, 124
conjunctivitis 22, 32, 49, 51, 53, 65
conjunctivitis, acute 32, 49, 53, 65
conjunctivitis, epidemic 22
constipation 7, 13, 14, 31, 32, 34-37, 55, 66, 67, 139, 162, 173, 177, 184
constipation, habitual 35-37
constipation, postpartum or post-surgical 35
convulsions 63, 107
cor pulmonale 82, 112
corneal ulcers 53, 166
coronary artery disease 85, 94, 167
coronary heart disease 82
costochondritis 82, 193
cough 12, 19, 22-24, 28, 29, 67, 69, 70, 77-79, 110-112, 131-133, 165, 167, 172, 173, 181, 187, 190, 192
cough which will not stop, dry 111
cough with no phlegm, dry 110
cough with profuse phlegm 28, 70
cough with profuse, white phlegm 29
coughing 14, 19, 28, 57, 77-79, 97, 112, 121, 133, 172, 188
counterflow chilling of the extremities 48
coursing & scattering external wind formulas 102
cramps in the hands and feet 177
Crohn's disease 44
crying and irritability in teething infants 147
cystitis, acute 53

D

dampness-dispelling medicines 113
dampness-drying, phlegm-transforming medicines 131
dampness-drying, stomach-harmonizing medicines 114
dermatitis 67, 104
dermatomycoses 105
diabetes mellitus 48, 158, 162, 165, 192, 193, 199
diaphragm, pain and palpable lumps below the 83
diarrhea, chronic 124
diarrhea, recurrent, with pain 44
digestive disorders, stress-related 72
disorientation 150
dizziness, postpartum 174
dosages 15, 49
drinks, desire for chilled 58
drooling from the corners of the mouth 96
dry heaves 45, 82
dryness-treating medicines 109
duodenal ulcers 62, 63, 76, 179
dysentery, bacterial and amebic 56
dysentery, bacterial 44
dysentery, initial stage 27
dysentery, red and white 56, 139
dysmenorrhea 82-84, 89, 91, 92, 173, 177
dysmenorrhea, primary 92, 177
dyspnea on minor movement 166
dystonia, autonomic 151, 156, 158
dysuria 121

E

ears, swelling of the 53
eclampsia 107, 132
eclampsia, puerperal 107
eczema 53, 104, 118, 195
edema 17, 18, 70, 113, 114, 121-124, 195, 200
edema during pregnancy 122
edema, generalized 122
edema, menopausal 122
edema, chronic nephritic 121
effusion of heat 18, 33, 50, 92, 116, 124
emaciation 59, 141, 165, 171, 183, 184
emission of heat 19, 29, 55, 57
emotional depression 134, 167
encephalitis B 23, 32
endometriosis vii, 34, 83-85, 89, 91, 142
enriching & nourishing spirit-quieting medicines 147
enriching yin, moistening dryness medicines 111
enteritis, acute 49
enuresis 151, 157
epididymitis 53, 74
epigastric, abdominal distention and fullness 115
epilepsy 39, 107, 108, 146
epistaxis 32, 49, 97
eructation 72, 73, 77, 115, 137
erysipelas 49, 51, 67
esophageal, stenosis, neurotic 70
esophagitis, acute hemorrhagic 97
essence-astringing, loss-stopping medicines 156
exterior-interior dual resolving medicines 65
exterior-resolving medicinals 17, 69
exterior-securing, perspiration-stopping medicines 155
extremities, chilled 166
extremities, lack of strength of the four 162
extremities, heavy, sagging feeling in the 115
eye aching 26
eye pain 27, 67
eyelids, pallor on the undersides of the 36
eyes, deviation of the mouth and 96, 107
eyes, distention in the head and 108
eyes, dry, astringent 37
eyes, dry, scratchy 187
eyes, easy tearing of the 187
eyes, itchy 189
eyes, red 8, 32, 53, 67, 189
eyes, redness and swelling of the 29
eyesight, decrease in 195

F

face and head, redness, swelling, and burning pain of the 50
face, swelling of the 19, 55
facial complexion, dark, sooty 85, 94
facial complexion, lusterless 62, 173
facial complexion, lusterless, yellow 129
facial complexion, flushed red 32, 108
facial complexion, pale 174, 176, 184
facial complexion, red 32, 48, 58, 108
facial complexion, sallow yellow 165, 180
facial complexion, withered, white 162
fatigue vii, 42, 59, 91, 115, 132, 141, 162, 164, 166, 167, 169, 170, 179-181, 183, 184, 190, 198, 200, 204
fatigue, easy 115
fatigue of the body and limbs 132
fear of cold 196
feet, and heart, heat in the hands, 112, 186
feet, cold 182, 195, 197, 198
feet, enduring cold hands and/or 64
fever 12, 17, 22-24, 27, 34, 39, 40, 48, 49, 58, 59, 62, 63, 71, 82, 102, 108, 113, 121, 129, 147, 151, 162, 166-168, 173
fever, afternoon tidal 59
fever and chills, alternating 12, 40, 71
fever and chills with shivering 129
fever, enduring low-grade 59
fever, extreme 17
fever, high 27, 48, 49, 162, 168
fever with macular eruptions, high 49
fever with profuse sweating, high 48
fever, lingering 39
fever of unknown origin 62, 151
fever, postpartum 108
fever, puerperal 39
fever, slight 17, 22
fever, tidal 58, 59, 82
fibrocystic breast condition 41, 75
fibromylagia vii
flooding and leaking 43, 98, 99, 173, 181
flus 22, 23, 52, 102
food allergies 143
food or drink, no thought for 76, 115, 200
food poisoning 67
food stagnation 14, 72, 73, 76, 112, 137-139, 170-172, 186
food-dispersing, stagnation-abducting medicines 137
formulas, acrid, cool, exterior-resolving 17
formulas, acrid, warm, exterior-resolving 17
formulas, coursing & scattering external wind 102

formulas warm precipitating 31
formulas, water-dispelling precipitating 31
formulas which warm the center and dispel cold 61
formulas which warm the channels and scatter cold 61
fright palpitations 150
fright, susceptibility to 134, 146
frostbite 64
functional neurosis 82
functional uterine bleeding vii, 63, 92, 97, 98, 166, 179, 186
furuncles 49, 51, 53

G

gallstones 39
gastrectasis 63, 114, 121
gastric neurosis 114
gastric ulcer 39, 45, 62, 114, 142
gastritis 39, 41, 42, 45, 62, 63, 72, 73, 76, 97, 114, 121, 132, 134, 137, 142, 146, 161, 165
gastritis, chronic 42, 45, 63, 72, 73, 114, 132, 134, 137, 142, 161, 165
gastroenteritis, acute 44, 56, 116, 121
gastrointestinal flu 137
gastrointestinal neurosis 70
gastrointestinal weakness and dysfunction 161
gastroptosis 63, 121, 132, 161, 166
generalized bodily aching and heaviness 19
genital itching 53, 101, 179
genital sores 118
genital sweating 53
genital swelling 53
genitourinary tract infections 121
glaucoma 53, 195
glaucoma, acute 53
globus hystericus 70
glomerulonephritis 57, 117, 123, 186
glomus and fullness below the heart 45
goiter 132
gonorrhea 117, 166, 179, 195
gouty arthritis 129
groin, lymphadenitis of the 53
gums, bleeding 40, 48
gynecological diseases 32

H

hair, falling 87, 174
hair, premature greying of the 177
half exterior/half interior evils 39
hands and feet, cold 8, 162, 204

hands and feet, cramps in the 177
hands and feet, insensitivity of the 103
hands and feet, inversion chill of the 142
hands and feet, numbness of the 127
hands and/or feet. enduring cold 64
hands due to stress, cold 42, 71
hands, feet, and heart, heat in the 112, 186
hangover 132
harmonizing & resolving medicines 39
head and eyes, distention in the 108
head distention 25
head, hot feelings in the 108
headache 7, 8, 17, 22-27, 40, 42, 48, 53, 65, 66, 82, 87, 95, 101, 102, 107, 108, 110, 116, 121, 173
headache, frontal 25
headache, migraine 53, 82, 95, 102
headache, neurogenic 102, 173
headache, tension 102
hearing, loss of 53
heart and abdominal distention and fullness 122
heart disease 82, 108, 123, 124, 149, 153, 167, 179, 184
heart disease, rheumatic 82, 123, 167, 184
heart disease, rheumatic valvular 124
heart palpitations 62, 82, 132, 134, 145, 147-150, 153, 173, 179, 180, 183-185, 197
heart palpitations, rapid 147
heart, racing 150, 180
heart vexation 26, 40, 110, 142, 192
heat in the hands, feet, and heart 112, 186
heat stroke 48
heat-clearing medicinals 47, 65, 165, 185
heat-clearing, dampness-eliminating medicines 117
heat-clearing, phlegm-transforming medicines 132
heavy, settling spirit-quieting medicines 145
hemafecia 34, 99, 173, 179
hemangiomas 36, 87, 89, 94
hemangiomas, small 36, 89
hematemesis 97
hematuria 58
hemiplegia 96, 103, 106, 126
hemoptysis 49, 97, 112
hemorrhagic febrile diseases 97
hemorrhoidal leakage 67
hemorrhoids 35, 98, 99, 166
hemorrhoids, bleeding 98, 99
hepatic disease, chronic 124
hepatitis 39, 41, 42, 45, 49, 52, 53, 62, 72, 73, 76, 121, 134, 137, 165, 166, 193
hepatitis, acute icteric 49, 53

hepatitis, chronic 42, 45, 62, 72, 73, 76, 134, 165, 166
hepatitis, infectious 121
herpes genitalia 53
herpes zoster 53
hot flashes 197
hydrocele, scrotal 121
hypertension 32, 40, 49, 53, 65, 66, 82, 107, 108, 124, 146, 185, 186, 193, 195
hypertension during pregnancy 193
hypertension, essential 107, 108, 193
hypertension, primary 124
hypertensive encephalopathy 107, 108
hyperthyroid condition 156
hyperthyroidism 44, 53, 146, 184, 186
hyperaldosteronism, primary 124, 195
hypochondral pain 75
hypoglycemia 62, 143
hypotension 195
hypothyroidism 124, 195, 199
hysteria 49, 70, 146, 151

I

impotence 39, 53, 166, 179, 186, 195, 196, 199
incontinence, stress 158, 159
indigestion, pediatric 114
infections, acute suppurative 23
infertility vii, 92, 175, 181, 182, 194
influenza 27, 67, 110, 116
insomnia 26, 42, 49, 59, 107, 134, 142, 145-148, 150, 154, 177, 179, 184, 190, 198
intercostal neuralgia 39, 53, 82, 177
Interferon 40
interior-warming medicines 61
intermenstrual bleeding 92
internal heat but cold extremities 41
intestinal abscesses 33
intestinal cramping 37
intestinal dysbiosis 143
intestinal flu 116
intestinal spasm 73
intestinal tuberculosis 124
intestinal wind 67, 99
irascibility 43
irritability 32, 41, 42, 48, 55, 58, 59, 108, 147, 175, 177, 184, 190, 204
irritable bowel syndrome 44, 63, 162
ischemic attacks, transitory 106
itching 53, 101, 105, 106, 118, 177, 179, 195

J, K

jaundice 39, 40, 49, 54, 55, 113, 114
jaundice, acute 54, 55
joint soreness and pain 120, 127
joints, difficulty bending and stretching the 103
joints, redness, swelling, heat, and pain in the 129
keratitis 195
kidney stones 195
kidney tuberculosis 195
knee soreness and weakness, low back and 127, 186, 187, 190, 194, 197
knees, weak 191, 195
Ko, Richard 205

L

lactation, scanty 173
laryngitis 52, 70, 112
larynx, carcinoma of the 112
leaky gut syndrome 143
leg and knee aching and heat 192
leukemia 62, 179
leukopenia 166
leveling & extinguishing internal wind medicines 106
Li Dong-yuan 148, 167, 194
lie down flat, inability to 19
limbs, aching and weakness of the four 157
limbs and body, puffy swelling of the 124
limbs, heavy, encumbered 122
limbs, lack of strength of the four 42
limbs, pain and soreness of the four 27
limbs puffy swelling of the face and four 19
lips and mouth, dry 92
lips and nails, pale 176, 184
lips, pale 36, 174, 176, 184
lips, red 32, 59
liver cirrhosis 73, 84, 121, 124
liver failure 40
liver spots 94
lochia, postpartum retention of 174
lochioschesis 85, 91, 166
low back and knee aching and pain 126
low back and knee limpness and weakness 196
low back and knee soreness and weakness 127, 186, 187, 190, 194, 197
low back and lower leg heaviness and weakness 103
lower abdominal aching and pain, right-sided 33
lower abdominal cramping 44
lower abdominal distention 31, 71
lower abdominal masses 84
lower abdominal pain 75, 84, 85, 89, 173, 174

lower abdominal pain, chilly 84
lower abdominal pain, possibly radiating to the testicles 75
lower abdominal tension and fullness 117
lower limb wilting and atrophy 96
lumbago 186, 195
lumbar intervertebral disc herniation 126
lumbar strain 126
lumps below the diaphragm, pain and palpable 83
lumps within the abdomen, palpable 91
lymphadenitis 39, 53
lymphadenitis of the groin 53

M

macules, static spots and 83
malabsorption syndromes 165
malar flushing 59
malaria 39, 59, 166, 177
malaria, persistent 166
malaria, taxation 59
malnutrition 165
mastitis 39, 41, 51
Mayway Corp viii, 1, 3, 4, 206
McBurney's point 34
measles 23, 27, 52, 57
measles, initial stage 27
medicines for clearing heat from the qi division 47
medicines for exterior conditions with interior vacuity 27
medicines, harmonizing & resolving 39
memory, impaired 147, 149, 150, 153, 158, 179, 183, 200
Meniere's disease 124, 132, 134, 146
meningitis 23, 32, 48
meningitis, epidemic 23
menopausal edema 122
menopausal syndrome 82, 92, 146, 149, 151, 153, 169
menorrhagia 175, 176, 179, 181, 182
menses, dark 83
menses, dark-colored containing clots 84
menstrual blood dark, purple 86
menstrual blood dark, purplish, black 91
menstrual pain 75, 89-91
menstruation, delayed 193, 194
menstruation, early 43, 86, 179
menstruation, excessively profuse 98, 179
menstruation, irregular 42, 82, 85, 173
menstruation, painful 71, 83-86, 89, 174, 193
menstruation, profuse 43, 86, 98, 179
mental instability in children 39
migraines 53, 82, 95, 102

miscarriage, habitual 166
miscarriage, threatened 98, 171, 173, 175, 176, 181, 182
mitral valve prolapse 184
mitral valve stenosis 184
morning sickness 70
mouth and throat, dry 42, 49, 185, 186, 193, 195
mouth and tongue sores 32, 153
mouth, bitter taste in the 40, 43, 53, 55, 70, 134
mouth, bland taste in the 115
mouth and eyes, deviation of the 96, 107
mouth, dry, and parched throat 183, 191
mouth, dry lips and 92
mouth odor, foul 137
mucus, yellow-green 26
multiple sclerosis vii
mumps 23, 39, 50, 52
muscular atrophy 120
myasthenia gravis 157, 166, 179
myelitis, acute 96

N

nails, brittle 176, 184
nails, pale 36, 174, 184
nasal blockage 87
nasal congestion 20, 21, 23-25, 28, 102
nasal discharge, clear 17
nasal mucus, copious 25
nasal mucus, green 25
nasal mucus, yellow, sticky 17
nasal obstruction 24, 25, 87
nasal obstruction, chronic 87
nasosinusitis 23, 133
nausea 55, 63, 69, 72, 113, 115, 132, 134, 137, 171
nausea and vomiting 63, 132, 171
nausea on eating 137
neck and upper back stiffness and rigidity 18
neck, pain and stiffness of the head and 27, 29
neck, shoulder, and upper back stiffness 18, 128
neck, stiff 48
nephritic edema, chronic 121
nephritis, chronic 62, 121, 123, 124, 165, 166, 186, 199
nephroatrophy 186
nephrosclerosis 195
nephrotic syndrome 125
nervous exhaustion 147
neurasthenia 42, 49, 62, 70, 147, 149, 153, 157, 166, 179, 184, 186, 192, 193, 195
neurogenic bladder syndrome 121
neurosis 39, 42, 70, 82, 107, 114, 132, 142, 146,

151
neurosis, functional 82
neurotic esophageal stenosis 70
night sweats 59, 112, 147, 150, 169, 170, 179, 186-188, 191, 192, 197, 198
nightmares 134, 147
nocturia 182, 186, 195, 197, 200
nodulations 33, 52, 70, 74, 135, 204
nose, dry 26, 110
nose, runny 20, 21, 23, 24
Nuherbs Co. viii, 2-4, 206
numbness of the extremities 177
numbness of the hands and feet 127

O

obesity 67, 114, 134
optic nerve atrophy 42, 186
optic neuritis 186
oral herpes 63
oral thirst 32, 48, 50, 58, 59, 110, 111, 167
orchiditis, chronic 193
orchitis 53, 74
osteoarthritis 103, 126
otitis media 39, 53
ovarian cysts 89, 91

P

pain and palpable lumps below the diaphragm 83
pain, chronic 94
palpitations 49, 62, 70, 82, 117, 121, 124, 126, 132, 134, 145, 147-150, 153, 173, 179, 180, 183-185, 197
palpitations, fright 150
palpitations, recurrent 70
pancreatitis, acute 65, 66, 137
pancreatitis, chronic 114
panting 14, 19, 57, 67, 69, 77-79, 110, 122, 172, 187, 190
panting and coughing 19
panting and wheezing 57
parasites 15, 105, 141
parasitic diseases 114
parasitosis 141, 143
parotitis, epidemic 29
pediatric indigestion 114
pediatric pneumonia 32
pelvic inflammation, acute 49, 53
pelvic inflammatory disease 89, 91, 92, 125, 177
pelvic inflammatory disease, chronic 89, 91, 92, 125, 177
peptic ulcer bleeding 97

peptic ulcers 41, 64, 98, 134, 193
peripheral nerve disorders 103
peritonitis 166
pernicious anemia 62, 166
perspiration, spontaneous 156, 168, 169, 172, 173, 183, 191
perspiration which does not flow easily 23
pertussis 57, 70, 110
pharyngitis 52, 112
phlegm, profuse, which is clear and white in color 20
phlegm, profuse, thin 19
phlegm, thick, yellow-colored 77
phlegm, yellow-colored 24, 77
phlegm-dispelling medicines 131
pleuritis 39
plum pit qi 70
pneumonia 22, 32, 39, 48, 49, 57, 110, 133
pneumonia, bronchial 57
pneumonia, lobar 48, 57
pneumonia, pediatric 32
pneumonitis 57
pneumothorax, spontaneous 112
poliomyelitis, sequellae of 96, 126
poly/dermatomyositis 129
polycystic ovarian disease 92
polymyositis/dermatomyositis vii
postpartum dizziness 174
postpartum fever 108
postpartum lower abdominal pain 174
postpartum or post-surgical constipation 35
postpartum retention of lochia 174
postpartum urinary retention 195
postpartum weakness 173
post-concussion syndrome 82, 146, 179
post-gastrectomy syndrome 142
post-surgical infections 27
pox 17, 18
pregnancy 32, 35, 70, 72, 82-85, 88, 89, 91, 96, 98, 103, 114, 115, 117, 122, 126, 141, 171-173, 175, 181, 193
pregnancy, hypertension during 193
pregnancy, pain in the midline and back during 126
pregnancy, vaginal bleeding during 98, 175
pregnancy, vomiting during 171
premature ejaculation 157
premenstrual tension 42
prostatitis, acute 53, 117
prostatitis, chronic 118, 125
protein-deficiency edema 122
pruritus 49, 195

pruritus, senile 195
puerperal eclampsia 107
puerperal fever 39
pulmonary emphysema 132
pulmonary tuberculosis 39, 97, 110, 112, 167, 184, 186, 193
pyelitis 195
pyelonephritis 39, 51, 53, 117, 125
pyelonephritis, acute 51, 53, 117

Q

qi-downbearing medicines 14, 76
qi-rectifying medicines 69
qi-supplementing medicines 161

R

rashes 17, 18, 32, 67, 101, 202
rashes, dark, macular 32
rectum, prolapsed 166
renal failure chronic 121
renal tuberculosis 199
resolving the exterior and attacking the interior formulas 65
resolving the exterior and clearing the interior formulas 65
resolving the exterior and warming the interior formulas 65
respiratory tract infections, upper 27, 32, 57
restless fetus 173
restlessness 62, 91, 145, 146, 175, 181
retinitis, central 42, 53, 186
rheumatic fever 129
rheumatic heart disease 82, 123, 167, 184
rheumatic sciatica 126
rheumatoid arthritis vii, 64, 103, 124, 126, 128, 129
rhinitis, acute and chronic 25, 102
rhinitis, allergic 20, 21, 25, 156
rib-side distention and pain 71, 72, 193
rib-side pain 42, 53, 71, 110

S

safety of Chinese patent medicines 205
salpingitis, chronic 91
scabies 105
scarlatina 23
schizophrenia 134, 146, 147
schizophrenia, early stage 134
sciatica, rheumatic 126
sores, early stage 23
scrotal hydrocele 121

securing & astringing medicines 155
seminal discharge 157, 191
seminal incontinence 158
senile pruritus 195
senile vaginitis 125
senility 186
septicemia 49
sexual desire, decreased 197-199
sexual taxation 109
shivering 27, 124, 129
shoulders, nape of the neck, stiffness and pain in the upper back, 18
silicosis 112
sinusitis 25, 39, 95, 102
six environmental excesses 17
skin, dry 36, 37, 173, 174, 176, 183
skin lesions, wet, red, itchy 104
sleep, scanty 149, 150, 153
sneezing 20
Song and Yu, Profs. 152
speak, disinclination to 166, 180
speech, delirious 32, 49, 146
speech, difficult, slurred 96
spermatorrhea 158, 186, 195
spider nevi 36, 94
spirit abstraction 150, 151, 158
spirit, dimming of the 48
spirit, lassitude of the 42, 149, 153, 157, 196, 200
spirit-quieting medicines 145, 147
splenomegaly 83
spots and macules, static 83
steaming bones 58, 112
sterility 196
stomach duct and abdominal aching and pain 116
stomach duct and abdominal fullness and distention 76
stomach duct glomus, fullness, and distention after eating 164
stomach duct glomus, fullness, distention, and pain 137
stomach pain 71, 153
stomachache 39, 62
stools, bloody 63
stools, dry, bound 34-37, 149, 153, 184
stools, loose 7, 162, 165, 166, 172-174, 192, 204
stools, white-colored 55
strangury, bloody 117
strength, loss of 157, 190
stuttering 39
sudden turmoil 63, 116
supplementing & boosting medicines 161
sweating 12, 17-19, 23, 26, 27, 48, 53, 57, 67,

109, 113, 123, 124, 155, 156, 166-169
sweating, no 18, 19, 23, 26, 27
sweating, spontaneous 156, 166
swelling of the ears 53
swelling of the face 19, 55
swelling of the limbs and body, puffy 124
swelling, puffy 19, 121, 124, 196

T

tachycardia, supraventricular 179
taste, lack of 115, 164
taxation fatigue 59
taxation malaria 59
tenesmus 56, 92, 139, 178
testicular swelling 74
thirst 17, 22, 23, 32, 48, 50, 58, 59, 63, 110, 111, 121, 124, 146, 162, 166, 167, 186, 191
thirst, severe oral 48
thirst, vexatious 121, 146, 162
throat, dry 40, 59, 62, 111, 147, 167
throat, dry, painful 112
throat, dry, parched 62, 110
throat, inhibited 50, 67
throat, red, sore 22
throat, sensation of something stuck in the 70
throat, sore 12, 17, 22, 23, 50-52
thrombocytopenic purpura 179, 193
tinnitus 65, 66, 87, 101, 108, 148, 157, 173, 186, 190, 194, 197
tinnitus, chronic 87
tinnitus, continuous, cicada-like 190
tongue and mouth sores 58
tongue, dry 50, 110
tongue, sores on the tip of the 58
tongue, swollen 32
tonsillitis 22, 23, 32, 39, 50, 52
tonsillitis, acute 22, 23
toothache 48, 55, 186
torpid intake 163, 164, 192
torticollis 39
toxemia during pregnancy 70
tracheitis 22, 70, 132, 133
tracheitis, acute 22
traumatic injury 81, 88, 100
treatment outcomes 16
treatment principles 9-13, 21, 52
trichomoniasis 118, 125
trigeminal neuralgia 55, 82, 107, 177
tuberculosis of the lungs, kidneys, and/or bones 192
tumors 83

U

umbilicus, throbbing palpitations below the 121
U.S. Customs Department 205
U.S. Food & Drug Administration 205
ulcerative colitis 56
ulcers 7, 41, 45, 49, 53, 62-64, 76, 98, 134, 149, 153, 166, 179, 193
upper abdominal distention and pain 66
upper respiratory tract infections 27, 32, 57
urethritis 53, 57, 117, 195
urinary blockage 117
urinary incontinence 96, 158, 166, 195, 196
urinary retention 121, 195
urinary retention, postpartum 195
urinary strangury 53
urinary tract infection 51, 117, 186
urinary tract infections, acute 49
urination cloudy and red 117
urination dark, scanty 32, 129
urination, dark, scanty, painful, astringent 58
urination, excessive 109, 195
urination, red, astringent 67
urination, scanty 32, 37, 129, 190
urination, short, frequent 35
urine, dark 55
urine, turbid 53, 125, 158
urticaria 49, 64, 67, 82, 101, 104, 105, 122, 149, 153, 195
urticaria, chronic 64, 149, 153
uterine bleeding vii, 42, 63, 82, 92, 93, 97, 98, 155, 166, 173, 179, 186
uterine myomas vii, 91
uterine prolapse 158, 166
uveitis 53

V

vaginal bleeding during pregnancy 98, 175
vaginal candidiasis 118, 125
vaginal discharge, abnormal 42, 53, 118, 119, 155, 166, 177, 179, 199
vaginal discharge, enduring, clear, chilly 198
vaginal discharge, enduring white, watery 125
vaginal discharge, red and white 119, 120
vaginal inflammation, external 105
vaginal itching 53, 118, 195
vaginitis 53, 125
vaginitis, senile 125
varicose veins 36
varicosities 85, 87, 89, 94
vertigo 22, 40, 67, 87, 102, 107, 108, 121, 132, 134, 147, 186, 190, 191, 200
vexation and agitation 49, 55, 145, 184, 197

vexatious heat in the hands and feet 62, 92
vexatious thirst 121, 146, 162
vision, blurred 101, 173, 177, 180, 187, 189, 190, 194
vision, dimming of 87
vocal cords, polyps on the 112
voice, faint, lethargic 162
vomit, desire to 40
vomiting 18, 40, 45, 55, 62, 63, 66, 67, 69, 70, 72, 73, 97, 109, 113, 115, 116, 121, 132, 134, 137, 138, 141, 142, 153, 162, 163, 165, 171
vomiting during pregnancy 171
vomiting frothy saliva 121
vomiting of food containing roundworms 142
vomiting of undigested food 137

W

waking from sleep in a terror 134
walking, difficulty 128
wasting thirst 186
weakness, postpartum 173
welling abscesses 32, 33, 51, 52, 106
wheezing and panting 77
whole body encumbrance and heaviness 146
wind cold, slight aversion to 23
wind-treating medicines 101
Wiseman, Nigel viii, ix
worms 105, 141, 142
worm-killing medicines 141

OTHER BOOKS ON CHINESE MEDICINE AVAILABLE FROM BLUE POPPY PRESS

A Division of Blue Poppy enterprises, Inc.
3450 Penrose Place, Suite 110, Boulder, CO 80301
For ordering 1-800-487-9296 PH. 303\447-8372 FAX 303\245-8362
Email: bpeinc1@cs.com www.bluepoppy.com

A NEW AMERICAN ACUPUNCTURE by Mark Seem, ISBN 0-936185-44-9

ACUPOINT POCKET REFERENCE ISBN 0-936185-93-7

ACUPUNCTURE AND MOXIBUSTION FORMULAS & TREATMENTS by Cheng Dan-an, trans. by Wu Ming, ISBN 0-936185-68-6

ACUPUNCTURE PHYSICAL MEDICINE: An Acupuncture Touchpoint Approach to the Treatment of Chronic Fatigue, Pain, & Stress Disorders by Mark Seem, ISBN 1-891945-

ACUTE ABDOMINAL SYNDROMES: Their Diagnosis & Treatment by Combined Chinese-Western Medicine by Alon Marcus, ISBN 0-936185-31-7

AGING & BLOOD STASIS: A New Approach to TCM Geriatrics by Yan De-xin, ISBN 0-936185-63-5

AIDS & ITS TREATMENT ACCORDING TO TRADITIONAL CHINESE MEDICINE by Huang Bing-shan, trans. by Fu-Di & Bob Flaws, ISBN 0-936185-28-7

BETTER BREAST HEALTH NATURALLY with CHINESE MEDICINE by Honora Lee Wolfe & Bob Flaws ISBN 0-936185-90-2

THE BOOK OF JOOK: Chinese Medicinal Porridges, An Alternative to the Typical Western Break- fast by B. Flaws, ISBN 0-936185-60-0

CHINESE MEDICAL PALMISTRY: Your Health in Your Hand by Zong Xiao-fan & Gary Liscum, ISBN 0-936185-64-3

CHINESE MEDICINAL TEAS: Simple, Proven, Folk Formulas for Common Diseases & Promoting Health by Zong Xiao-fan & Gary Liscum, ISBN 0-936185-76-7

CHINESE MEDICINAL WINES & ELIXIRS by Bob Flaws, ISBN 0-936185-58-9

CHINESE PEDIATRIC MASSAGE THERAPY: A Parent's & Practitioner's Guide to the Prevention & Treatment of Childhood Illness by Fan Ya-li, ISBN 0-936185-54-6

CHINESE SELF-MASSAGE THERAPY: The Easy Way to Health by Fan Ya-li ISBN 0-936185-74-0

THE CLASSIC OF DIFFICULTIES trans. by Bob Flaws ISBN 1-891845-07-1

A COMPENDIUM OF TCM PATTERNS & TREATMENTS by Bob Flaws & Daniel Finney, ISBN 0-936185-70-8

CONTROLLING DIABETES NATURALLY WITH CHINESE MEDICINE by Lynn Kuchinski ISBN 1-891845-06-3

CURING ARTHRITIS NATURALLY WITH CHINESE MEDICINE by Douglas Frank & Bob Flaws ISBN 0-936185-87-2

CURING DEPRESSION NATURALLY WITH CHINESE MEDICINE by Rosa Schnyer & Bob Flaws ISBN 0-936185-94-5

CURING HAY FEVER NATURALLY WITH CHINESE MEDICINE by Bob Flaws, ISBN 0-936185-91-0

CURING HEADACHES NATURALLY WITH CHINESE MEDICINE, by Bob Flaws, ISBN 0-936185-95-3

CURING INSOMNIA NATURALLY WITH CHINESE MEDICINE by Bob Flaws ISBN 0-936185-85-6

CURING PMS NATURALLY WITH CHINESE MEDICINE by Bob Flaws ISBN 0-936185-85-6

A STUDY OF DAOIST ACUPUNCTURE & MOXIBUSTION by Liu Zheng-cai ISBN 1-891845-08-X

THE DIVINE FARMER'S MATERIA MEDICA (A Translation of the Shen Nong Ben Cao) by Yang Shou-zhong ISBN 0-936185-96-1

THE DIVINELY RESPONDING CLASSIC: A Translation of the Shen Ying Jing from Zhen Jiu Da Cheng, trans. by Yang Shou-zhong & Liu Feng-ting ISBN 0-936185-55-4

DUI YAO: THE ART OF COMBINING CHINESE HERBAL MEDICINALS by Philippe Sionneau ISBN 0-936185-81-3

ENDOMETRIOSIS, INFERTILITY AND TRADITIONAL CHINESE MEDICINE: A Laywoman's Guide by Bob Flaws ISBN 0-936185-14-7

THE ESSENCE OF LIU FENG-WU'S GYNECOLOGY by Liu Feng-wu, translated by Yang Shou-zhong ISBN 0-936185-88-0

EXTRA TREATISES BASED ON INVESTIGATION & INQUIRY: A Translation of Zhu Dan-xi's Ge Zhi Yu Lun, by Yang Shou-zhong & Duan Wu-jin, ISBN 0-936185-53-8

FIRE IN THE VALLEY: TCM Diagnosis & Treatment of Vaginal Diseases ISBN 0-936185-25-2

FU QING-ZHU'S GYNECOLOGY trans. by Yang Shou-zhong & Liu Da-wei, ISBN 0-936185-35-X

FULFILLING THE ESSENCE: A Handbook of Traditional & Contemporary Treatments for Female Infertility by Bob Flaws, ISBN 0-936185-48-1

GOLDEN NEEDLE WANG LE-TING: A 20th Century Master's Approach to Acupuncture by Yu Hui-chan and Han Fu-ru, trans. by Shuai Xue-zhong

A HANDBOOK OF TRADITIONAL CHINESE DERMATOLOGY by Liang Jian-hui, trans. by Zhang & Flaws, ISBN 0-936185-07-4

A HANDBOOK OF TRADITIONAL CHINESE GYNECOLOGY by Zhejiang College of TCM, trans. by Zhang Ting-liang, ISBN 0-936185-06-6 (4th edit.)

A HANDBOOK OF MENSTRUAL DISEASES IN CHINESE MEDICINE by Bob Flaws ISBN 0-936185-82-1

A HANDBOOK of TCM PEDIATRICS by Bob Flaws, ISBN 0-936185-72-4

A HANDBOOK OF TCM UROLOGY & MALE SEXUAL DYSFUNCTION by Anna Lin, OMD, ISBN 0-936185-36-8

THE HEART & ESSENCE OF DAN-XI'S METHODS OF TREATMENT by Xu Dan-xi, trans. by Yang, ISBN 0-926185-49-X

THE HEART TRANSMISSION OF MEDICINE by Liu Yi-ren, trans. by Yang Shou-zhong ISBN 0-936185-83-X

HIGHLIGHTS OF ANCIENT ACUPUNCTURE PRESCRIPTIONS trans. by Wolfe & Crescenz ISBN 0-936185-23-6

HOW TO WRITE A TCM HERBAL FORMULA: A Logical Methodology for the Formulation & Administration of Chinese Herbal Medicine in Decoction by Bob Flaws, ISBN 0-936185-49-X

IMPERIAL SECRETS OF HEALTH & LONGEVITY by Bob Flaws, ISBN 0-936185-51-1

KEEPING YOUR CHILD HEALTHY WITH CHINESE MEDICINE by Bob Flaws, ISBN 0-936185-71-6

THE LAKESIDE MASTER'S STUDY OF THE PULSE by Li Shi-zhen, trans. by Bob Flaws, ISBN 1-891845-01-2

Li Dong-yuan's TREATISE ON THE SPLEEN & STOMACH, A Translation of the Pi Wei Lun by Yang Shou-zhong & Li Jian-yong, ISBN 0-936185-41-4

LOW BACK PAIN: Care & Prevention with Chinese Medicine by Douglas Frank, ISBN 0-936185-66-X

MASTER HUA'S CLASSIC OF THE CENTRAL VISCERA by Hua Tuo, ISBN 0-936185-43-0

MASTER TONG'S ACUPUNCTURE: An Ancient Alternative Style in Modern Clinical Practice by Miriam Lee 0-926185-37-6

THE MEDICAL I CHING: Oracle of the Healer Within by Miki Shima, OMD, ISBN 0-936185-38-4

MANAGING MENOPAUSE NATURALLY with Chinese Medicine by Honora Lee Wolfe ISBN 0-936185-98-8

PAO ZHI: Introduction to Processing Chinese Medicinals to Enhance Their Therapeutic Effect, by Philippe Sionneau, ISBN 0-936185-62-1

PATH OF PREGNANCY, VOL. I, Gestational Disorders by Flaws, ISBN 0-936185-39-2

PATH OF PREGNANCY, Vol. II, Postpartum Diseases by Bob Flaws. ISBN 0-936185-42-2

THE PULSE CLASSIC: A Translation of the *Mai Jing* by Wang Shu-he, trans. by Yang Shou-zhong ISBN 0-936185-75-9

THE SECRET OF CHINESE PULSE DIAGNOSIS by Bob Flaws, ISBN 0-936185-67-8

SEVENTY ESSENTIAL TCM FORMULAS FOR BEGINNERS by Bob Flaws, ISBN 0-936185-59-7

SHAOLIN SECRET FORMULAS for Treatment of External Injuries, by De Chan, ISBN 0-936185-08-2

STATEMENTS OF FACT IN TRADITIONAL CHINESE MEDICINE by Bob Flaws, ISBN 0-936185-52-X

STICKING TO THE POINT 1: A Rational Methodology for the Step by Step Formulation & Administration of an Acupuncture Treatment by Bob Flaws ISBN 0-936185-17-1

STICKING TO THE POINT 2: A Study of Acupuncture & Moxibustion Formulas and Strategies by Bob Flaws ISBN 0-936185-97-X

A STUDY OF DAOIST ACUPUNCTURE by Liu Zheng-cai ISBN 1-891845-08-X

TEACH YOURSELF TO READ MODERN MEDICAL CHINESE by Bob Flaws, ISBN 0-936185-99-6

THE SYSTEMATIC CLASSIC OF ACUPUNCTURE & MOXIBUSTION (*Jia Yi Jing*) by Huang-fu Mi, trans. by Yang Shou-zhong & Charles Chace, ISBN 0-936185-29-5

THE TAO OF HEALTHY EATING ACCORDING TO CHINESE MEDICINE by Bob Flaws, ISBN 0-936185-92-9

THE TREATMENT OF DISEASE IN TCM, Vol I: Diseases of the Head & Face Including Mental/Emotional Disorders by Philippe Sionneau & Lü Gang, ISBN 0-936185-69-4

THE TREATMENT OF DISEASE IN TCM, Vol. II: Diseases of the Eyes, Ears, Nose, & Throat by Sionneau & Lü, ISBN 0-936185-69-4

THE TREATMENT OF DISEASE, Vol. III: Diseases of the Mouth, Lips, Tongue, Teeth & Gums, by Sionneau & Lü, ISBN 0-936185-79-1

THE TREATMENT OF DISEASE, Vol. IV: Diseases of the Neck, Shoulders, Back, & Limbs, by Philippe Sionneau & Lü Gang, ISBN 0-936185-89-9

THE TREATMENT OF DISEASE, Vol. V: Diseases of the Chest & Abdomen, by Philippe Sionneau & Lü Gang, ISBN 1-891845-02-0

THE TREATMENT OF DISEASE, Vol. VI: Urological Diseases & Proctology, by Philippe Sionneau & Lü Gang, ISBN 1-891845-05-5

THE TREATMENT OF EXTERNAL DISEASES WITH ACUPUNCTURE & MOXIBUSTION by Yan Cui-lan and Zhu Yun-long, ISBN 0-936185-80-5

630 QUESTIONS & ANSWERS ABOUT CHINESE HERBAL MEDICINE: A WORKBOOK & STUDY GUIDE by Bob Flaws ISBN 1-891845-04-7

230 ESSENTIAL CHINESE MEDICINALS by Bob Flaws, ISBN 1-891845-03-9

160 ESSENTIAL CHINESE PATENT MEDICINES by Bob Flaws ISBN 1-891845-12-8

630 Questions & Answers About Chinese Herbal Medicine

A WORKBOOK & STUDY GUIDE

by Bob Flaws

This book is a study guide and exam preparation workbook for Chinese herbal medicine. Comprised of 630 questions and answers, it covers all aspects of the theory and practice of Chinese herbal medicine, including:

Materia Medica (*ben cao*)
Medicinal Combinations (*dui yao*)
Processing (*pao zhi*)
Formulas and Prescriptions (*fang ji*)
Additions and Subtractions (*jia jian*)

No matter your degree of expertise, answering the questions in this book can help you reach a higher level of Chinese herbal practice. This book is also extremely useful for preparing for school, state, or national Chinese herbal exams.

ISBN 1-891845-04-7 $29.95 US

Yes! Send me ____ copy(ies) of *630 Questions & Answers About Chinese Herbal Medicine*

Name ....
Address ....
....
City, State, Zip ....
Phone/fax ....
Email ....
Credit Card # ....
Expiration Date ....

Send to: Blue Poppy enterprises, Inc.
3450 Penrose Place, Suite 110, Boulder, CO 80301
For ordering 1-800-487-9296 PH. 303\447-8372 FAX 303\245-8362
Email: bpeinc1@cs.com www.bluepoppy.com

Teach Yourself to Read Modern Medical Chinese
A WORKBOOK & GUIDE

by Bob Flaws

Teach yourself to access valuable Chinese medical information that will never be translated into English. In this workbook you will learn:

How to look up C*hinese* characters in
a Chinese-English dictionary.
How to interpret the cha*racters* you have looked up.
How to use q*uick "c*heat sheets" for identifying:
Chinese acupuncture point na*mes*
Chinese medicinal names
Chinese formula names
How to purchase Chinese medical texts by mail.
How to subscribe to Chinese medical journals from China.
How these books and journals are set up and what and
what not to translate as a beginner.

ISBN 0-936185-99-6 $39.95 US

Yes! Send me _____ copy(ies) of *Teach Yourself to Read Modern Medical Chinese*

Name ....
Address ....
....
City, State, Zip ....
Phone/fax ....
Email ....
Credit Card # ....
Expiration Date ....

Send to: Blue Poppy enterprises, Inc.
3450 Penrose Place, Suite 110, Boulder, CO 80301
For ordering 1-800-487-9296 PH. 303\447-8372 FAX 303\245-8362
Email: bpeinc1@cs.com   www.bluepoppy.com